T0306066

Construction and Application of Property Price Indices

The importance of house prices to households, real estate developers, banks and policy-makers cannot be overemphasised. House price changes affect consumer spending and business investment patterns, which in turn affect the wider macro economy and the entire business cycle. Measuring and understanding house prices is therefore essential to a functioning economy, but researchers continue to disagree on the best methodological approach for constructing real estate indices.

This book argues the need for more accurate house price indices, outlines the various methods used to construct indices and discusses the existing house price indices around the globe. It shows how the raw data of property transactions can be prepared for the purpose of constructing indices, discusses various applications of property price indices and empirically demonstrates how the index numbers can be used to model the supply of new houses and to estimate the price elasticity of supply.

Essential reading for economists, real estate professionals and researchers, and policy-makers.

Anthony Owusu-Ansah (PhD) is a Senior Lecturer and Coordinator of Graduate Programmes at the Business School of the Ghana Institute of Management and Public Administration (GIMPA), Accra. He has published extensively in the areas of house price index construction, housing market dynamics, hedonic modelling and the role of real estate in portfolio management. He is a professional member of the Ghana Institution of Surveyors and an Associate of the British Higher Education Academy.

Routledge Studies in International Real Estate

The Routledge Studies in International Real Estate series presents a forum for the presentation of academic research into international real estate issues. Books in the series are broad in their conceptual scope and reflect an inter-disciplinary approach to Real Estate as an academic discipline.

Construction and Application of Property Price Indices

Anthony Owusu-Ansah

Routledge
Taylor & Francis Group

LONDON AND NEW YORK

First published 2018
by Routledge
2 Park Square, Milton Park, Abingdon, Oxon OX14 4RN

and by Routledge
605 Third Avenue, New York, NY 10017

First issued in paperback 2021

Routledge is an imprint of the Taylor & Francis Group, an informa business

British Library Cataloguing-in-Publication Data
A catalogue record for this book is available from the British Library

Library of Congress Cataloging-in-Publication Data
Names: Owusu-Ansah, Anthony, author.
Title: Construction and application of property price indices / Anthony
Owusu-Ansah.
Description: Abingdon, Oxon ; New York, NY : Routledge, 2018. |
Series: Routledge studies in international real estate | Includes
bibliographical references and indexes.
Identifiers: LCCN 2018006273 | ISBN 9781138104709 (hardback : alk.
paper) | ISBN 9781315102085 (ebook)
Subjects: LCSH: Price indexes—Methodology. | Housing—Prices—
Statistics. | Real property—Prices—Statistics. | Real estate business.
Classification: LCC HB225 .O98 2018 | DDC 333.33/823—dc23
LC record available at https://lccn.loc.gov/2018006273

Typeset in Goudy
by Keystroke, Neville Lodge, Tettenhall, Wolverhampton

ISBN 13: 978-1-03-209507-3 (pbk)
ISBN 13: 978-1-138-10470-9 (hbk)

Contents

Acknowledgements

This book is the product of research begun in September 2009 at the University of Aberdeen in the UK. I have received a lot of feedback on earlier drafts from many great academics and industry players. I wish to single out and acknowledge the staff at the Centre for Real Estate Research at the University of Aberdeen, especially Dr Rainer Schulz, Professor Deborah Roberts, Professor Norman Hutchison and Professor Bryan McGregor for the guidance, encouragement, feedback and negotiating the data access during the research process. To them, I am most grateful.

I also wish to thank the Aberdeen Solicitors Property Centre for providing their housing transaction data for the research and also to all the other data providers. I also wish to thank Professor Stanley McGreal (University of Ulster, UK), Professor Mats Wilhelmsson (Royal Institute of Technology, Sweden), Dr Raymond Abdulai (University of Newcastle, UK) Professor Samuel Azasu (University of Witwatersrand, South Africa), Dr Franklin Obeng-Odoom (University of Technology Sydney, Australia), Dr Steven Devaney (University of Reading, UK), Professor Paul Asabere (Temple University, USA) and Dr Cynthia Holmes (Ryerson University, Canada) for critical comments which have helped to strengthen this book.

I thank my family and very close friends for the encouragement and different suggestions during the research process – especially Mrs Amma Serwah Owusu-Ansah, Francis Owusu-Ansah, Hillary Owusu-Ansah, Mr Francis Ohemen, Dr Eric Yeboah, Dr Kenneth Soyeh, Dr Wilfred Anim-Odame, Mr Joseph Abbey and all the colleagues and students at the Ghana Institute of Management and Public Administration, Accra.

Finally, I thank all the anonymous reviewers and editors of *Journal of Property Research*, *Property Management*, the *International Journal of Housing Markets and Analysis*, and Routledge for the useful comments and suggestions during earlier versions of chapters of this book.

1 Introduction

The setting

Real estate is so important a subject that it cannot be left out in any serious macroeconomic deliberation and the collective quest for wealth creation and economic development. This is true whether in the advanced or developing world. Land, for example, is a primary commodity that provides space for human and economic activities. Thus, for many people around the world it is a very strategic economic asset. It is, therefore, not surprising that in many countries in the developing world, landed property accounts for about 50% to 75% of the national wealth (Bell, 2006).

Real estate can be broadly grouped into residential real estate and non-residential real estate (Brueggeman and Fisher, 2001). Residential real estate includes flats, single-family houses and multi-family properties such as apartment blocks. This real estate provides accommodation for households and is often called "housing". The non-residential real estate includes commercial real estate such as hotels, factories, offices, warehouses and retail buildings, agricultural real estate, land and corporate real estate like hospitals and universities. The focus of this book is largely on residential real estate or housing.

Housing forms a major component of the real estate market. In the UK, the most valuable asset of the nation's wealth is residential real estate with a total value of £6.8 trillion in January 2017, representing about 3.7 times the country's GDP (Financial Times, 2017). According to the statistics, the figure is nearly half the value of all companies on the London Stock Exchange, with London and the South East accounting for almost half of the total value. Various studies, including Green (1997) and Coulson and Kim (2000), have established the effects of housing investment on a country's economic growth. These studies note that residential real estate investment for instance may stimulate GDP growth more than other types of investment because a lot of jobs, both direct and indirect, are created by the sector. Real estate has played a major role in shaping the business cycles of countries like the USA, Britain, New Zealand, Australia and Canada (Hale, 2008).

Furthermore, the price of real estate has an impact on the net wealth of people who own it. In Britain, home-ownership has grown rapidly between 1971 and

2010 from about 49% to 68.5% (ONS, 2011). Since about 75% of house purchases in the UK are financed with a mortgage loan, and the average mortgage repayment accounts for almost 19% of the average household income in the early 2000s (ONS, 2004), a change in house price can affect the value of home-owner wealth and consumption expenditure. As Tsatsaronis and Zhu (2004) observe, since the behaviour of house prices affects individual expenditure, the aggregate expenditure is also affected. House price changes affect consumer spending and business investment patterns through the wealth effect, which in turn affects the wider macro economy and the entire business cycle dynamics. The importance of accurate information on house prices to households, real estate developers, banks and policy-makers therefore cannot be over-emphasised.

Measuring of house prices is, however, not easy. This is because real estate in general has a set of unique characteristics with regard to location, structural composition as well as neighbourhood and environmental quality. That is, unlike the stock market for instance, the real estate market is highly heterogeneous in the sense that there are different market segments and property types and so no two properties can be considered as being the same. Two residential properties can be similar with regard to some of the physical characteristics but they can never be the same because no two properties can be located at the same place. Also, there is no central location or trading place where properties are transacted, and there are also high transaction costs associated with the selling or buying of a real estate. The heterogeneity that exists in the real estate market, the lack of a central trading place and the high transaction costs have made gathering of information on the property market difficult.

Transaction data in the property market is very difficult to come by. Commercial real estates for instance are hardly sold on the market. Renting is therefore the common way of transferring commercial property from one person to the other. As a result of this, there is insufficient information available on transaction prices of commercial properties. The construction of price indices for commercial properties therefore is largely based on appraisals. Examples of such commercially available indices include the NCREIF (National Council of Real Estate Investment Fiduciaries) Index, JLW (Jones Lang Wootton) and the IPD (Investment Property Databank). These and other available commercial indices are mentioned in Chapter 2. Appraisal data is also mostly used to construct indices for residential properties in emerging markets. In such housing markets, property transactions are not frequent and the properties that are transacted are mostly done in secret and so transaction databases rarely exist in such markets. Most of the housing market analysis that involves an examination of market values or prices use the appraisal data (Owusu-Ansah, 2012a). In such housing markets and all commercial property markets, the work of the appraisers are very important in order to obtain reliable results. The appraiser's task is to assess the market value of the properties at a given point in time using any of the commonly accepted methods of valuation. These methods are discussed in Chapter 2.

In situations where raw data about real estate transactions exists, it is normally difficult to understand and easily make use of such data because of the real estate market heterogeneity. One way in which raw real estate data can be meaningful and useful is to transform the data so as to construct property price indices (showing price movements over time). However, real estate, like other capital assets, is a composite asset and so it is sold wholly as one unit. When the factors that cause the changes in real estate prices are uncovered, it helps to understand house price changes. The factors that may cause changes in real estate prices may be due to shifts in the relationships between demand and supply; and may also be caused by differences in dwelling characteristics and/or differences in or quality of locational and neighbourhood attributes of the properties sold. It is therefore necessary to remove the effect of the different and mixed physical and locational attributes on real estate prices and to efficiently measure the variation in real estate prices caused by inflation on a standardised basis. In the UK, the main sources of house price information are the Halifax, Nationwide, HM Land Registry and the Council of Mortgage Lenders (CML). Each provides price indices of the private housing market at regional and national levels. The HM Land Registry and the CML indices are based on the repeat-sales and mean prices of the transactions respectively. Therefore, the CML price information is likely to be influenced by the differences in physical characteristics and locational attributes and so they are not constant-quality. Both the Nationwide and the Halifax indices are constructed using the hedonic regression technique but their indices do not exist at local levels, only at national and the twelve regional levels, including Scotland. The existing house price indices that exist in the UK and some other international markets are discussed and compared in Chapter 2.

In terms of real estate price index construction, there are three main quality-controlled index construction approaches: the hedonic, repeat-sales and the hybrid, which is a combination of the first two approaches. With the hedonic technique, the price of the property is regressed on the characteristics of the property and may be applied on a period by period basis or estimated on pooled transaction data with time dummies as additional regressors. In each case, however, objections have been raised as to the difficulties involved in identifying all the relevant price influences and the correct functional form (Case and Quigley, 1991; Shiller, 1993).

Due to the difficulty involved in identifying and gathering all the physical and locational characteristics, the repeat-sales method standardises the characteristics of the properties with reference only to themselves, by confining the analysis to properties which have been sold at least twice (Bailey et al., 1963). The method is however criticised as it discards all the single-sale transactions, thereby wasting a lot of transaction data. Thus, the fraction of properties which are repeat-sales is likely to be small in any market (Palmquist, 1982; Mark and Goldberg, 1984; Case, 1986; Case and Shiller, 1987, 1989).

The hybrid method utilises the desirable features of both the hedonic and the repeat-sales techniques to estimate real estate price indices. It uses all available information on property sales, whether single or repeat transactions, and also capitalises on the added precision when multiple transactions exist, by comparing transaction prices for the same properties. The method is therefore used to estimate the real estate prices for a standardised unit by combining data from single transactions where one sale is observed; multiple where the physical and locational characteristics are the same; and multiple transactions where the physical and locational characteristics of the property have changed between sales. The hybrid method has however been rarely used in practice. This book discusses these methods in detail and empirically uses transaction data to demonstrate how index numbers can be produced using all these methods.

The literature has reached no firm conclusion as to which index construction method performs best in terms of accuracy (see for example, Case and Quigley, 1991; Quigley, 1995; Haurin and Hendershott, 1991; Thibodeau, 1997). Case et al. (1991), for instance, find repeat-sales indices increase more slowly than those constructed using other methods. They also do not find any clear efficiency gains from using the hybrid method. This is in contrast with Case and Quigley (1991) who find the hybrid method to be more reliable. This inconsistency may be due to the way in which the index accuracies are measured. An average index is usually used as a benchmark index against which the index from the other methods are measured. This is clearly problematic since the average index does not control for property heterogeneity. There is therefore the need for further empirical studies on the examination of index accuracy. This book provides an alternative way of measuring index accuracy, and these various methods have been empirically compared with respect to accuracy in different situations.

Beyond the issues of index construction technique selection and the need to monitor real estate prices at the local level is the pooling of data across time in analysing trends and volatilities in prices. Most studies in the literature have arbitrarily pooled data into broader representations of time to estimate indices. The perception is that pooling data helps overcome the problem of small sample size, a common problem encountered in studies using real estate transaction data. In doing this, however, they implicitly assume that the pooled sample will produce index numbers that are statistically equivalent to those that would have been obtained from their constituent sub-samples. Since factors such as buyer preferences and supply conditions play a crucial role in determining real estate prices, and these may vary across time, it is necessary to test if pooling of data alters predictive performance. This book contributes by testing the temporal aggregation effect.

The analysis of real estate markets can be at national, regional or local level depending on the data required. If it is at the macro level, then crude data aggregates might be sufficient. But an index aggregated from reliable local information would be better. Reliable local information is necessary when the level of analysis is local (Hwang and Quigley, 2006; Maclennan, 1977). In examining the British housing market for instance, Meen (1999) notes that the housing market in the UK may be best described as a series of different local markets that are interlinked rather than characterising it as a single national market. One of the important features of real estate price indices is that they should be local in terms of spatial coverage (Costello and Watkins, 2002). Indeed, making assumptions based on the aggregate nature and behaviour of markets when constructing house price indices at the neighbourhood level may make the resulting index unreliable (Munro and Maclennan, 1986). The book shows why real estate market analysis should be confined to the local level instead of using an aggregated market to analyse the various local markets.

In the literature, constant-quality house price indices have been applied in several areas. These areas include asset pricing, empirical tests of housing market efficiency, hedging mechanisms for house price volatility, estimating real estate derivatives and home equity insurance, estimating the relationship between house prices and housing demand, as well as modelling the supply of housing. This book demonstrates how index numbers can be applied to estimate housing supply and the price elasticity of supply.

Based on the discussions above, the aim of this book is to demonstrate how to construct and apply property price indices so as to benefit academics, practitioners and policy makers. In order to accomplish this aim, three objectives are pursued and set out as follows: *(i) to establish the state of current knowledge on house price index construction methods and identify areas where further knowledge or research is required; (ii) to apply the different methods to the same dataset, empirically examine the accuracy of the various methods and examine the effect of aggregating observations on house prices across time; (iii) to use the house price index series to learn more about the supply side of the Aberdeen housing market.*

Structure of the book

Chapter 2 discusses the various traditional property valuation methods. These include the comparison sales approach, the replacement cost method, the income method, the profits method and the development or residual method. Some of the existing appraisal based indices around the world are presented in the chapter. These include the NCREIF index, JLW and the IPD.

Chapter 3 provides a global tour of the existing transaction-based property price indices. The chapter begins by discussing the meaning and importance of property price indices. The attributes which determine the quality of a property price index are also discussed in this chapter. Some of the indices existing around the globe are discussed. The scope, methodology and the level of index construction are all discussed. Notably, the Halifax and Nationwide indices produced for the UK housing market are discussed as well as the S&P/Case-Shiller indices in the USA.

Chapter 4 discusses the hedonic pricing theory. All the property price index construction methods directly or indirectly draw inspiration from this theory. The chapter begins with an overview of the hedonic theory. It also identifies the various property characteristics that affect that price of the property and how to include them during the modelling processes. Next, the various functional forms and how to select a functional form to fit a hedonic model are discussed. Finally, the main sources of hedonic problems and how to control or deal with them during the modelling process are identified and discussed.

Chapter 5 discusses the various property price index construction methods. These methods are the average method, the hedonic method, the repeat-sales method and the hybrid method. The advantages and disadvantages of these methods and how the methods have been compared in the literature are all discussed. The issue of temporal aggregation (i.e. pooling data across time) and how that can affect the index numbers is also discussed.

Chapter 6 introduces, prepares and describes the data used for demonstrating how property price index construction is done. The source of the data and the raw dataset and its limitations are all discussed. The data cleaning exercise is described in this chapter. By doing this, some variables are dropped and new variables are generated to aid the analyses, and the final dataset is presented and described.

Chapter 7 begins with the empirical analyses. Five models from the three main house price index construction methods are implemented at various levels of temporal aggregation. The models are the explicit time variable (ETV) hedonic model, strictly cross-sectional (SCS) hedonic model, ordinary repeat-sales (ORS) model, weighted repeat-sales (WRS) model and the Quigley's hybrid (Q-hybrid) model. The implicit prices of the housing and locational attributes are tested to find out if they are constant over time. The out of sample technique is used in this chapter to measure the mean squared error (MSE) of the various index construction models to examine the accuracy of the different index models. The effect of temporal aggregation on house price indices is also examined.

Chapter 8, the penultimate chapter, focuses on an application of house price indices. The chapter uses constant-quality house price indices for the Aberdeen City district together with other variables to examine the determinants of housing construction and to estimate the price elasticity of supply for the Aberdeen local housing market using different model specifications. The chapter compares the price elasticities of supply for the Aberdeen local market with the price elasticities of supply for other local areas in the UK and also highlights the need for housing market analysis to be confined to local or district levels.

Chapter 9 summarises and concludes, providing several conclusions that are drawn from the research. The main findings are presented in relation to the research objectives. This is followed by policy implications and contributions the research makes to knowledge. Finally, limitations of the research as well as the potential areas for future research are provided to conclude the book.

2 Property valuation and appraisal indices

Introduction

The measurement of house prices is not easy due to the fact that real estate in general has a set of unique characteristics with regard to location, structural composition as well as neighbourhood and environmental quality. Two residential properties can be similar with regard to some of the physical characteristics but they can never be the same because no two properties can be located at the same place. Also, there is no central location or trading place where properties are transacted, and there are also high transaction costs associated with the selling or buying of real estate. The heterogeneity that exists in the real estate market, the lack of a central trading place and the high transaction costs have made gathering of information in the property market difficult. Real estate transaction data is very difficult to come by in order to measure house price movements accurately.

Commercial real estates for instance are hardly sold in the market. Renting is therefore the common way of transferring commercial property from one person to the other. As a result of this, there is insufficient information available on the transaction prices of commercial properties. The construction of price indices for commercial properties therefore is largely based on appraisals. Examples of such commercially available indices include the NCREIF Index, JLW and the IPD. These and other available commercial indices are discussed in this chapter. Appraisal data is also mostly used to construct indices for residential properties in emerging markets. In such housing markets, property transactions are not frequent and the properties that are transacted are mostly done in secret and so transaction databases rarely exist in such markets. Most of the housing market analysis that involves an examination of market values or prices use the appraisal data. In such housing markets and all commercial property markets, the work of the appraisers is very important in order to obtain reliable results. The appraiser's task is to assess the market value of the properties at a given point in time using any of the commonly accepted methods of valuation. In the second section of the chapter, the various traditional property valuation methods such as the comparisons sales approach, the replacement cost method, the income method, the profits method and the development or residual method are discussed. The third section also presents some of the existing appraisal-based indices around the world and the fourth section concludes the chapter.

Property valuation types

Valuation is defined as the process of ascribing values to land and landed properties. The basis of valuation is mostly the open market value. The International Valuation Standards Council (2017) defines the market value as:

> The estimated amount of money for which an asset should exchange on the date of valuation between a willing buyer and a willing seller in an arm's-length transaction after proper marketing wherein the parties had each acted knowledgeably, prudently and without compulsion

That is, the price at which an interest in real property might reasonably be expected to be sold by private treaty assuming:

   i   a willing seller and a willing buyer, neither of them being under any compulsion to participate in the market;
  ii   a reasonable period within which to negotiate the sale, taking into account the nature of the subject property and the state of the market;
 iii   both parties are well informed or well advised about what they consider their own best interest;
  iv   values would remain reasonably stable throughout the period;
   v   no account is taken of an additional bid by a special purchaser;
  vi   that the property is put to its highest and best use; and
 vii   that the transaction is based on cash or cash equivalent consideration.

The estimation of the market value can be conducted using different methods. The five traditional methods that are known are the (i) comparison sales approach, (ii) depreciated cost approach, (iii) income approach, (iv) profits method and (v) development or residual method.

The sales comparison approach

The sales comparison approach (SCA) is the process in which the market value is estimated by analysing the market for similar properties and comparing these properties to the subject property. Analysis focuses on similarities and differences, which affect the property value.

> *Value of the property = prices for comparable and competitive properties ± adjustments for difference.*

The SCA relies on the principle of substitution. This is because a property is worth the same as another property with similar utility. The method is applied when the property or similar ones appear frequently on the market.

Procedure

i   *Find comparable properties:* The SCA relies heavily on comparisons. The accuracy of the method therefore is a direct function of the comparability of the properties being used in comparing prices. The comparables must therefore be the subject matter of recent transactions. There should also be enough comparables to improve the quality of the method.

ii *Identify characteristics of value of the subject property and comparables:* There are two sets of characteristics that the valuer must consider – property characteristics and non-property characteristics. The property characteristics are the physical and the locational elements of the properties such as the size of the property or plot, the constructed space of the two properties, the type and quality of the construction as well as the location of the properties. As much as possible, the subject property and the comparables must be similar with regards to the characteristics above. The non-property characteristics must also be considered and these include the date of sale, unusual conditions to sale like the relation between the parties and the type of interest encumbered on the property, whether freehold or leasehold.

iii *Make adjustments to reflect the differences between the subject properties and the comparables:* The purpose of the adjustments is to estimate the price at which the comparable property would be sold if it were the same as the subject property. Adjustments are used when the subject property and comparable sales have differences in the following:

- locations;
- physical characteristics of the property, such as size, age, quality of construction, conditions of the property, attractiveness etc;
- lease contracts and quality of tenants;
- external factors, given by market etc.

Here is an example of the adjustment: If the subject property has a better location than comparable sales and other factors are equal, then it should have a higher value than the comparable sales. If this is the case, appraisers adjust the price of the comparable sales upwards to estimate the market value of the subject property.

iv *Do a collation of the results to get a value for the subject property.*

The comparisons sales approach is useful so far as there are more recent comparables and appropriate adjustments are made to the comparables to reflect the subject property. That is, there is some element of subjectivity which makes the role of the valuer very important.

The depreciated cost approach

The cost method proposes that the value of a property is approximately the cost of replacing the improvement, less accrued depreciation plus site value. Using this method, the market value is estimated assuming that the rational investor will not pay more than the cost of replacing the property with the one which is equally productive on a comparable site.

Value of the property = land value + the replacement cost of the building – depreciation

---

Like the sales comparison approach, the method is premised on the principle of substitution because it is presumed that a buyer will not pay more for a site than the amount it will cost to make improvements on an equal plot.

Where the land value is estimated by means of the sales comparison approach; replacement cost is a composition of the property size and the replacement cost per unit of the size; depreciation is the negative difference between the value of the subject property and the value of a new property.

Procedure

i *Estimate the replacement cost:* The replacement cost is the cost of replacing the existing improvement with another one offering equal utility. There are four methods to assess the replacement cost. These are: the (a) unit-in-place method. With this method, the structure is broken down into its components and the cost of each component is established. Examples are the superstructure, substructure etc. The estimated cost must be the current cost; (b) quantity survey method. This method is more detailed than the first one. Instead of units, the structure is broken down into components which are analysed on their own. Because of the details, there is a possibility of ending up with a higher figure than using the first method; (c) comparative unit method. This is a simpler version of unit-in-place method. This method involves looking at the estimated cost of the entire building. After arriving at the cost, it is divided by the floor space to obtain the cost per square metre; (d) construction cost services method. This method involves a ready reckoning of costs on construction of property. It is a list that gives an idea as to the amount that will be needed to construct a building.

ii *Assess depreciation:* Depreciation is a measure of the loss of utility due to the present condition of the improvements as compared to a completely new one. Depreciation therefore represents the reduction in value of the improvements due to physical, functional and economic features. The physical depreciation is the loss of value due to wear and tear and the effect of other elements over time. Every manmade improvement suffers from being used up. This is called physical depreciation. Physical depreciation is curable when the curable cost is equal to or less than the value added to the property. The functional depreciation or obsolescence is the loss attributable to the improvements' inability to give similarly efficient utility that a new improvement with possible new design will give. Functional obsolescence reflects taste and type of design. The economic depreciation, also known as external or locational depreciation, results indirectly from the negative environmental factors or conditions in the neighbourhood. It is a loss of utility from the negative environmental conditions.

iii   *Find the depreciated replacement cost:* This is arrived at by deducting the depreciation (ii) from the estimated replacement cost (i).

iv   *Estimate site value:* We apply the market data approach to estimate the value of the land per se.

v   *Estimate property value:* Add the depreciated replacement cost (iii) to the estimated site value (iv) to get the estimated property value.

The cost method is applied in the valuation of properties which scarcely change hands in the open market. This includes specialised properties such as schools, hospitals, libraries, community centres, churches etc. It is used where the subject property is relatively new and authentic data relating to cost of construction are available. In using the method, however, we assume that cost is equal to value. Cost may be approximated to value but most of the time it is not equal to value, and this is one of the greatest weaknesses of this method.

The income approach

The income method estimates the market value by taking into consideration future incomes from the property. The approach normally requires a discounted cash flow analysis, but in practice simplified models are used. An appraiser estimates the market rent for the property, the impact of lease terms, and expenses for the property. One of the methods is to divide net operating income of the first year by the capitalisation rate.

> *Value of the property* = *Net Operating Income (year 1) / Required return − growth rate + depreciation rate*

The principle underlying this method is that the market value of the property is equivalent to the price the purchaser will pay. Therefore, the capital value of the property reflects the income generated by the property and the rights to the income generated by the property. Availability of accurate information on the net income and the required rate is a key determinant of the correctness of the method.

The profits method

This method is also known as the accounts method. The profits method proceeds by establishing the profit that the hypothetical tenant/operator will make out of the premises in order to determine what he is likely to give to enable him have the opportunity of making the profit. In other words, the tenant will pay for a place provided the business on the premises generates some profits from which a reasonable portion will be paid as rent. The principle here is that capital value is related to the turnover or volume of trade from the business that is being operated on the premises which forms the subject of valuation.

Procedure

i   Estimate the gross receipts or earnings from the business being operated on the premises. In doing this, care should be taken to ensure that only earnings or revenues related to the business are considered.

ii   Estimate the working expenses incidental to the earnings. That is only expenses that are directly related to the business are considered.

iii Work out the divisible balance. This is difference between the gross receipts and the working expenses. The divisible balance comprises the interest on capital which the operator uses to run the business and the remuneration for the tenant operator for the risk incurred in running the enterprise.

iv   Establish the gross rental value. To arrive at this, deduct from the divisible balance an amount representing the interest on the capital and remuneration.

v   Estimate the net rental value by deducting items like rates, tax etc.

vi   Capitalise the net rental value at the appropriate rate to get the capital value of the premises.

The method is an indirect approach to the valuation. It works best when the business records are available to facilitate accurate estimates. Where a particular operator has special skills that enable him to have extra profit, then this should be ignored. This is because we look at a situation where an average person is operating under reasonable conditions and make reasonable profits.

The development or residual method

This method is used solely in the valuation of development properties. A development property is that property which is capable of giving higher income if capital is spent on its development, refurbishment or redevelopment, or change in user or both. The value of the property therefore is said to be latent. The development or change of user may however be subject to planning permission.

The principle is that the prospective purchaser will pay for such development property the equivalent of the surplus after he has met his costs out of the proceeds from the sale of the completed development. The costs may include the cost of construction, cost of finance, allowance, risks etc.

Procedure

i   Conduct a preliminary study: This is to determine the type of development best suited for the land. Availability for planning permission for that use must also be considered. Again, the appraiser must estimate the period of time for the development.

ii Estimate the market value of the property. That is, the capital value of the increased incomes that goes with the proposed user.

iii Estimate all costs which include cost of construction, cost of finance, development profit etc.

iv Estimate the value of the property by deducting the total costs from the proceeds of the sale of the property.

All the methods mentioned above will give different values to the appraiser. After that the appraiser has to make a decision about the final figure. This process is called a reconciliation of value estimates. Boykin and Ring (1986) give the following definition:

> *Reconciliation is the careful weighing of the initial value results on the basis of accuracy and completeness of data and in light of market conditions that prevail on the date of the appraisal.*

The usage of one or another valuation approach depends on the available data and the type of valued property. If there is a significant difference between the values, the models should be checked for accuracy.

Existing appraisal indices around the world

The appraisal-based indices mostly exist for commercial properties since the amount of information available on transaction prices in the commercial property market is insufficient, as already discussed in Chapter 1. The appraisal indices are constructed as an average of the current appraised values of the properties at each period of time in which the index is reported. Like the transaction-based indices, the appraisal-based indices can be constructed for national, regional or local markets, and for a particular property types.

It is not possible to consider the whole market when constructing an index, whether appraisal-based index or transaction-based index. Thus, appraisal-based indices rely on a sample of properties. The main task here is to collect as much representative data for the sample as possible. As the properties are transacted on an irregular basis, their values in the sample have to be estimated regularly. For example, if the index is reported quarterly, the properties included in the index have to be reappraised quarterly. This regular estimation of the property values requires a large amount of work. There could therefore be some instance where the period of the index construction and the property valuations are different. An example of such indices is NCREIF Index, which is compiled and reported quarterly, but in fact, most properties are reappraised just once a year. Thus, it is more accurate to rely on it as on annual index, partially updated each quarter. In contrast, JLW and IPD are truly quarterly indices, because each property included in an index is reappraised every period in which the index is compiled and reported.

Some appraisal-based indices exist in the following countries:

USA
NCREIF Property Index (NPI) is the most widely used index of investment performance of income property. It has been constructed since the fourth quarter of 1977. NPI is based on the appraisal values of properties held for tax-exempt institutions by members of the National Council of Real Estate Investment Fiduciaries. The index is computed and reported on a quarterly basis. NPI now contains almost 35,000 institutionally owned properties valued at over $543.5 billion. It also consists of over 150 open-end and closed-end funds. The objective of the NPI is to provide a historical measurement of property-level returns to increase the understanding of, and lend credibility to, real estate as an institutional investment asset class. The property return is weighted by its market value. Even though it includes properties with leverage, all returns are reported on an unleveraged basis. The index includes apartments, hotels, industrial, offices and retail properties, and sub-types within each type. The NPI is a composite index defined by the membership of NCREIF and the index is analogous to the New York Stock Exchange (NYSE) composite index based on the stocks listed on that exchange. Geographically, the index is available by region, division, state, CBSA and Zip Code.

UK
The most widely used indices in UK are Investment Property Databank Index (IPD), Jones Lang Wootton (JLW) and Investors Chronicle Hillier Parker Index (ICHP). The IPD Index was established in 1984. Now it is the main property index in the UK. IPD is computed and reported on a monthly, quarterly and annual basis and has several sub-indices (including office, industrial and retail). The index tracks the performance of 22,530 property investments and 970 portfolios with a total capital value of £202.2 billion as at the December 2016. The IPD Index also exists in many countries including Australia, Austria, Belgium, Canada, Czech Republic, Denmark, France, Germany, Hungary, Ireland, Italy, Japan, Korea, Netherlands, New Zealand, Poland, Portugal, South Africa, Spain, Sweden, the UK and the USA.

Other countries
Appraisal-based indices are also compiled in:

- Canada (the Russell Canadian Property Index, RCPI) since the beginning of 1985
- Australia (Property Council of Australia, PCA)
- Germany (Deutsche Immobilien Index, DIX) since 1996
- Hong Kong (JLW Hong Kong Index)

- New Zealand (BOMA New Zealand)
- South Africa (Richard Ellis and IPD).

Conclusion

In this chapter, we have demonstrated that real estate transaction information, even though is important, is difficult to come by. This is true especially when it comes to non-residential real estate. This is because the non-residential properties are hardly sold – the common form of property transfer with these real estate markets is through renting. Transaction data by definition is virtually not in existence in these markets. In most developing residential markets, too, transaction data is virtually not in existence in these markets. The concept of property valuation and the role of the value in estimating the capital value of properties, both residential and non-residential, cannot be overemphasised. This chapter has discussed the various traditional methods and has identified some of the existing appraisal-based indices across the globe. The chapter has indicated the weaknesses involved in using any of the traditional valuation methods to estimate the value of the property. The focus of this book is on transaction data-based and residential property indices. In the next chapter, a global tour of residential property indices is provided.

3   A global tour of transaction property price indices

Introduction

Index numbers are used to aggregate detailed information on prices and quantities into scaler measures of price and quantity levels or their growth (Diewert, 2008). Presenting this detailed information in the form of indices makes it easy to see how the prices and quantities have changed over time and also to facilitate comparisons of series with different units of measurement (Brooks and Tsolacos, 2010). Index numbers are widely used to display series for gross domestic product (GDP), consumer prices, stock prices, exchange rates, house prices etc. It is very important to ensure that the index numbers relied upon are accurate, timely and robust. Obviously, the methodology used to construct the indices will determine how accurate and robust the index numbers are. All the transaction property price indices discussed in this chapter are residential and this is the focus of this book.

This chapter discusses the uses of residential real estate price indices as well as the existing indices in some selected countries such as the USA, Sweden, Germany, New Zealand, Australia and the UK. Among other indices, the S&P/Case-Shiller indices in the USA are discussed. The second section discusses the attributes of good property price indices. In the third section, the existing property price indices in some selected markets are highlighted and the discussion is narrowed down to the UK market in the fourth section: notably, the Halifax, the Nationwide, the Land Registry and the Aberdeen house price indices are the main existing indices discussed here. The coverages and methodologies of these indices as well as their limitations are all discussed. The aim is to show the gap that exists in the market. The chapter concludes with a summary of the EU directive on national house price indices and standard methodologies in the fifth section.

Uses of residential real estate price indices

Individuals and organisations use real estate price indices for different purposes in many areas of society. The different uses of the index numbers can influence the coverage, frequency and the methodology to employ when estimating the index numbers. From the perspective of most individuals or households, real estate represents the single largest in their portfolios. It accounts for the largest share of wealth for most nations. The implications for changes in house prices on individuals and households cannot be overemphasised. The levels of and changes in house prices influence home improvement and expenditures incurred on reno-vations. Thus, changes in house prices affect overall consumer spending through the wealth effect. In the measurement of the affordability of homeownership, house prices play a major role.

Policy-makers, analysts and players in the financial markets also depend on house price information for decision-making. They use it to measure the sound-ness and financial stability of their mortgages as well as to monitor the impact on economic activities. The various uses of residential real estate price indices are discussed in this section.

Inflation and monetary policy targeting

In most countries, inflation targets are directly linked to property price indices. The monetary conditions index (MCI) utilised by some central banks also includes some measure of house prices because house prices play an important role in controlling inflation and ensuring economic development (Jarocinski and Smets, 2008). Inflation targets based on the consumer price index (CPI) will indirectly consider the movement in house prices when setting interest rates. An inflation target is used by many countries to define and operate their monetary policy ranges (Fenwick, 2013). As a result of this, residential property prices are likely to play an increasing role in the conduct of monetary policy.

Financial stability indicators

Financial stability indicators (FSIs) show the current health and soundness of the financial system and institutions of a country. All the indicators that represent the markets in which the financial markets and institutions operate are considered together in measuring the soundness. These include statistics on real estate prices. The International Monetary Fund (IMF) developed FSIs so as to monitor and strengthen the global financial system and also to increase financial stability following the financial market crises in the 1990s. This is seen as a way of pre-venting such global financial crises. In order to provide such financial stability indicators, a compilation of accurate and reliable house price indices is needed (Fenwick, 2013). When house prices fall sharply, the health and stability of the financial sector is greatly affected and especially so in developed countries. Many studies have documented that real estate cycles and economic/business cycles are directly related (see for example Pholphirul and Rukumnuaykit, 2010). The role of real estate in financial crises especially in the developed world is well documented since most residential purchases are done through mortgages (see for example Wu et al., 2015).

Macroeconomic indicator of economic growth

The studies that have examined the relationship between house prices and the economic cycle, such as Hofmann (2006), have established that rising house prices are often associated with periods of economic expansion. During periods of economic contraction, however, house prices fall. Reinhart and Rogoff (2009) have noted that most of the major crises in the financial sector are the result of bubbling and bursting of the housing market. When house prices increase, the balance sheet of households will also increase, through the wealth effect, and this will increase household spending on consumption and investment (Campbell and Cocco, 2007). As a result of this, the entire economy will expand. Several studies including Owusu-Ansah's (2014) have established that there is a positive relationship between house prices and housing supply. As a result, an increase in house prices will also stimulate an increase in construction activities. When construction activities increase, there will be more employment and higher incomes for the employed workers in the construction sector. When the income increases, the purchasing power will also increase and so the workers will be able to make an effective demand for more goods and services, including new homes and making renovations on existing homes (Fenwick, 2013). Through the multiplier effect, there will be an increase in economic growth. Closely related to this, as house prices increase and both construction and demand for housing increase, government tax revenue will also increase. This will lead to an increase in government spending and, in effect, an overall expansion in the economy.

Input into buy (or sell) decision-making

One of the biggest financial decisions households and individuals may enter into is the decision to buy or sell a house. In making this decision, households and individuals are mostly influenced by the level of and changes in house prices. In fact, the budget plans and savings decisions of the prospective homebuyers are all influenced by the changes in property prices. Most individuals and households consider the purchase of a house as a capital investment and also as a means of providing shelter. When it is purchased because of its potential to generate capital gains in the future, then monitoring of house prices will become important. That is, the decision to buy (or sell) now or in the future will depend on, among other things, the price levels and changes and the trends (both past and estimated future) of house prices. For this reason, house price indices are important.

Input for estimating the value of housing as a component of wealth

Real estate is one of the major asset classes in the economy. When measuring the aggregate wealth of the economy, the values of houses is included. It is therefore necessary to constantly monitor the changes in house prices. In order to do this effectively, construction of house price indices becomes important.

Use in making regional, national and international comparisons

When computing the cost of living index (CLI) and comparing across cities, regions and countries, house price indices play a major role. Housing forms the greatest percentage of household expenditure and so forms a major component in the calculation of CLI. When including housing into the CLI calculation for city, regional, national and international comparisons, it is required that the properties to be included are comparable across the city, regional, national and international areas being used for the comparison. In ensuring this, constant-quality house price indices are required.

Attributes which determine the quality of a property price index

The features of a good property price index method should include but are not limited to the following (Bourassa et al., 2006):

Data requirement

The first attribute considered here is that data is difficult to come by, and so an index method should not require huge amounts of data. If the data requirement is huge, then the application of that index method would become difficult. If the method requires specific property characteristics and such variables are absent, it may cause bias in the estimated index numbers. More so, the subset of properties that form the basis for the construction of the index should be representative of the inventory of properties. That is, there should be no sample selection bias in the construction of price indices.

Standardisation

Secondly, one of the most important features for any property price index is that it should be able to track price changes for a property that has the same set of characteristics over time. That is, they should be standardised to account for changes in the stock and neighbourhood mix of transactions in different time periods. In this case, the price changes would only result from changes in the market prices of characteristics, and not from differences in the characteristics of properties that have transacted in the various periods. The index method therefore should be able to produce constant-quality indices.

Implementation

Another attribute to be considered is that an index method should be transparent and easy to construct or implement and it should not require complex estimation techniques or technical skills. This is because when an estimation technique is very complex, it becomes very difficult to identify when a mistake is made, and it will be difficult for people without such technical knowledge to replicate and implement the model. Easy methods therefore facilitate transparency and make replication easily possible.

Revision

The fourth attribute is the stability of the index numbers when they are revised. Index numbers are typically revised periodically when either the method used to incorporate the data or the data themselves are updated (Clapham et al., 2006). Information does not come in all at once and so when new data arrives after an index has already been published, the index has to be re-estimated to incorporate the new information (Shiller, 1993). In doing this, the extent to which the index numbers change as additional data are included in the index estimation is a great concern. That is, the property price index construction method should not change the historical index values when new transaction data arrives. When historical index numbers change after the arrival of new information, it becomes a big concern for investors and policy-makers when these numbers are relied upon for policy formulation, investment decisions and economic modelling. For example, if government agencies use the property price index to construct a cost of living index that serves as a basis for wage and benefits adjustments, the accuracy of the previous wage and benefits adjustments will be questioned when the index numbers are changed (Owusu-Ansah, 2012b). Again, when the price indices are used to hedge against property risk, then changes in the historical index numbers will be a big problem for all the users. Therefore, the particular index construction method should not change the historical or already published index numbers significantly.

Thus, the desirable properties of an index computation method are that the method should: (i) require less data in its implementation; (ii) use data which is representative of the inventory; (iii) be standardised for quality (constant-quality); (iv) be easy to implement; (v) not change the historical numbers when revised. It is expected that at least one of the methods to be reviewed fulfils the criteria best.

Property price indices in some selected markets

Property price indices have been constructed in different countries by various governmental and private organisations so that the indices become available for research and decision-making. This section summarises some of these indices in selected international property markets. These markets include the USA, Sweden, Germany, New Zealand, Australia and Canada. Commercially established property price indices in developing property markets are virtually non-existent. In the USA, commercially available house price indices for metropolitan areas have been reported monthly by the National Association of Realtors (NAR) since 1968. The NAR series are from transactions reported by members on existing single-family homes in metropolitan areas. The index is for the median transaction price with no adjustment for quality. The National Association of Home Builders reports mean and median prices of existing and new houses from county records. Clearly, better quality houses may tend to sell during booming markets, while lower quality houses may dominate sales in downturns. In this case, the median index will overstate the volatility of house prices. Constant-quality hedonic price indices are also available in the USA for new houses. The US Bureau of the Census C-27 index (Current Construction Reports) is for newly constructed houses sold quarterly for the nation and annually for the four census regions of Midwest, Northeast, South and West. The volume of new houses covered is only one-third of the total due to the sample selection rule (Calhoun et al., 1995). Another hedonic house price index is for a standardised 1977 house.

The S&P/Case-Shiller Home Price Indices exists in the USA and it is the leading measure for the US residential housing market (Standard and Poor, 2012). The indices track changes in the value of residential real estate, both nationally as well as in twenty metropolitan regions. The metropolitan indices are calculated monthly and the US national index is calculated quarterly. The monthly indices use the repeat-sales method and the quarterly US national index aggregates nine quarterly US Census division repeat-sales indices. The indices originated in the 1980s by Case and Shiller (1987, 1989). The data for the index construction is managed by Fiserv Inc., a leading provider of information technology which receives sale price information from multiple sources and then crosschecks all the data points before including them in the database. A modified version of the weighted repeat-sales method is used by the US Office of Federal Housing Enterprise Oversight to construct quarterly house price indices for single-family detached properties.

In Sweden, the SCB index is constructed using the assessed value of properties (which are based on hedonic regressions). Based on the assessed values, the statistical office divides the houses into 12 assessed-value classes within each region. Weights are calculated using all properties in the housing stock (not just the sold properties) within the value classes. By using the weights, the mean sale prices in different value classes can be calculated and the price index is estimated (Englund et al., 1998). This method is similar to the SPAR method suggested by Bourassa et al. (2006). The method, as indicated above, is a combination of transaction-based and appraisal-based methods in that it forms a ratio between the transaction price and appraisal value. The average ratio is then used to construct the index numbers. One clear problem of using this method is that the appraisals will need frequent updates with the help, presumably, of a hedonic regression.

The Nasdaq OMX Valueguard-KTH housing index exists in Sweden. This is a private and commercialised transaction-based price index for single-family houses and condominiums. The index exists for three metropolitan areas in Sweden, namely, Stockholm, Gothenburg and Malmö. The method used for the index construction is the explicit time variable (ETV) hedonic method. The base period for the index is January 2005 (2005M1=100) and is updated on a monthly basis. The objective of this index is to provide a consistent and reliable benchmark for the traded private real estate house and apartment markets.

The Hypo Real Estate Index (HypIndex) exists in Berlin, Germany. This index was established in December 2008. It came to operation on 1st July 2009. The purpose of the index is to meet the need for market information especially as the German Banking Act (KWG) stipulates that the value of mortgaged properties must be monitored on an ongoing basis. They use the Association of German Pfandbrief Banks (vdp) transaction data from both property and market-related perspectives. The vdp has maintained a property transaction database since 2004 and the database contains information on more than 427,000 properties from data submitted by a total of 13 financial institutions. The indices are constructed for apartments and single-family houses as well as for Germany as a whole and for smaller geographical areas such as cities, towns or administrative districts. They use the explicit time variable hedonic approach and the indices are constructed on quarterly basis.

In New Zealand, the sale price appraisal ratio (SPAR) method has been used since the early 1960s to produce semi-annual price indexes for regions and cities in New Zealand. The main purpose of the index is to measure the affordability of home-ownership over time and relative to renting (Bourassa et al., 2006).

The Australian Bureau of Statistics (ABS) produces quarterly house price indices for eight capital cities of Australia, as well as weighted average of them. These cities are Sydney, Melbourne, Brisbane, Adelaide, Perth, Hobart, Darwin and Canberra. The indices also exist separately for Established Houses and Project Homes. The median method is used to construct the indices but control for compositional change in the sample of houses used to compile the house price indices each quarter. They do this by stratifying houses according to two characteristics: the long-term level of prices for the suburb in which the house is located, and the neighbourhood characteristics of the suburb.

In Canada, Teranet and the National Bank of Canada produce house price indices which provide price indicators to the public. Teranet is an international leader in electronic land registration and is the exclusive provider of online property search and registration in Ontario and The Property Registry in Manitoba. Teranet facilitates the delivery of electronic land registration services on behalf of the Province of Ontario and is widely recognized as one of the most advanced, secure and sophisticated electronic land registration systems in the world. The Teranet–National Bank House Price Index is an independent representation of the rate of change of Canadian single-family home prices. The index is estimated by tracking the observed or registered home prices over time. Properties with at least two sales are required in the calculations. Such a "sales pair" measures the increase or decrease of the property value in the period between the sales in a linear fashion. That is, the repeat-sales methodology is employed to construct the price index. The index covers eleven Canadian metropolitan areas namely, Victoria, Vancouver, Calgary, Edmonton, Winnipeg, Hamilton, Toronto, Ottawa, Montréal, Québec and Halifax and the index is produced on monthly frequencies.

Having discussed the existing house price indices in some international markets, the next section discusses the existing house price indices in the UK with the Halifax and the Nationwide as the main index providers. The UK housing market has been distinguished here from the other housing market because data for the empirical demonstration is from one of the UK cities, Aberdeen.

Existing property price indices in the UK

This section provides an overview of existing house price indices in the UK. Notably, the Halifax and the Nationwide house price indices are discussed. Both the Halifax and the Nationwide are mortgage lenders and their indices are available at the regional and national levels only. Apart from these two indices, the Land Registry also provides information about house price trend indicators in the UK.

The Land Registry House Price Index measures changes in the value of residential properties. The house price index is published by Land Registry using completed sales data collected on all residential housing transactions, whether for cash or with a mortgage, in England and Wales since January 1995. The index is based on the repeat-sales methodology. The Land Registry database does not contain information about the physical characteristics of the properties and so the repeat-sales method readily lends itself as the method suitable for estimating quality adjusted indices by the Land Registry. The indices exist at the England and Wales level as well as the regional levels within England and Wales. In addition, there are some county level indices and an index for London boroughs. That is, specific local indices are not produced by the Land Registry. The lack of local indices may be due to the fact that the sample size of properties transacted at the local level may not be enough to support indices at the local level.

The Halifax and Nationwide indices are discussed and compared in the next three sub-sections. These two are the main house price indices usually relied on in the UK (Leishman and Watkins, 2002).

Halifax Index

Background

The Halifax House Price Index is a standardised index of house prices launched by the Halifax in April 1984. It is claimed to be the longest running house price series that covers the whole of the UK from January 1983. There are a number of national indices that cover different categories of houses (all, new and existing) and buyers (all, first-time buyers and home-movers). These indices are produced on a monthly basis. In addition, regional indices are produced on a quarterly basis and exist for the twelve standard planning regions of the UK. The Halifax Index is derived from the mortgage data of the country's largest mortgage lender, which provides a robust and representative sample of the entire UK market. All these indices are adjusted so as to account for seasonal variation effect on house prices.

The indices calculated are "standardised" and they represent the price of a typically transacted house. "Standardisation" is very important because no two houses are identical and may differ according to a variety of quantitative and qualitative characteristics relating to the physical attributes of the houses themselves or to their locations. Thus, analyses of average house price differences between one region and another, or of changes in average prices over time, are not based on the comparison of like with like if the "characteristics-mix" of houses traded is not adjusted for the quality differences. The methodology employed by the Halifax to estimate their index series is discussed below.

Methodology

The strictly cross-sectional (SCS) hedonic model, discussed in Chapter 5, is employed by the Halifax to construct the house price indices. The standard set of housing characteristics that pertained in a base period (year 1983) is used by the Halifax to estimate the index numbers. Thus, the Halifax Index numbers represent the movement in average prices for houses possessing the same characteristics as those bought in 1983. The index numbers themselves are computed by comparing the weighted (i.e. mix-adjusted) prices in each current period with the weighted average price in the base period. Even though we do not know the average characteristics of properties transacted in 1983, it is most likely that these characteristics have changed over time.

One important decision to make when using the hedonic method is to determine the appropriate form of the functional relationship between the variables. The semi-logarithmic functional form (with the dependent variable, price, measured in natural logarithms) is used by the Halifax to construct the index numbers.

Data

The database employed for the construction of the Halifax house price indices was established by the Halifax at the beginning of 1983. The data refer to mortgage transactions at the time they are approved, rather than completed. The database therefore has the disadvantage of covering some cases which may never proceed to completion. The database covers about 12,000 house purchase transactions per month after the necessary cleaning exercise. Even though this seems to be a large figure, it is less than 1% of the total housing stock figure of 26.3 million in the UK. Thus, sample selection bias is likely to be a problem. Also, qualitative factors relating to the standards of repair of existing (non-new) houses, the quality of workmanship, the nature of fixtures and fittings, environmental quality of the neighbourhood etc. are not reflected in the database.

Information is obtained about the following house characteristics: purchase price; location (region); type of property (house, sub-classified according to whether detached, semi-detached or terraced, bungalow, flat); age; tenure (freehold, leasehold, feudal); number of rooms (habitable rooms, bedrooms, living-rooms, bathrooms); number of separate toilets; central heating (none, full, partial); number of garages and garage spaces; garden; land area if greater than one acre; and road charge liability.

The definition of these variables is presented in Table 3.1. It is clear from the table that the database covers most of the physical housing characteristics.

Table 3.1 Definitions and code names of variables included in the model for estimating the Halifax indices

House characteristic	Code	Definition
House Type:		
Detached	DH	Five dummy variables taking the
Semi-detached	SDH	value of 1 if the property corresponds
Terraced	TH	to a particular type. Otherwise 0.
Bungalow	BUNG	
Flat	FLAT	
Number of bathrooms	NOBATHS	Actual number of bathrooms.
Number of separate toilets	NOTOILET	Actual number of separate toilets.
Number of garages	NOGARAGE	Actual number of garages.
Number of garage spaces	NOGSPACE	Actual number of garage spaces.
Presence of a garden	GARDEN	Dummy variable taking the value of 0 if the property has a garden. Otherwise 1.
Number of acres	A1	Dummy variable taking the value of 1 if the property has one acre or more. Otherwise 0.
Central heating:		
Full	CHF	Three dummy variables taking the value of
None	CHO	1 according to central heating provision.
Partial	CHP	Otherwise 0.
Location:		
North	EPR1	Twelve dummy variables taking the value
Yorkshire & Humberside	EPR2	of 1 according to the region in which the
North West	EPR3	property is located. Otherwise 0.
East Midlands	EPR4	
West Midlands	EPR5	
East Anglia	EPR6	
Wales	EPR7	
South West	EPR8	
South East	EPR9	
Greater London	EPR10	
Northern Ireland	EPR11	
Scotland	EPR12	
Road charge liability	ROADCHRG	Dummy variable taking the value of 1 if the property is liable to a road charge. Otherwise 0.
Number of habitable rooms	NOHABS	Actual number of habitable rooms.
Age of property	PROPAGE	Actual age of property in years.

However, locational characteristics are not fairly represented as there is no neighbourhood information relating to a specific house.

Nationwide Index

Background

The Nationwide Building Society has a long history of recording and analysing house price data. Average house price information has been published by the Nationwide since 1952, and these have been published on an annual basis. In 1974, quarterly average prices were published for the first time. In 1989, the quality of the various houses that were used to estimate the average figures were standardised and so quality adjusted house price indices became available by the Nationwide from this year. These indices were initially produced on a quarterly basis but from 1993, the UK indices became available also on a monthly basis. Apart from the monthly indices for the entire UK, the Nationwide also publishes on a quarterly basis, house price indices for thirteen regions (the twelve regions identified by the Halifax above as well as the Outer Metropolitan) and the entire UK as a whole. These regional and national indices exist for four types of property (detached, semi-detached, terraced and flats), two types of buyer (first-time buyer and former owner occupiers) and three property ages (new, modern and old). Thus, they have a total of 140 separate series, all of which are published quarterly.

Methodology

The methodology used by the Nationwide to produce the index numbers is similar to the one used by the Halifax. That is, the strictly cross-sectional method illustrated in Chapter 5 is also employed by the Nationwide to estimate their index numbers. They use the same functional form as the Halifax (semi-log functional form) and also uses the initial period's average set of characteristics to estimate the index. Like the Halifax, the Nationwide also adjusts for the effect that seasons may have on house prices.

Data

The source of data for the Nationwide House Price Index series is the Nationwide Mortgage Data. Like the Halifax, the data is extracted monthly for mortgages that are at the approval stage and after the corresponding valuation report has been completed. Using approval date instead of completion date has the advantage of giving an earlier signal of current trends in prices in the housing market. However, should the buyer later withdraw the transaction, then the transaction would not be completed and so the inclusion of such approval transaction will lead to sample selection bias.

The housing characteristics that are included in the regression equation for the estimation of the Nationwide house price indices are the following: UK location (that is, part of country); type of neighbourhood (the Nationwide Index uses an established demographic system that classifies areas in the UK into 54 categories based on the type of people who live there. Two examples include retirement and council areas); floor size; property design (detached house, semi-detached house, terraced house, bungalow, flat etc.); tenure (freehold/leasehold/feudal) except for flats which are nearly all leasehold; number of bath- rooms (1 or more than 1); type of garage (single garage, double garage or none); number of bedrooms (1, 2, 3, 4 or more than 4); and whether property is new or not.

A comparison of the Halifax and Nationwide Indices

This sub-section compares the Halifax and the Nationwide Indices with regards to the methodology, quality of data and the final index numbers.

Methodology and quality of data

INADEQUATE LOCATIONAL CONSIDERATION

The information on location is very limited in both the Halifax and the Nationwide databases. In the construction of the national house price indices, regional area dummies are used to control for the locational differences. At the regional level, however, there is no explicit locational measure in their databases. Even though the Nationwide database includes neighbourhood-type dummies, it is still inadequate since neither specific information about the neighbourhood quality nor the georeference coordinates are present in the database. Differences between the different local areas in the various regions are therefore not appropriately considered in both indices. For example, the absence of the locational measures implies that in the construction of the Scotland Index series, for instance, the Aberdeen, Edinburgh and Glasgow housing markets are assumed to be similar. Also, within Glasgow, for instance, all the areas are assumed to be similar. This assumption inherent in the Halifax house price indices is questionable since house prices are expected to vary from one area to the other. The failure to include locational measures in estimating the regional indices may therefore reduce the standardisation or quality adjusted nature of the house price indices.

AGE VARIABLE

The age variable is absent in the Nationwide database but present in the Halifax database. The age variable is used to control for the depreciation effect on house prices. It is very important especially when heterogeneous markets like the national and regional housing markets are considered. This is therefore a clear advantage of the Halifax database over that of the Nationwide.

THE APPLICATION OF THE SCS MODEL

It was discovered from the previous chapter that when constructing property price indices at the lower level of temporal aggregation (monthly and quarterly levels), then statistically, the explicit time variable (ETV) hedonic model is preferred to the strictly cross-sectional model. This is because at the lower levels of temporal aggregation, the sample size is relatively small and so pooling the data together over time using the ETV hedonic model improves the estimates. Both the Halifax and the Nationwide however use the SCS hedonic model to estimate the monthly and quarterly house price indices. The precision of the Halifax and the Nationwide Index series may therefore not produce the most accurate index series.

NO REVISION OF INDEX

Both the Halifax and the Nationwide estimate the Laspeyres House Price Index by using the initial period's weight of the housing characteristics to produce the index numbers. The initial period of the Halifax and the Nationwide indices are the years 1983 and 1993. Even though the average characteristics of Halifax's 1983 and Nationwide's 1993 "standard" homes are not known, it is most likely that between those periods and the current period (2012), the average characteristics of the housing attributes have changed and so are likely to bias the index numbers since the initial weight no longer represents the average characteristics of the housing attributes. More so, there is no indication of revision of the indices after 1983 and 1993 for the Halifax and Nationwide, respectively. Index revisions make it possible for the weights to be adjusted and the lack of index revisions undermine the quality of the indices.

NO LOCAL-LEVEL INDICES

The Halifax and the Nationwide indices are available at the national level and the twelve regional levels. County and local-level indices are not produced by both the Halifax and the Nationwide. Due to the fact that neighbourhood and environmental factors affect house prices and these differ from county to county, and from local area to local area, the regional indices cannot be employed for analysis and decision-making at the local level. This lack of local house price indices does not promote efficient decisions taken by home owners at the local level.

INDEX SERIES

The comparison of the methodology and quality of data above has shown some similarities between the way both the Halifax and the Nationwide calculate their house price index numbers. First, both the Halifax and the Nationwide produce their indices at only the national and regional levels. They do not produce local indices. Second, they both use similar methodology – the SCS hedonic method – in the computation of the index numbers, and they both control for seasonality effect on the house price indices. Third, they both use mortgage data to construct the house price indices. The mortgage data they use represent mortgages at the approval stage and not completed sales, and they both claim that their databases are a fair representation of the inventory of housing stock in the UK.

Based on the similarities identified above, it is expected that the house price indices produced by the Halifax and Nationwide should track changes in house prices in similar patterns. This sub-section compares some of the index series produced by the Halifax and the Nationwide. The UK national index series and the Scottish regional index series are used for this comparison. The analysis is done using the quarterly seasonally adjusted index numbers for a seven-year period, from the first quarter of 2005 to the last quarter of 2011, a total of twenty-eight quarters.

Figures 3.1 and 3.2 show the comparison of the Halifax and the Nationwide Indices at the National and the Scottish regional levels. It is clear from Figure 3.1 that the pattern of house prices estimated by the two institutions at the national level are different. While the house price index by the Halifax is always above that of the Nationwide between the second quarter of 2005 and the first quarter of 2008, the Nationwide Index is above the Halifax from the second quarter of 2009 to the fourth quarter of 2011. The difference between the two indices is much greater and even diverge during the latter part of 2011. Even though the two indices exhibit a similar pattern between the second quarter of 2008 and the first quarter of 2009, the overall pattern shows that the two indices are not similar.

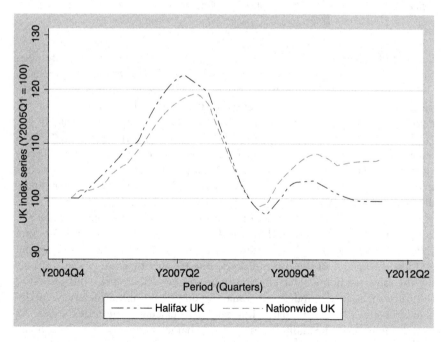

Figure 3.1 A Comparison of the Halifax and Nationwide Index Series at the National Level

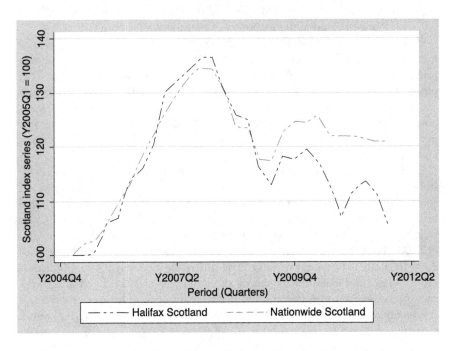

Figure 3.2 A Comparison of the Halifax and Nationwide Index Series at the Scottish
Regional Level

The differences between the indices at the Scottish regional level are even
worse than at the national level. Figure 3.2 clearly shows these differences.
Particularly, during the fourth quarter of 2010, there is an approximate 14%
difference between the two indices and the Halifax Index falls sharply during that
period. The volatile nature of the Halifax Index as compared to that of the
Nationwide between the first quarter of 2010 and the fourth quarter of 2011 is
also worthy of note. The conflicting signals about the magnitude and pace of price
changes produced by the Halifax and the Nationwide is a great concern for actors
in the housing market (Leishman and Watkins, 2002). One reason for the periodic
divergence has been suggested to be the consequence of each institution's share
of the mortgage market. The Nationwide Index is said to be influenced by the
South East, while the Halifax Index is driven by the North East and Scotland
(Nicol, 1996). This sample selection bias is one of the possible reasons for the
periodic divergence of the two indices despite the fact that the two institutions
use the same methodology in the construction of the house price indices. Also,
the differences in the index series may be due to possible differences in the
characteristics of the "standard" home used to calculate the index series. As
already mentioned, the Halifax uses the 1983 characteristics of a "standard" home
while the Nationwide uses the 1993 characteristics. The "standard" home for the
Halifax may be different from the "standard" home for the Nationwide and hence

the characteristics may be different. Clearly, indices constructed with different housing characteristics are expected to be different.

The Aberdeen House Price Index

This book uses raw data from the Aberdeen (in Scotland) housing market to do the empirical demonstrations in Chapters 7 and 8. It is therefore important to review the house price indicators existing in this town. As noted above, quality-adjusted local house price information is lacking in the UK. In 2009, the University of Aberdeen, through its Centre for Real Estate Research (CRER), collaborated with the Aberdeen Solicitors' Property Centre (ASPC) to produce local house price indices to fill this gap. Through its CRER, the University produces quarterly indices and market reports on the Aberdeen housing market. The purpose of the index project is to provide quality adjusted house price information for policy-makers, investors, home owners, banks, estate agents and academics, for decision-making as well as teaching and research purposes. The index project is a collaboration between the CRER in the Business School of the University of Aberdeen, ASPC and Aberdeen City Council. A modified version of the ETV hedonic model based on a five-year rolling window approach is used for the index project. The rolling window approach is particularly important because as established in Chapter 7, the implicit prices of the housing attributes do not stay constant over time. Since the index project is expected to be in existence for a long period of time, changes in the implicit prices over such a long period of time will question the quality of the indices and hence the need for the rolling window approach to control for this. The coefficients of the housing and locational attributes together with the time dummies for each specific period are used in estimating the index number for each period, while either only the time dummy or only the property and locational attributes are considered in the ETV hedonic or SCS hedonic, respectively. As a result of using this approach, the form of the hedonic model for the index project differs from what has been provided in Chapter 7.

Conclusion

Recently, a handbook on Residential Property Price Indices (RPPI) funded by Eurostat has been drafted that seeks to provide guidance for those wishing to set up RPPI in view of international harmonisation (Eurostat, 2011). In the draft handbook, it is stated that it is not possible to construct a "perfect" RPPI. Any index construction is an "approximation to the theoretically ideal index" for a specific purpose. The handbook therefore provides some guidelines for individuals, institutions and organisations that seek to construct RPPI. Issues discussed in the handbook include the conceptual basis of the particular index, the scope of the index, the fact that the index should be constant-quality and the statistical methods for compiling such constant-quality indices. The methods identified are the stratification "mix adjustment" methods, the hedonic methods, the repeat-sales methods and the appraisal-based methods. It is noted that general recommendation cannot be made as to the best method that should be used internationally and that the method will vary considerably among countries. It is, however, recommended that the statistical agencies should provide evaluations of the resulting indices of the various methods, as done in Chapter 7 of this book, so that the best method can be used for the particular market.

As a result of these guidelines, the UK National Statistician has provided a review of house price indices so as to ensure that official house price statistics meet user needs and that the relevant information is available for users to inform their use (Government Statistical Service, 2010). It is therefore expected that when these guidelines and review become operational, there will be more transparency in the property market.

4   The theory of hedonic
    pricing modelling

Introduction

Five property valuation methods, namely the comparison sales method, the depreciated replacement cost method, the income method, the profit method and the development or residual method, have been discussed in Chapter 2. These five methods are classified as the traditional valuation methods. This chapter discusses the hedonic pricing theory. The hedonic pricing theory is considered as an advanced form of valuation. This is important because most of the house price index construction methods directly or indirectly rely on the hedonic regression analysis. This chapter is structured into nine sections. Following this introduction, the second section provides an overview of the hedonic method. The history and definition of the hedonic model are provided in this section. The parametric, nonparametric and semi-parametric hedonic modelling approaches are discussed in the third, fourth and fifth sections, respectively. In the sixth section, the property characteristics that are included in hedonic modelling, both the physical characteristics and location, are discussed. The seventh section discusses the functional forms that are normally employed in hedonic analysis and the penultimate section discusses the problems that are often encountered during hedonic modelling. Issues such as heteroscedasticity, multicollinearity and omitted variable bias are discussed. The last section concludes and summarises the chapter.

An overview of the hedonic method

It has been suggested by several scholars that A.T. Court (1939), an automobile industry analyst, was the first to estimate a hedonic model, price as a function of commodity attributes (see Griliches, 1958; Goodman, A.C., 1998; Malpezzi, 2003). However, before the 1939 study by Court, other studies had applied the hedonic model. Berndt (1991) mentions Waugh (1928) as one of the first researchers to apply the hedonic model in the area of agricultural economics to find out that quality variation existed among lots of asparagus. Aside this, Colwell and Dilmore (1999) also mention Haas (1922) as the first researcher to apply the hedonic model. According to Colwell and Dilmore (1999), Haas (1922) applied the hedonic model in the area of land economics to value farm lands. Even though several early contributions exist, they are mostly applied.

Lancaster (1966) began the theoretical foundation of the hedonic pricing theory in his consumer theory studies where he provides a micro economic foundation for estimating the value of utility generating attributes. This was followed by another study in 1974 by Rosen who focused on housing characteristics. Rosen (1974) used the hedonic pricing model to estimate the implicit prices associated with housing characteristics. The study of Rosen, therefore, is often cited to have developed the theoretical framework of the hedonic pricing model and provides the foundation for non-linear hedonic pricing models (Sirmans et al., 2005).

Housing is bought as a bundle of attributes, and each of these attributes contributes to the price of the property. A property is therefore purchased not for the property's sake but for the attributes that make up the property. However, since the individual attributes do not have explicit prices, the price one pays for a particular property is the sum of the implicit prices the market gives to the various attributes that make up the bundle (Rosen, 1974). Since most of these housing characteristics are not traded explicitly and their prices could not be observed directly on the market, the hedonic pricing model is applied to estimate the marginal contribution of each property and neighbourhood characteristic to the house price. The hedonic price function theory therefore provides the framework for the analysis of differentiated goods such as housing, whose individual features we do not have observable market prices for (Pagourtzi et al., 2003).

The hedonic technique involves the estimation of some regression relationship between the transaction prices P_t, of properties at time t, and their physical and locational characteristics, X:

$$P_t = f(X) \tag{4.1}$$

Most of the studies using the hedonic pricing model use the parametric approach. By this approach, the regression curve, $f(.)$, is assumed to have some pre-specified functional form that is fully described by a finite set of parameters, which are usually coefficients of the independent variables (Härdle, 1990). However, studies using a nonparametric approach have also evolved (see Meese and Wallace, 1991). The nonparametric approach is flexible and does not pre-specify the model in advance. It, however, assumes a smooth population regression function (Härdle, 1990) and therefore provides an adaptable method of exploring a general relationship between the dependent and the independent variables. The nonparametric regression techniques include the kernel regression method, the nearest neighbour method, the local polynomial regression or locally weighted regression (see Härdle, 1990). A combination of the parametric and the non-parametric approaches, called the semi-parametric approach, has also been used to construct house price indices (see Clapp, 2004).

Parametric hedonic pricing models

The parametric hedonic model is a type of hedonic model in which the regression curve is assumed to have some pre-specified functional form which is fully described by a finite set of parameters which are usually the coefficients of the independent variables (Härdle, 1990; Horowitz and Lee, 2002; Fox, 2004). For example, a multiple parametric hedonic function can take the form of the following:

$$y = \beta_0 + \beta_1 x_1 + \beta_2 x_2 + \ldots + \beta_v x_v + u \tag{4.2}$$

where y is the dependent variable and x_1 through to x_v are the independent variables which explains the value of y or on which y depends. The betas (β_0 through to β_v) are the unknown parameters to be estimated from the equation and u is the error or the disturbance term, which is assumed to be normally distributed with a mean of zero and a constant variance, σ^2. The most commonly known parametric models are discussed below:

The log-linear OLS model

The log-linear functional form has been greatly employed in hedonic price analysis especially in constructing price indices and analysing housing price determinants (Sirmans et al., 2005). With this, the natural logarithm of the transaction price of the property is taken as the dependent variable and the housing and locational characteristics are taken as the independent variables. That is, instead of taking the absolute values of the transaction prices, we take a natural logarithm of them. A log-linear model can take the form

$$\ln Y_i = \beta_0 + \beta_1 X_i + \beta_2 Z_i + u_i \tag{4.3}$$

where: $\ln Y$ represents the transaction price of the property; X represents a vector of housing characteristics; Z also represents a vector the two locational variables (latitude and longitude); and u is the error term which is assumed to normally distributed with a mean of 0 and a constant variance σ^2.

A lot of studies have used and stressed the advantages of the semi-logarithmic form over the other linear functional forms. Follain and Malpezzi (1980) particularly find that the semi-logarithmic form makes the interpretation of the regression coefficients easy – as the percentage change in the price given a unit change in the housing attribute; allows for variations in the currency value of each housing characteristic; and finally helps to minimise the problem of heteroskedasticity.

The Box-Cox OLS model

Box and Cox (1964) have developed a statistical test for the functional form providing the "best fit" based on likelihood ratio tests and most studies now employ this in choosing the functional form (Wooldridge, 2009). According to the formal Box-Cox model,

$$V(\alpha) = b_0 + \Sigma\, b_i Z_i\,(\beta) + {}_i\Sigma\,\Sigma_{j \neq i}\, C_{ij}\, Z_i\,(\beta)\, Z_j\,(\beta) \tag{4.4}$$

where

$$V(\alpha) = (V^{\alpha} - 1)/\alpha \qquad \alpha \neq 0$$
$$V(\alpha) = \ln(V) \qquad \alpha = 0$$
$$Z_i(\beta) = (Z_i^{\beta} - 1)/\beta \qquad \beta \neq 0$$
$$Z_i(\beta) = \ln(Z_i) \qquad \beta = 0$$

The Box-Cox methodology has been used in studies by Goodman (1978), Linneman (1980), Blomquist and Worley (1981), Halvorsen and Pollakowski (1981), Eberts and Gronberg (1982) and Casssel and Mendelsohn (1985). In comparing the linear functional forms with the Box-Cox transformation, Goodman (1978) rejects the linear functional forms. He notes that the linear functional form is "overly restrictive" and so the Box-Cox transformation provides a better estimate than the linear functional forms. Halvorsen and Pollakowski (1981) also recommend the use of a Box-Cox transformation. Cassel and Mendelsohn (1985) note that the Box-Cox functional form is attractive when the goodness of fit criterion is used but the fact that the best fit criterion is used to choose functional form does not necessarily mean that the estimates of the housing characteristics are more accurate. Particularly, they note that the accuracy of the Box-Cox estimates is reduced when the number of coefficients to be estimated is extremely large. They also argue that the coefficients of a non-linear transformation are "cumbersome" to use properly and also the Box-Cox transformation may not be suitable when the dataset contains negative numbers. This is because "any negative number raised to a non-integer real power is imaginary". Finally, Cassel and Mendelsohn (1985) note that the Box-Cox methodology may be inappropriate for prediction.

The OLS models explained above usually calls for five sets of assumptions (usually called the Gauss-Markov assumptions) to make the estimates valid. Among them are the zero conditional mean assumption, the homoscedasticity assumption and the linearity in parameters assumption (Wooldridge, 2009). If the five sets of assumptions hold, then the ordinary least squares (OLS) is seen as the best linear unbiased estimator (BLUE).

One major criticism of the OLS models that has also received particular attention in the literature is the problem of heteroskedasticity. As highlighted above, for the OLS to be BLUE we assume that the variance of the unobservable error, u, conditional on the independent variables is constant (homoscedasticity assumption). That is, $\text{Var}(u/ x_1, x_2 \ldots, x_k) = \sigma^2$. However, it has been found in a lot of studies that the homoscedasticity assumption mostly fails in multiple regression analysis (White, 1980; Fleming and Nellis, 1984; Robinson, 1987; Fletcher et al., 2000a; Stevenson, 2004). That is, the variance of the error term changes across different segments of the population – a situation called heteroskedasticity.

It should be noted that the homoscedasticity assumption is needed to justify the usual t and F tests, as well as the confidence intervals for OLS estimation of the multiple linear regression model. Therefore, in the presence of heteroskedasticity we cannot make inferences since the standard errors and for that matter the F and t statistics are invalid. The estimates, however, are not biased or inconsistent. Fletcher et al. (2000a) also confirm this by saying that when heteroskedasticity is present in economic models, OLS estimators are still unbiased but not the best. According to Robinson (1987) also, the presence of heteroskedasticity in economic models leads to "inefficient point estimators and hypothesis tests with suboptimal asymptotic local power". Heteroskedasticity can lead to both changes in the estimated standard errors of the coefficients and changes to the value of the coefficients themselves (Stevenson, 2004).

The weighted least square (WLS) models

The WLS models are another set of models that researchers mostly rely on. Like the OLS models, the WLS models are also specified in advanced. With the OLS models, we assume that the error variance is identical for all the variables in the population and so the OLS gives the same weight to each observation. Instead of given equal weights to all the observations as in the case of the OLS, the WLS gives different weights to different observations. Less weight is therefore given to observations with higher error variance (see for example Park, 1966; Harvey, 1976; Lardaro, 1992; Goodman and Thibodeau, 1995, 1997; Fletcher et al., 2000a).

If the heteroskedasticity in the OLS models are known up to a multiplicative constant, then the generalised least squares (GLS) proposed by Davidian and Carroll (1987), which is a type of WLS, have the potential of giving better estimates than the OLS (Stevenson, 2004). With this model, the initial OLS model is re-estimated with WLS using the reciprocals of the normalised predicted values from the absolute residual model.

Fletcher et al. (2000a) find that in the presence of heteroskedasticity of unknown form, the estimated generalised least square (EGLS) estimators are consistent and asymptotically efficient than OLS estimators. The model uses the residuals from the original OLS model. Fletcher et al. (2000a) stress that EGLS gives a forecast closer to the actual *ex post* forecasting. This means that the confidence intervals for forecasts are narrower. However, they indicate that the EGLS estimators are efficient in large samples. Therefore, in case of small samples, the procedure may not be the best. Stevenson (2004) notes that the corrected models have the desired effect of reducing the standard errors of the hedonic coefficients. Unlike the iterative GLS that attribute the cause of heteroskedasticity to a particular variable like age of a property, and so has the ability to remove all heteroskedasticity from the hedonic model, the EGLS does not assume that heteroskedasticity is caused by a single specified variable and hence does not eliminate all evidence of heteroskedasticity.

Merits and demerits of the parametric model

The major advantage of the parametric model is its simplicity in estimating and interpreting the coefficients – no wonder it still remains one of the popular approaches in hedonic modelling.

The approach has, however, come under serious criticisms in the literature. Härdle (1990) indicates the preselected parametric model might be too restricted or too low-dimensional to fit unexpected features. This is also confirmed by Anglin and Gencay (1996) who argue that parametric model involves implicit restrictions. The parametric approach has also been strongly criticised for imposing strong assumptions such as the linearity of the parameters of the dependent variable (y) to the independent variables (x's) as discussed above, which in many cases lead to inefficiency in the estimates (Fox, 2004).

Nonparametric hedonic pricing models

The nonparametric approach is a flexible approach that does not pre-specify the model in advance and relaxes the strong assumptions imposed by the parametric model approach (see for example Fix and Hodges, 1951; Watson, 1964; Cover, 1968; Stone, 1977; Li, 1984; Robinson, 1987; Meese and Wallace, 1991; Hastie and Loader, 1993). It however assumes smooth population regression function (Fox, 2004; Härdle, 1990) and therefore provides an adaptable method of exploring a general relationship between the dependent and the independent variables.

Unlike the parametric regression approach which specifies the regression (f) in advance, the nonparametric traces the dependence of the explained variable (y) on the explanatory variables (x's) without pre-specifying the regression function (f) that relates the explained to the explanatory variables (Fox, 2004). The mean curve is therefore estimated without a reference to a specific form and this therefore offers a flexible tool in analysing unknown regression relationships (Härdle, 1990). Like the parametric approach, a weighted sum of the y observations is usually used to obtain the fitted values for the nonparametric regression approach. However, instead of using equal weights as in the case of the OLS or weights proportional to the inverse of variance as in the case of the WLS, with the nonparametric approach, the independent variables closest to the focal independent variable (x_0) are given more weight than those more remote from it. There is therefore a decreasing function of the distances of the location of the independent variables from the focal independent variable (x_0). There are many types of nonparametric regression techniques and these include the spline method (Reinsch, 1967), the nearest neighbours method (Fix and Hodges, 1951; Cover and Hart, 1967; Stone, 1977; Li, 1984), the kernel estimates (Watson, 1964; Nadaraya, 1964) and the locally weighted regression (LWR) or local polynomial regression (LPR) approaches (Cleveland et al., 1988). The next subsection describes some of these techniques.

The Kernel regression method

The Kernel estimation method is one of the famous methods used in nonparametric regressions (see for example Watson, 1964; Nadaraya, 1964). The method aims to obtain and use appropriate weights to yield the fitted values. The general idea is that in estimating $f(x_0)$, it is appropriate to give greater weight to observations that are close to the focal value x_0. It is argued that the kernel smoothing technique is one of the simplest ways of computing a weight sequence. According to Nadaraya (1964, 1965) and Watson (1964), the kernel weight sequence $\{Wni(x)\}$ $^n i=1$ can be represented by describing the shape of the weight function $Wni(x)$ by a density function with a scale parameter that adjusts the size and the form of the weights near x. This is defined by:

$$W_{ni}(x) = \frac{K_h(x - X_i)}{n^{-1}\Sigma K_{hn}(x - X_i)} \tag{4.5}$$

where $Khn(u)$ is a decreasing function of $|u|$ and hn>0 is called the bandwidth. By studying the above equation carefully, it can be noticed that the weighting scenario is different for the observations with observations at locations close to x having more weight than observations remote from it. The kernel estimate, $mh(x)$ is defined as a weighted average of the response variables in a fixed neighbourhood around x, determined in shape by the kernel K and the bandwidth h. It is worth mentioning that the kernel is a continuous, bounded and symmetric real function K, which integrates or sums up to one. Since Nadaraya (1964) and Watson (1964) propose the kernel weights of the form $Whi(x)$, the result from the kernel estimate

$$m_h(x) = \frac{n^{-1}\Sigma_{i=1}^n K_h(x - X_i)Y_i}{n^{-1}\Sigma_{i=1}^n K_h(x - X_i)} \tag{4.6}$$

is often called *Nadaraya-Watson estimator*.

The bandwidth, h, determines the rate at which the weights decrease as the distance from x_0 increases. Since the rate at which the weights decrease relative to the locations of the x's controls the smoothness of the resulting estimate of $f(.)$, the choice of the bandwidth becomes very necessary to the efficient performance of the nonparametric fit (Härdle, 1990). In a scenario where the bandwidth is small (h close to zero), the closest point to the focal x_0 will have the majority of the weight with only the other closest observations to this point receiving the remainder of the weight. The resulting fit would therefore connect the dots formed by the observed data points and will therefore make it undersmoothed with possibly high variance.

On the contrary, if the bandwidth is very large (equal or close to equal to the entire range in x values), then instead of concentrating the weights on a few data points, the weight is now evenly distributed across all the observations. This therefore makes the fit oversmoothed and possibly with a high bias because it essentially fits the value of y at each data point. Stock (1991) however shows that the choice of kernel function can significantly affect the estimates but the estimates are relatively insensitive to the choice of bandwidth. Where the bandwidth is a standard deviation of a normal distribution centred at the focal x_0, it is called the Gaussian or Normal kernel and when the bandwidth is a half-width of a window centred at the focal x_0, it is called the tricube kernel (Fox, 2004).

As pointed out already, the kernel and, for that matter, their weights should be symmetrical. However, when the x approaches a boundary of the data, whether to the left or to the right, the kernel weights can no longer be symmetric. For example, if the focal point x_0 is located at or very close to the right boundary, only points to the left of x_0 are capable of receiving kernel weights. This is because there are simply no (few if any) points to the right of x_0 to receive any weight. This is considered as the main problem of the kernel method.

The nearest neighbour method

The nearest neighbour (NN) method was instigated by Fix and Hodges (1951) and since then has been extensively employed in nonparametric density and regression estimation and discrimination (see for example Cover and Hart, 1967; Cover, 1968; Stone, 1977). The kernel regression estimation as discussed above can be seen as a way in which the weighted averages of the response variables in a fixed neighbourhood around x can be computed with the width of the neighbourhood being governed by the bandwidth h. The k-nearest neighbour (K-NN) estimator can also be viewed as a weighted average of the response variables in a neighbourhood x. The importance difference is that while the neighbourhood width is fixed with the kernel regression, the neighbourhood width is not fixed but variable in the case of the nearest neighbour estimate. That is, the values of Y used in computing the average are those which belong to the k observed values of x that are nearest to the point x, at which we would like to estimate $m(x)$.

Härdle et al. (2004) note that if the modeller is confronted with sparse data and wants to estimate $m(.)$ at a point of x, it may be the case that the k-nearest neighbours are rather far away from x and farther from each other as well. Therefore, the neighbourhood around x for which the average of the corresponding y values is computed will be wide. Like the kernel estimation, k is the smoothing parameter of the estimator. When k is increased, the estimate becomes smoother and vice versa.

The k-nearest neighbour can be viewed as a kernel estimator with uniform kernel, $K(u) = \frac{1}{2} I(|u| \leq 1)$ and variable bandwidth R=R(k). The bandwidth, R(k), is the distance between x and its furthest k-nearest neighbour. In this case, the nearest neighbour estimator can mathematically be written as:

$$\hat{m}_k(x) = \frac{\sum_{i=1}^{n} K_R(x - X_i) Y_i}{\sum_{i=1}^{n} K_R(x - X_i)} \tag{4.7}$$

Robinson (1987) indicates that the use of nonparametric nearest neighbour (NN) regression estimators of σ^2, in place of kernel estimators, avoids the technical problems imposed by the random denominator of the kernel estimators.

The local polynomial regression (LPR) or locally weighted regression (LWR)

Cleveland and Devlin (1988) and Cleveland, Devlin and Grosse (1988) have given a detailed description of the local polynomial regression. The local polynomial regression is a technique for estimating a regression surface in a moving average manner. As discussed earlier, the Nadaraya-Watson kernel regression corresponds to a local constant least squares fit. The local polynomial regression however helps "to fit a polynomial in a neighbourhood of x". The underlying principle is that instead of fitting only local constant least square fit, with the LPR, the smooth function can be well approximated by a low or high degree polynomial in the neighbourhood of any point, x. The LPR varies with x and hence can be described as a really local regression at the point x (Härdle et al., 2004).

The local polynomial estimator of the regression function m is $\hat{m}_{p,h}(x) = \hat{\beta}_0(x)$. By running the local polynomial regression with varying x, the curve $\hat{m}_{p,h}(.)$ can be obtained. Härdle et al. (2004) show that when p=0, $\hat{\beta}$ reduces to $\hat{\beta}_0$, which means that the local constant estimator is the same as the Nadaraya-Watson estimator. That is,

$$\hat{m}_{0,h}(x) = \hat{m}_h(x) = \frac{\sum_{i=1}^{n} K_h(x - X_i)Y_i}{\sum_{i=1}^{n} K_h(x - X_i)} \tag{4.8}$$

As discussed in the kernel regression section above, the Nadaraya-Watson estimate has a problem in that we typically observe one-sided neighbourhoods at the boundaries. This is because in local constant modelling, almost the same points are used to estimate the curve near the boundary. The LPR overcomes this by fitting a higher degree polynomial.

Again, the LPR fit can improve the function estimation in regions with sparse observations (Härdle et al., 2004), a problem commonly encountered with the k-NN estimate. The nonparametric regression approach has been used to estimate house price index by researchers like Meese and Wallace (1991) and was combined with a parametric component by Clapp (2004) to estimate local house price indices.

Merits and demerits of nonparametric regression

The nonparametric regression approach provides an adaptable method of exploring a general relationship between the dependent and the independent variables. It also has the ability of giving predictions of observations yet to be made without a reference to a fixed parametric model. The approach is also flexible and works well even with small dataset and even when the dataset has missing values. Also, the approach provides an objective estimation of the regression curve as compared to the parametric regression where the underlying assumptions are unreliable.

One major criticism of the nonparametric regression analysis is the problem of "curse of dimensionality". Since nonparametric regression estimates are based on local averaging, in higher dimensions, the observations become sparsely distributed even for large sample sizes and so the estimators perform unsatisfactorily. Again, unlike parametric regression estimate, there are no parameters to describe in nonparametric regression. It is therefore very difficult to make quantitative statements about the actual difference between two or more populations. Nonparametric regression has also not received the needed attention because of the technical and cumbersome nature of its estimation. The estimates are very quantitatively intensive and very technical and cumbersome. There is difficulty in assigning weights and also in choosing the appropriate kernel function and smoothing parameter (bandwidth) in nonparametric regression. All these make the approach difficult to test complex and sophisticated statistical models. Finally, Ullah (1988) finds that even though the nonparametric models increase the robustness of the estimates, it tends to be less precise.

Semi-parametric model

The semi-parametric model incorporates some parametric information into a nonparametric regression so as to get the advantages of both models and reduce the problems in the estimation. The semi-parametric regression is seen as a useful alternative to the pure nonparametric regression.

Robinson (1987) is seen as the originator of this idea. Stock (1989, 1991) subsequently uses this semi-parametric approach to estimate the effect of removing hazardous waste on house prices. This Robinson-Stock model is further illustrated and applied by Anglin and Gencay (1996) to estimate a hedonic price function using data from the UK. This model, together with two other varieties proposed by Yatchew (1997, 1998) and Clapp (2004), are discussed below:

The Robinson-Stock model

A semi-parametric model is of the form:

$$y_i = z_i\beta + f(x_i) + u_i \qquad (i = 1, 2, ..., n) \tag{4.9}$$

where y_i is the ith observation on a dependent variable, z_i and β are $1 \times p$ vectors, x_i is a $1 \times k$ vector and the error term u_i, has a mean of zero and conditional variance $\sigma^2(u_i \mid z_i, x_i)$. It is therefore the functional form which is unknown to the researcher and so the $z_i\beta$ and $f(x_i)$ forms the parametric and the nonparametric parts of the equation, respectively. According to Robinson (1987), the above model can be rewritten as

$$p_i - E(p_i \mid x_i) = (z_i - E(z_i \mid x_i))\beta + u_{i...} \tag{4.10}$$

Robinson (1987) and Stock (1989) show that β can be estimated in a two-step procedure. Firstly, a nonparametric technique is used to estimate the unknown conditional means, $E(p_i \mid x_i)$ and $E(z_i \mid x_i)$, and secondly, the estimates are substituted in place of the unknown functions in the equation. The parametric OLS model is then used to estimate β. Robinson (1987) shows that the resulting estimate of β is asymptotically equivalent to those where the true mean functions are known and used in the estimation. Various nonparametric techniques explained above can be applied to estimate the unknown conditional means, $E(p_i \mid x_i)$ and $E(z_i \mid x_i)$. Robinson (1987) for instance suggests the nearest neighbour (NN) technique. Anglin and Gencay (1996) however apply the nonparametric kernel estimator to estimate the conditional means. In applying the Robinson-Stock semi-parametric model, Anglin and Gencay (1996) enter all the dummy variables such as driveway, recreation room, finished basement, gas heating, central air, garage and neighbourhood dummy variables in the parametric or linear part of the model; and enter the discrete and continuous variables into the nonparametric part or the unknown $f(.)$. They note that the curvature of the function will not be affected if the dummy variables are included in the nonparametric part but would only cause scale effects.

Yatchew's differencing model

Another type of the semi-parametric approach is the differencing method proposed by Yatchew (1997, 1998). Like the other semi-parametric model of the form,

$$Y_i = z_i \beta + f(x_i) + u_i, \tag{4.11}$$

the differencing model also assumes the function f to be smoothed. In addition to this, the model assumes that the function f is single-valued with a bounded first derivative (Lokshin, 2006). Yatchew (1997, 1998) indicates that it is very imperative that the data is rearranged in ascending order such that $x_1 \leq x_2 \ldots \leq x_T$, where T is the number of observations in the sample. After the data is sorted, the above equation is then first differenced to obtain:

$$y_{i(n)} - y_{i(n-1)} = \{z_{i(n)} - z_{i(n-1)}\}\beta + [f\{x_{i(n)} - x_{i(n-1)}\}] + $$
$$u_{i(n)} - u_{i(n-1)} \quad n = 2, \ldots, T \tag{4.12}$$

It should be noted that because the derivative of f is bounded, when the sample size increases, $[f\{x_{i(n)} - x_{i(n-1)}\}]$ approaches zero and so the nonparametric effect is removed. Yatchew notes that so far as z and x are not correlated, the OLS model can be used to estimate β using the differenced data. In this case, the vector of estimated parameters β_{diff} has the approximate sampling distribution. Efficiency of the β estimate can be improved substantially by using higher order differencing (Yatchew, 1997).

Clapp's local regression model

One difficulty in hedonic models is how to accurately model house prices over space. According to Clapp et al. (2002) and Clapp (2003, 2004), house prices vary dramatically over space and most at times are difficult to model. Researchers most often omit a lot of unmeasured spatial variables from the hedonic equation by attempting to include some neighbourhood and accessibility variables (see for example Dubin, 1992; Gillen et al., 2001). Gillen et al. (2001) indicate that most of the omitted spatial variables can be modelled with spatial autocorrelation. Clapp's LMR combines this spatial autocorrelation approach with nonparametric technique to model the omitted spatial variables (Clapp et al., 2002). According to Clapp (2004), the model, like other data mining methods, requires the assumption that the underlying space-time surface is smooth and, also, the model does not assume information on distances to the CBD or other points of interest such as an airport. This makes the model more efficient since consistent identification of these points may not be available.

The LRM has two parts – an OLS model to hold constant for the housing characteristic, and a nonparametric smoother (LRP) which calculates location value as a function of longitude and latitude. In using the LRM, the coefficients on housing characteristics and measurable spatial variables are estimated using a linear function such as the log-linear model. A non-linear function of latitude and longitude is used to estimate the unmeasured spatial variables, and specifically, the local polynomial regression (LPR). Both the parametric and nonparametric parts of the mean function are jointly estimated. Let's consider a semi-parametric model:

$$Y_i = x_i\beta + f(w_i) + u_i, \tag{4.13}$$

where y_i is the log of house price, x_i is a vector of housing characteristics and w_i is a two dimensional vector of latitude and longitude. According to Clapp (2003, 2004), in using the LRM, firstly, the log of sale price is regressed on a vector of housing characteristics, x_i, and a vector of physical location variables of latitude and longitude, w_i. This is represented by the equation below:

$$y_i = x_i\beta_1 + w_i\beta_2 + \varepsilon_i \tag{4.14}$$

Secondly, the residuals, η, are calculated from the β estimates of the above equation. That is,

$$\eta = y - x\beta.$$

The calculated residuals are then used to estimate the nonparametric part:

$$F(W) = D = smooth\,(\eta/w)$$

where w has 2 column vectors of equally spaced latitude and longitude coordinates and D can be interpreted as a matrix of location values. The function that produces the smooth is the local polynomial regression (LPR). The LPR produces a local average by down-weighting observations that are more distant from the fixed point. Assuming we want to estimate a weighted average of D in the local neighbourhood around (w_0), then

$$D(w_0) = \Sigma_{i=1}^{q} \frac{K_h(W_i - w_0)(\eta_i)}{\Sigma_{i=1}^{q} K_h(W_{i-w_0})} \tag{4.15}$$

This is the Nadaraya-Watson estimator discussed under the nonparametric regression. The weighting function, $K_h(.)$ is an inverse function of distance and h is the bandwidth. Lesser weight is therefore given to more distant points. Clapp applies the kernel weights to estimate this equation. The product kernel gives,

$$K_h(W_i - w_0) = K_{hwi}(W_{i1} - w_{01}) \, K_{hw2}(W_{i2} - w_{02}),$$

where the subscripts 1 and 2 on the W variables indicate latitude and longitude.
The LPR takes the form:

$$D_i = \gamma_0 + (W_i - w_0) \, \gamma_1 + (W_i - w_0)^2 \gamma_2 + \ldots + (W_i - w_0)^p \gamma_p + \xi_i \ldots \tag{4.16}$$

where $w_0 = (w_{01}, w_{02})$ represents a specific point on space, and $W_i = (W_{i1}, W_{i2})$ represents the location variables. The subscripts 1 and 2 on the W and w variables indicate latitude and longitude, γ_j $(j=1,\ldots,p)$ are column vectors with number of elements equal to the column of Wi, γ_0 is a scaler quantity and D_i represents the unobserved location values to be estimated. Clapp indicates that w is a rectangular grid of equally spaced latitude and longitude points that span the data and the level of D is estimated conditional on each knot. Both the parametric and nonparametric parts of the semi-parametric equation must be estimated simultaneously and both must be consistent estimators of the underlying functions.

It is seen from this model that while the log-linear OLS model capture measurable effects, the LPR capture the effects on price of unmeasurable spatial variables. There is a common usage of the LPR and models of the form of the LRM in the field of medicine (see for example Wand and Jones, 1995; Fan and Gijbels, 1996; Hastie et al., 2001) but Clapp is one of the few researchers to apply this to the housing sector.

According to Clapp (2004), the semi-parametric approach of LRM offers greater flexibility and so allows the identification of space-time asymmetries which other models are not able to identify. He also finds the model increases the explanatory power and also improves out of sample prediction when compared to the hedonic OLS model. The LRM also efficiently uses scarce neighbourhood data to estimate the evolution of house prices at each point on the grid. The model does not require knowledge of the neighbourhood boundaries. Clapp indicates that the model's inability to forecast house prices is the main drawback of the LRM.

Merits and demerits of semi-parametric regression

The semi-parametric approach as indicated above combines the advantages that both the parametric and the nonparametric approaches possess. They keep the easy interpretability of the parametric approach and retain some of the flexibility of the nonparametric approach. These two features are well combined to produce an accurate and robust estimate for the regression model. In testing the semi-parametric and parametric models, Anglin and Gencay (1996: 634) find that the semi-parametric model outperforms their benchmark parametric model even though the benchmark parametric model "passes most of the specification tests that researchers use to reassure themselves that the parametric specification is reasonable". Again, the problem of the "curse of dimensionality" is reduced drastically if not eliminated since most of the regressors enter into the parametric part.

However, as with the parametric approach, if the underlying assumptions are violated, the model can produce inconsistent estimates. Again, the computational problems associated with the nonparametric regression are still associated with the semi-parametric model (Owusu-Ansah, 2011).

The hedonic method and property characteristics

There are two main variables included in hedonic modelling. These are the dependent and the independent variables. The dependent variable is usually the price of the property. However, depending on the availability of the transaction price information and the nature of the studies' undertaking, measures such as asking price, assessment value or even rent can be used. The independent variables are numerous. Wilhelmsson (2000) identifies four main factors that affect demand for properties and hence the price to include the property's structural attributes, its location or neighbourhood amenities, its environmental attributes and macro attributes like gross domestic product (GDP) and interest rate. The macro attributes like GDP and interest rate affect the entire economy and are discussed in Chapter 8. Only the structural or physical property characteristics, and its location in terms of neighbourhood characteristics and accessibility, are considered in this section.

Physical characteristics

The physical characteristics of a house influence the price to be paid for the house. Table 4.1 shows the structural physical characteristics employed in previous studies. While the studies and the variables in the table are not exhaustive, the table is very useful in that it serves as a guide in selecting the physical housing characteristics for the study. These physical characteristics can be grouped as: accommodation and size; structural improvement and materials used; and age and condition of the structure.

Accommodation and size

The level of accommodation provided by a house can influence the value or price to pay for the house. Such factors include the number of bedrooms and other rooms, the number of floors, floor size, land area etc. Generally, individual buyers have their own needs, tastes and preferences concerning the amount of accommodation. Such accommodation needs, tastes and preferences are influenced by the size of the family, prestige and status of the individual etc. They therefore restrict their enquiries to properties having the number of rooms or size of property that they want. If individuals get the amount and size of accommodation they want, they will be willing to pay a higher value for it than they would pay for property with more than or less than the amount of accommodation they require. The number of rooms (bathrooms, public rooms and bedrooms) dominantly affects price in a positive direction (Sirmans et al., 2005). This means that, all other things being equal, as the number of rooms increase, the price of the property also increases. Rationally, as the number of rooms increases, the utility of homebuyers is expected to increase as well because they will be able to allocate new rooms for other uses and ease the pressure on existing rooms. However, from theory, the utility should diminish beyond a certain number of rooms (Wooldridge, 2009).

Structural improvement and materials used

The materials that go into the construction of a property and the structural improvement made to the property affect the price paid for the property. Physical factors such as the type, style and quality of floor finishes, roof, ceilings etc. will influence the amenity to be derived from living in a particular property and hence the price to paid that property. Structural improvements like the availability of garage, swimming pool, gardens, fence wall etc. all affect the value of residential accommodation. Usually, the availability of improvements like swimming pool, garages and gardens in a property will make rational buyers pay a higher price for such a property than they will pay for similar property without such improvements, all other things being equal (Sirmans et al., 2005).

Age and condition of structure

The age and condition of a property will also influence the price paid for the property. In examining the factors that are mostly included in hedonic models to determine house prices, Sirmans et al. (2005) find that the age of a property influences the value of the property, mostly in the negative direction. This is not surprising because as the age of the property increases, the economic value of the property decreases and hence the utility to be derived from the property decreases. Furthermore, homebuyers would have to spend additional money on maintenance when properties are old. They are, therefore, willing to pay a price lower than a new property of similar but new attributes. Apart from the age, the condition of the structure also affects the value of the property. If a property is old but has seen

Table 4.1a Property characteristics included in previous studies

Authors	Lot size	Floor area	Living area	Other area	Age of property	Dwelling type	Presence of garden	Pool	Heating system	Condition of dwelling	Double glazing	No. of bedrooms	No. of bathrooms	No. of other rooms	Garage/on-site parking	Fireplace	Basements
Palmquist (1980)	X	X			X					X			X		X	X	X
Case and Quigley (1991)	X		X	X	X												
Adair et al. (1996)	X	X			X	X			X	X		X	X		X		
Anglin and Gençay (1996)	X								X			X			X		X
Hill et al. (1997)			X	X	X												
Henneberry (1998)			X						X		X	X			X		
Englund et al. (1998)	X	X				X			X	X					X	X	X

Table 4.1b Property characteristics included in previous studies

Authors	Lot size	Floor area	Living area	Other area	Age of property	Dwelling type	Presence of garden	Pool	Heating system	Condition of dwelling	Double glazing	No. of bedrooms	No. of bathrooms	No. of other rooms	Garage/on-site parking	Fireplace	Basements
Bourassa et al. (1999)					X	X				X		X					
Des Rosiers et al. (2000)		X			X			X	X	X							
Fletcher et al. (2000a)	X				X	X				X		X	X	X	X		
Fletcher et al. (2000b)	X		X		X	X			X			X	X		X		
McCluskey et al. (2000)		X			X	X			X			X	X		X		
Wilhelmsson (2000)	X		X		X					X							
Stevenson (2004)	X		X		X			X				X	X	X	X		X
Bourassa et al. (2006)	X	X			X										X		
Wilhelmsson (2009)			X	X	X	X				X							

a lot of refurbishment, it will demand a higher price than a similar property that has not been refurbished. Furthermore, the time the property was constructed also affects the vintage or the quality and style of the dwelling.

As shown in Table 4.1, lot size, floor area, age of property, dwelling type, heating system, quality of dwelling, number of bedrooms, number of bathrooms, as well as the availability of garage are among the physical property variables mostly included in hedonic models.

Location

The importance of location in real estate is well known. There is a real estate adage that states that the three most important factors which determine property values are: (i) location, (ii) location and (iii) location. Spatially, no two properties are the same and, indeed, there is a consensus among valuers that location is the most important factor in property value determination (McCluskey et al., 2000). The importance of location is evident by the fact that location physically fixes a property in a space and thereby defines its distance from features such as commercial, transportation and leisure activities. Again, in cases where houses within a particular submarket or neighbourhood are homogeneous, many of the amenities that are common to those properties are best represented by location (Gelfand et al., 1998). Location is an inherent attribute of a house which directly determines the quality and hence the market value of the house.

The locational influences on the value of residential property may arise from a number of sources. These are grouped under neighbourhood quality and accessibility (McCluskey et al., 2000). Table 4.2 presents some of the neighbourhood and accessibility factors that have been used in previous studies.

Neighbourhood quality

Can (1990) defines neighbourhood in an economic sense as an area within which relatively the same prices prevail for properties that permit approximately the same types of uses and socioeconomic status. In his extensive review of literature to determine the existence of neighbourhoods or submarkets, Jones (2002) concludes that there is little consensus on how neighbourhoods or submarkets should be identified. Neighbourhood quality can be argued as an unobservable variable (Dubin and Sung, 1987). However, subjective assessments can be made about some of these perceived quality indicators. The neighbourhood quality factors that influence residential property values include: (a) exposure to adverse environmental factors; (b) neighbourhood amenities; (c) perceived levels of neighbourhood security etc. Depending on the presence or absence of these amenities, residential properties may reduce or increase in value (Gallimore et al., 1996a).

Adverse environmental factors are those factors that impact negatively on the health and comfort of the inhabitants within the neighbourhood. Such adverse environmental factors include traffic noise, air pollution, vibration, noise level, aesthetic and barrier effects (Wilhelmsson, 2002). These factors have a negative relationship with residential property values. That is, because such factors directly affect the health of people, if such factors are high within the neighbourhood, the health and comfort of the people will be greatly at risk and so people will not be willing to live in such places. They will only be willing to live there when they are compensated by paying less to live there. For example, Wilhelmsson (2002) empirically examines the effect that traffic noise has on single-family houses in the Stockholm Municipality and finds that a single-family house that values at SEK 975,000 would be sold for SEK 650,000 if the property is located on or near a very noisy road. Traffic noise in this case reduces single-family property values by as much as 30%. Other empirical studies that have examined the effects of such environmental attributes on house prices and estimated the willingness-to-pay (WTP) for negative externalities include Hughes and Sirmans (1993) and Palmquist (1992). Similarly, positive environmental factors like clear air, good weather conditions etc. also affect property prices positively.

Neighbourhood amenities are the necessary services and attractions within the neighbourhood that make life easy and comfortable for the inhabitants. These amenities make living in a particular neighbourhood more satisfactory than other areas. A good neighbourhood has such amenities as the availability of schools, hospitals, shopping facilities, leisure facilities, road and other transportation networks. If a particular site generally has good and high levels of amenities, then it will be a more pleasant place to live than other sites with less amenities. Naturally, if a property is located in a neighbourhood with a higher amenity level, it becomes more desirable and valuable than one located in a neighbourhood with fewer amenities, all other things being equal. This is because if a neighbourhood has an amenity like good schools, children around the neighbourhood will not have to travel to other neighbourhoods to get to school. This will save time and resources for the parents as well since they do not have to pay extra for such services. The level of amenity in a neighbourhood is obviously a qualitative factor. It can therefore be determined subjectively by different individuals. Even though it cannot be measured directly, its value can be measured (Brigham, 1965).

The perceived levels of security in a neighbourhood also determine the quality of the neighbourhood (Gallimore et al., 1996b). What determines such perceived security levels include factors such as the level of crime, number of drug users in that neighbourhood etc. If there is low level of crime and drug users in a neighbourhood for instance, coupled with the presence of the police, the security level will be high and the individuals within the neighbourhood will live in comfort and peace. Property values in such neighbourhoods will therefore be higher than other neighbourhoods with less security. This is because, all things being equal, consumers are more willing to pay a premium for areas with higher security because of safety and comfort than for neighbourhoods with less perceived safety and comfort.

To sum up, if a particular neighbourhood is of a relatively higher quality, has many amenities like schools, hospitals, has less adverse environmental indicators like traffic noise and has a higher level of security, the demand for properties within that neighbourhood is expected to be high. This is because, all other things being equal, people prefer to live in places where there are high levels of amenities, high security levels and less adverse environmental factors. With the high demand of properties within that neighbourhood and supply remaining the same, the residential property values in that neighbourhood would rise. Neighbourhood quality therefore has a great impact on the values of residential properties.

Accessibility

Easy and convenient accessibility within a neighbourhood will determine the price of properties within a particular neighbourhood. Such accessibility measures involve property proximity to shops, desirable supporting facilities such as transportation, place of employment, shopping and leisure facilities etc. Generally, locations that afford relatively easy access to various desirable activities have higher property values than locations that do not have such easy access. Accessibility also relates to the convenience of moving people and goods from one site to the other by overcoming the use of time and cost. Brigham (1965: 326) notes that

> *if transportation were instantaneous and costless, then the urban population could spread out over all usable space.*

In this case, all property locations will have approximately the same value if all other factors are held constant. Since transportation is not instantaneous and involves cost, how easily and conveniently people can have travel to their place of work, recreational and social services will determine the value to pay for a particular location. Transportation services vary widely among various locations with areas that offer easier access to bus lines, freeways etc. having more accessibility value and hence higher property values than other areas with a lack of such bus lines and roads, for example. That is, social facilities should be close enough to be convenient, but not so close to become a nuisance to the quiet enjoyment of living amenities.

To examine the effect of accessibility on house prices, the most common approach is to include a distance variable from the central business district (CBD). This process of specifying accessibility effect on house prices implicitly assumes that location is monocentric (McCluskey et al., 2000). Indeed, the traditional monocentral model has predicted that properties that are closest to the city centre must have the highest value. This is a good predictor of land values when cities develop around a central port. This is because businesses that are located near the city centre or central port will pay less to move goods to and from the central port.

Again, before the introduction of modern transportation systems, most people preferred to live close to work. Businesses and residential users therefore competed for the limited central space and so increased the demand for land in the city centre. However, crime and congestion at the city centre have made people relocate to the suburbs. The increasing rate of people at the suburbs has made

Table 4.2 Neighbourhood and accessibility variables used in previous studies

Authors	Study area	Variables used
Palmquist (1980)	Washington, USA	Distance to nearest park, location to highway, access to recreational facilities
Case and Quigley (1991)	Hawaii, USA	Distance to shore
Rosiers and Theriault (1992)	Canada	Distance to highway exists, major work places, parks, primary schools, regional and neighbourhood shopping centres, welfare housing
Garrod and Willis (1992)	Britain	Approximate distance from nearest urban centre, post office and schools, the presence of pub, post office, river, canal etc.
Adair et al. (1996)	Ireland	Aggregate accessibility index
So et al. (1997)	Hong Kong	Walking distance to bus stations, availability of car parks, car sport facilities, shopping centre and swimming pool
McCluskey et al. (2000)	Northern Ireland	X and Y coordinates
Bateman et al. (2001)	Glasgow, Scotland	Neighbourhood variables like people who own cars, unemployment rate, number of young families, people who do not own property etc.
Frew and Wilson (2002)	Portland, USA	Distance to city centre, highway and highway intersection
Bourassa et al. (2003)	New Zealand	Distance to CBD and neighbourhood variables like population densities, % of unemployed, rooms per house, ethnic composition, % of people who receive support, homeownership rate etc.
Day (2003)	Glasgow, Scotland	Straight line distance to city centre, car travel time, walking distance
Wilhelmsson (2004)	Stockholm, Sweden	Distance from CBD
Rodriguez and Targa (2004)	Colombia	Shortest walking time to nearest BRT station, travel time to CBD, and other railway stations
Gibbons and Machin (2005)	London, UK	Straight line distance to nearest railway station
Bourassa et al. (2006)	New Zealand	Distance from CBD and distance from subcentre
Dehring and Dunse (2006)	Aberdeen, Scotland	Proximity to urban parks
Owusu-Ansah (2013)	Aberdeen, Scotland	X and Y coordinates

many retailers move to the suburbs to meet the requirement of their customers who moved. Other activities such as restaurants, shopping centres and entertainment centres can now be found at the suburbs as well. These trends have now made land at the suburbs valuable and have therefore reduced the attention on and the value of land in the city centre. Therefore, the relationship between land value and its proximity to the city centre have now changed. Such complexities indicate that using the distance of a house to the city centre or points of reference will reduce the model's ability to predict property values (see Hoyt, 1938; Harris and Ullmann, 1945; Frew and Wilson, 2002). The existence of such sub-centres therefore makes the multi-centre model more appropriate than the monocentric model (Dubin and Sung, 1987). Generally, therefore, support facilities should be close enough to be convenient, but not so close to become a nuisance to the quiet enjoyment of everyday amenities.

Figure 4.1 summarises the main property attributes that determine the value of properties and so need to be included in hedonic models.

Neighbourhoods within the geographical area may appreciate at substantially different rates. As a result of this, there is the need to apply methods that can model location in flexible and finely grained spatial detail. The ideal method

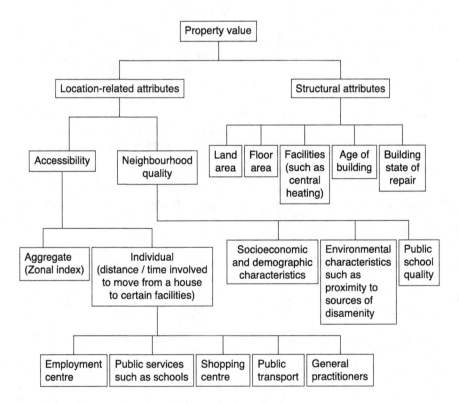

Figure 4.1 The property value tree by Kauko (2002)

therefore would be the application of a nonparametric model, as in the case of Meese and Wallace (1991), or a semi-parametric model as in the case of Clapp (2004). While the nonparametric models enable both the housing and locational influences on house prices to vary across space and time, the semi-parametric model permits the locational influences on house prices to be estimated in a flexible and continuous manner that enables it to also vary across space and time. In this book, however, parametric models are implemented. The reasons for implementing parametric models are two-fold – first, the parametric approach dominates the literature on the modelling of house prices and especially on the construction of house price indices. Therefore, in order to be consistent with the literature, this approach is used. Secondly, it is easy to estimate and interpret the estimated coefficients using the parametric approach and also easier for people to understand as compared to the nonparametric and semi-parametric approaches (Anglin and Gencay, 1996).

McCluskey and Borst (2007) identify five ways of modelling the locational effect on house prices. These are:

i   Neighbourhood delineation variable which is very common in mass appraisals. When neighbourhoods are delineated, a binary variable indicating neighbourhoods is included in the model to capture the neighbourhood effect.

ii Accessibility measures such as "distance to" important economic centres as discussed above. Table 2.2 shows that neighbourhood and accessibility measures seem to be the most popular way of modelling location. However, when the quality of the data obtained for some of these variables are in doubt, they may not be appropriate for empirical modelling.

iii Advanced model specification methods such as models with spatially varying parameters and spatial autocorrelation models. Studies that have considered advanced model specification like spatial autocorrelation include Figueroa (1999), Pace et al. (1998) and Dubin (1992).

iv Market segmentation which is based on the premise that two or more models are "better" than one overall model. There is a debate among housing researchers as to whether a housing market should be modelled as a single market or as a series of submarkets, and to whether spatial elements are important to be considered. Submarkets can be seen as the existence of the identification of significant price differences between the same property characteristics in a defined geographical area (Adair et al., 1996). Maclennan et al. (1998) note that understanding and considering the issue of submarkets allow housing planners to explore the geographical pattern of the housing market with regards to pressured markets. Submarket modelling also prevents the problems of non-linearity and interaction commonly associated with the housing markets (Adair et al., 1996). The market segmentation procedure may be either "spatially-based" or "characteristics-based" (McCluskey and Borst, 2007: 315). A lot of studies have been conducted on market segmentation and include White et al. (2009), Bourassa et al. (2007), Adair et al.

(1996) and Can (1990), and in the UK, through studies such as Fletcher et al. (2004) and Ball and Kirwan (1977).

v   Explicit use of location where linear, quadratic, cubic or higher order terms of the X and Y coordinates as well as their cross products like Y, X^2Y, XY^2, and X^2Y^2. The use of cubic function of the X and Y coordinates is the approach used for modelling location in this book. This approach, even though not as flexible as the nonparametric or semi-parametric models, allows the marginal price of the housing attributes to vary in a continuous manner (Jones and Casetti, 1992). This approach, however, can put restrictions on the pattern of spatial variation and peaks from area to area. Also, the presence of particular kinds of boundaries such as major communication routes and geographical barriers may lead to discontinuities in land values. Nevertheless, it has some flexibility and avoids averaging house prices over discrete geographic boundaries as is the case in the use of neighbourhood dummies, for instance (Can, 1990).

Hedonic modelling and functional form selection

The parametric, nonparametric and the semi-parametric hedonic approaches have been discussed in this chapter. The empirical hedonic modelling in this book follows the parametric approach and so it is important to discuss the functional form selection in this chapter. Functional form selection is one of the key issues in hedonic price modelling. The choice of functional form selected for a study has a great effect on the regression results. Graves et al. (1988) for instance note that their estimated parameters change significantly when the functional forms are changed. Economic theory provides little guidance and puts few restrictions on the functional form to use (Cropper et al., 1988; Anglin and Gencay, 1996; Tu, 2003) and as a result, researchers have employed and examined so many types of functional forms in hedonic price analysis (Basu and Thibodeau, 1998).

The functional forms are many and include:

Level-level model: This is where both the dependent and independent variables are expressed in levels. That is one unit increase in X increases price, Pt by $\beta 1$.

$$P_t = \beta_0 + \beta_1 X \qquad (4.17)$$

Log-level model: This is also known as the semi-logarithm model, where the dependent variable is transformed as a natural logarithm but the independent variables are untransformed

$$\ln P_t = \beta_0 + \beta_1 X \qquad (4.18)$$

Level-log model: This is where the dependent variable is expressed in absolute terms and the independent variables are transformed as natural logarithms

$$P_t = \beta_0 + \ln \beta_1 X \qquad (4.19)$$

Log-log model: With this, both the dependent and independent variables are transformed as natural logarithms

$$\ln P_t = \beta_0 + \ln \beta_1 \qquad\qquad (4.20)$$

Box and Cox (1964) have developed a statistical test for the functional form providing the "best fit" based on likelihood ratio tests and some studies now employ this in choosing the functional form. This is to consider the non-linearity aspect of housing. The formal Box-Cox model has already been presented in this chapter. The Box-Cox methodology has been used in studies by Goodman (1978), Linneman (1980), Bloomquist and Worley (1981), Halvorsen and Pollakowski (1981), Eberts and Gronberg (1982) and Cassel and Mendelsohn (1985). In comparing the linear functional forms with the Box-Cox transformation, Goodman (1978) rejects the linear functional forms. He notes that the linear functional form is "overly restrictive" and so the Box-Cox transformation provides a better estimate than the linear functional forms. Halvorsen and Pollakowski (1981) also recommend the use of a Box-Cox transformation. Cassel and Mendelsohn (1985) also note that the Box-Cox functional form is attractive when the goodness of fit criterion is used. However, the fact that the best fit criterion is used to choose a functional form does not necessarily mean that the regression estimates are more accurate. Particularly, they note that the accuracy of the Box-Cox estimates is reduced when the number of coefficients to be estimated is extremely large.

Selecting best functional form is however important when one wants to interpret individual implicit prices for the housing characteristics. This is because if the functional form is inappropriate, the estimated implicit prices will also be biased. For index construction, functional form selection is of less importance. This is because the overall prediction can be still unbiased even if all the estimates are biased (Wooldridge, 2009). The housing characteristics observed in the dataset for the empirical analysis are only discrete and so only the dependent variable is transformed (log price). This decision is also supported by previous index construction studies (see for example Wilhelmsson, 2009; Leishman and Watkins, 2002; Meese and Wallace, 1997), which have chosen the semi-logarithm functional form. The advantages of the semi-logarithm functional form over the other functional forms have been stressed in a lot of studies. Follain and Malpezzi (1980) particularly emphasise that the semi-logarithmic form makes interpretation of the regression coefficients easy – as the percentage change in the price given a unit change in the housing attribute; allows for variations in the currency value of each housing characteristic; and finally helps to minimise the problem of heteroskedasticity. For index construction, estimating the regression equation in semi-log form and including the intercept make it possible to interpret the parameter estimates concerning the time dummies as marginal changes.

Main sources of hedonic problems

The main source of hedonic problems includes heteroskedasticity, multicollinearity and omitted variable bias (Greene, 2000). These problems could cause a substantial portion of price variability to be unexplained by the model. Clear understanding of these problems, their causes, how to identify them in hedonic models and how to deal with them are imperative in hedonic pricing models.

Heteroskedasticity

Much research has been done on the existence of heteroskedasticity in multiple regression analysis (see for example White, 1980; Robinson, 1987; Fletcher et al., 2000a; Stevenson, 2004). That is, when the variance of the error or disturbance term of the hedonic model changes across different segments of the population, then the homoskedasticity assumption made on multiple regressions fails, and this gives rise to a phenomenon called heteroskedasticity (Hendry, 1995). Heteroskedasticity also arises when the variance of the error term is unequal (Fletcher et al., 2000a).

It should be noted that the homoskedasticity assumption is needed to justify the usual t and F tests, as well as the confidence intervals for OLS estimation of the multiple linear regression model. The failure of the homoskedasticity assumption however does not affect the unbiasedness of OLS regression estimates and so the presence of heteroscedasticity does not cause bias or inconsistency in the OLS estimators of the coefficients. However, such estimates cannot be efficient since their variances are no longer minimised. In this case, inferences cannot be made since the standard errors and for that matter the t- and F-statistics are invalid (Fletcher et al., 2000a). The problem may however be minimised if a large sample size is used (Greene, 2000). Heteroskedasticity can lead to both changes in the estimated standard errors of the coefficients and changes to the value of the coefficients themselves (Stevenson, 2004; Robinson, 1987).

Heteroskedasticity is commonly present when cross-sectional data is used for the hedonic analysis even though it can happen in time series data as well (Fletcher et al., 2004; Nguyen and Cripps, 2001). A lot of studies, such as Goodman and Thibodeau (1997), Goodman and Thibodeau (1995), Fletcher et al. (2000a) and Stevenson (2004), have been done to explore the causes of heteroskedasticity in hedonic models. Hendry (1995) groups the causes of heteroskedasticity into two main groups: statistical sources and economic behaviour of sample sources. Apart from these, the characteristics of the sample used for the analysis can also cause heteroskedasticity (Fletcher et al., 2000a). The statistical sources include variables omitted from the model, model specification, measurement errors and outliers. Fletcher et al. (2000a) particularly note that significant results from heteroskedasticity tests are sometimes an indication of model specification.

Fletcher et al. (2000a) also note that outliers in the model can spuriously show as heteroskedasticity. The use of inappropriate functional form can also cause heteroskedasticity. A typical example of the economic behaviour of a sample source of heteroskedasticity is the bargaining power of housing consumers. If the houses within a given sample are purchased by consumers who have high bargaining power, there is a high possibility for the house prices to be lower than they ought to be. Therefore, the variances would be higher and this could cause a more serious heteroskedasticity problem (Harding et al., 2003). The major property characteristic that has been found as a major cause of heteroskedasticity in economic models is age (Goodman and Thibodeau, 1997; Fletcher et al., 2000a; Stevenson, 2004). Fletcher et al. (2000a) again find that in addition to age, the external area of the property is a major cause of heteroskedasticity in hedonic models. They note that if houses become larger and larger, the differences in fittings, fixtures and designs also become larger and this can give rise to a greater spread of prices, which is heteroskedasticity.

Various tests are suggested in the literature to test for heteroskedasticity in hedonic models but none of them is accepted as a standard test (Stewart and Gill, 1998). The tests that have been mostly used include the Park Test (Park, 1966), the Glejser Test (Glejser, 1969), the Breusch-Pagan Test (Breusch and Pagan, 1979), the White Test (White, 1980) and the Goldfeld-Quandt Test (Goldfeld and Quandt, 1965). Greene (2000) also mentions the Likelihood Ration test as a means of testing for groupwise heteroskedasticity. Even though heteroskedasticity will not affect the index numbers to be estimated as noted above, the heteroskedasticity-robust procedure is used to adjust the standard errors and make the t and F statistics valid for inferences.

Multicollinearity

Multicollinearity is when two or more of the explanatory variables in a multiple regression model are very highly correlated. When the explanatory variables are highly correlated, they would be explaining the same thing and it becomes very difficult to determine the independent variable that is actually producing the effect on the independent variable (Wooldridge, 2009). According to Wilhelmsson (2000), multicollinearity describes a condition in the explanatory variables that occurs when multiple linear dependencies are present among the variables. One of the assumptions of the OLS is that in both the sample drawn and the population, none of the independent variables should be constant, and that there should be no exact linear relationships among them. The presence of multicollinearity violates the OLS assumption. More commonly, the issue of multicollinearity arises when there is a high degree of correlation (either positive or negative) between two or more independent variables. Even though perfect multicollinearity is very uncommon, the occurrence of imperfect multicollinearity is very common (Greene, 2000). A very typical example is number of rooms and floor area. All other things being equal, if the number of rooms increases, the floor area will also increase.

To the extent that the multicollinearity problem exists, the estimated regression coefficients may not be uniquely determined and the relative importance of the variables as indicated by the partial regression coefficients would be less reliable. The presence of multicollinearity only affects the calculations regarding individual predictors. The standard errors tend to be greater as multicollinearity gets greater, and the confidence intervals for the coefficients become very wide (Wooldridge, 2009). Rejecting a null hypothesis tends to be harder when multicollinearity is present. The predictive power or the reliability of the model as a whole is not affected by the presence of multicollinearity. Even when extreme multicollinearity exists, OLS estimates will still be the best linear unbiased estimators (Wooldridge, 2009). In the presence of multicollinearity also, the coefficient estimates may change inconsistently when there is a small change in the model or the data.

There are several ways in which the presence of multicollinearity in hedonic models can be detected. Firstly, if there are large changes in the estimated regression coefficients after an explanatory variable is dropped or added, then it is an indication of the presence of multicollinearity. Again, the sample can be randomly divided into two and analysed to see the stability of the coefficients if a different sub-sample is used. If there are dramatic changes in the coefficients, then the problem of multicollinearity is present. Also, one can examine the bivariate correlations between the independent variables. There may be the likelihood of the presence of multicollinearity when there are high correlation values. However, the magnitude of the correlation values is not well established in the literature (Wooldridge, 2009).

Omitted variable bias

Omitted variable bias is one common problem associated with the hedonic pricing model (Wilhelmsson, 2009). More often, it becomes very difficult to collect data on all the quality characteristics of the properties. In the case of the housing sector, some of the housing characteristics may be left out of the model and so the model will become biased (Hoesli and MacGregor, 2000). Omitted variable bias occurs in hedonic models when the specification of the hedonic model omits an independent variable that should have been in the model. For such bias to occur, the true regression coefficient of the variable that is omitted must not be zero and the omitted variable must be correlated with one or more of the independent variables included in the model (Greene, 2000). If the omitted variable bias exists then it means that the model is poorly specified and so the estimated parameters are likely to be biased.

If we include a variable in the specification that does not belong, there will be no effect on the parameter estimate, and so the OLS model will remain unbiased. However, even with the inclusion of dozens of independent variables in the model, the exclusion of even a single important explanatory variable will cause bias in the model (Greene, 2000). If the correlations between the omitted variable and the dependent variable, and between the omitted variable and any of the independent variables are in the same direction (either positive or negative), the bias will be positive. This means that the coefficient estimate of the included correlated variable will be high. However, if the correlations are in different directions, then the bias will be negative (Wooldridge, 2009). For example, if living area and lot size are positively correlated, and living area is positively correlated with price and is excluded from the model, the positive effect from the large living area will appear in the coefficient estimate of the lot size. The problem of omitted variable bias is also noted by Garrod and Willis (1992) and Wilhelmsson

(2002). According to Wilhelmsson (2002), omitted variable bias is very common in real estate regression models because real estate transaction varies in location and including all attributes in real estate regression models is almost not possible.

There is no known procedure to deal with the problem of omitted variable bias in hedonic models and in this study, effort will be made to include all important variables that are available in the dataset.

The reasons for using a hedonic model can be summed up, according to Maclennan (1977) as follows:

- To explain statistically the apparent determinants of house prices in static, cross-section, usually in aggregative studies.
- To determine statistically the relative importance of various elements, such as environmental or internal characteristics, in the house price regression equation, or to demonstrate how this equation varies over colour or income groups.
- To derive demand functions for housing.
- To test, indirectly, alternative theories of residential location.

The application of the hedonic method in this book is to construct house price indices. Thus, the first two purposes of hedonic modelling outlined by Maclennan above are more relevant in this book. The four main methods of house price index construction to be discussed are the average method, the hedonic method, the repeat-sales method and the hybrid method.

Conclusion

Hedonic pricing models have been extensively used in housing research and the simple parametric models seem to be the most well-known and the most commonly employed methods. The three broad hedonic modelling approaches, the parametric, nonparametric and semi-parametric approaches have been identified and discussed in this chapter. The advantages and problems in using each of the approaches have also been identified. The three broad approaches the hedonic pricing can be modelled; the parametric approach, the nonparametric approach and the semi-parametric approach are discussed. The parametric approach assumes the regression curve has a pre-specified functional form which is fully described by a finite set of parameters. The parametric models considered in this paper include the log-linear OLS model, the Box-Cox OLS model and the weighted least square models. The chapter shows that the WLS reduces the problem of heteroskedasticity which is a major problem in parametric models. The parametric approach has the advantage of accurately estimating and interpreting the model. Its major demerit is that when the assumptions underlying the model are violated, the model may give a misleading picture of the regression relationship. The nonparametric avoids specifying the regression function in advance and so prevents the strong assumptions underlying the parametric approach. The model is, however, criticised for its "curse of dimensionality" problem which makes the estimates inaccurate if the number of regressors is large. Again, it is very technical and complex and in computing the estimates and this makes it uncomfortable for most modellers in using the method. Some of the nonparametric models discussed include the kernel method, the nearest neighbour estimate and the local polynomial regression. The semi-parametric approach combines elements of the parametric and the nonparametric approaches. This approach has the advantage of reducing the problems associated with the parametric and the nonparametric approaches but at the same time maintain the advantages they possess. The hybrid approach has the advantage of making the estimate easy to interpret. It also reduces the "curse of dimensionality" problem because it reduces the number of regressors which enter into nonparametric part. The technical computational problem and some of the underlying assumptions of the parametric approach are however still present, though they are reduced.

The final and obvious question to ask from the above discussion is, "does the choice of the model depend on the advantages and the disadvantages of the model?" The answer is not necessarily yes. No particular approach is necessarily superior to the other. The nature and objective of the particular housing analysis to be done determine to a large extent the model to be employed. This is noted by Mertens (2003) and Creswell (2003, 2007) who generalised that the type of methodology to be employed in research depends on the research objectives and research questions and not on the merits or otherwise of a particular research approach.

5 Property price index construction methods

Introduction

This chapter provides an overview of the various house price index construction methods. These methods are the average method, the hedonic method, the repeat-sales method and the hybrid method. The various methods and models to be discussed are presented in Table 5.1. The second section covers the average index construction method, with the advantages and disadvantages inherent in using the method. In the third section, the hedonic method is described. The two variations of the hedonic price index construction method, the explicit time variable and strictly cross-sectional, are presented and discussed in this section. Finally, the advantages and disadvantages of using the hedonic method to construct house price indices are also discussed in this section.

The fourth section presents the repeat-sales methods of house price index construction. The unweighted or original repeat-sales (ORS) and the weighted repeat-sales (WRS) methods are discussed, as well as the advantages and disadvantages of using the repeat-sales method to construct house price indices. In the fifth section, the hybrid methods of constructing house price indices are presented. Notably, the methods proposed by Case and Quigley (1991), Quigley (1995), Hill et al. (1997) and Englund et al. (1998) are all discussed. The relative advantages and disadvantages of using the hybrid method are also discussed in this section. The sixth section compares the various house index construction methods based on previous empirical findings. It identifies and summarises the findings from some previous house price index construction studies and uses them to compare the various house price index methods. The absence of the appropriate proxy for the "true" unobservable house price trend and the issue of temporal aggregation are also briefly discussed. These two issues are of particular importance since they may influence or determine the accuracy of the various index methods. The seventh section concludes the chapter.

The average method

The average method is the simplest way of constructing house price indices. Even though it is sometimes ignored, the starting point of the method is to define a homogeneous segment of the market. Usually, a property type like a flat or a

Table 5.1 The various hedonic methods and models

	Methods	Models
Quality-adjusted	Hedonic regression	– Explicit time-variable
		– Strictly cross-sectional
	Repeat-sales	– Ordinary repeat-sales
		– Weighted repeat-sales
	Hybrid	– Case and Quigley's (1991)
		– Quigley's (1995)
		– Hill, Knight and Sirman's (1997)
		– Englund, Quigley and Redfearn's (1998)
Non-quality-adjusted	Average	– Mean
		– Median

detached house can be considered in a city or in a region. Definition of the market segment is very important because the property market is very heterogeneous. Therefore, defining a narrow segment will help to reduce the heterogeneity in the market by separating flats, for instance, from detached houses in the market. After defining the market segments, data would have to be collected on the transaction prices of the properties which have been sold during each time increment. If a monthly index is to be constructed, then the transaction prices have to be collected on a monthly basis. For quarterly indices also, the prices are collected for each quarter etc. When this data is available, then the average price per period or for each time increment can easily be computed. There are two ways of computing the average price per period. These are the mean method and the median method.

The mean price per period is also calculated by dividing the sum of all the transaction prices per period by the number of properties sold per period. Mathematically, the mean price for each period is computed as follows:

$$\overline{P}_t = \frac{1}{N_t}\sum\nolimits_{n=1}^{N_t} P_{t,n} \tag{5.1}$$

where

- $\overline{P}_t$ is the mean price at period t
- $\Sigma P_{t,n}$ is the sum of prices of properties sold in period t
- N_t is the number of observations at period t

The median price on the other hand refers to the average price indicated by the middle value or values in the house price series at period t. If N_t is odd, the median price is simply the central/middle value. However, if N_t is even, then the median price is the mean of the two central values. The index can then be simply constructed on the basis of the average price (whether mean or median) per period already computed. In doing this the first period's average price is normalised to 100 and the changes in the index series are computed based on this first period's average price.

Advantages and disadvantages of the average method

The average house price index method is easy to construct. The method does not require any technical regression specifications. The method also requires less data for its implementation. Only the transaction prices, selling dates and in some cases the living area per square metre or number of bedrooms, as the case may be, are needed to estimate the index numbers.

However, the method does not take account of the fact that the housing market is heterogeneous and that different types of properties are transacted at different periods. For example, detached houses are different from flats, and houses with garages are different from similar houses without garages. These differences influence the price paid for each property. These differences and the fact that housing characteristics can change over time are not controlled for by using the average method. The lack of standardisation or a constant-quality attribute of house price indices is therefore the main drawback of the average method of index construction.

The hedonic method

The hedonic method can be used to construct house price indices by employing two main models. These are the explicit time variable hedonic model and the strictly cross-sectional hedonic model.

Explicit time variable hedonic index (ETV) model

The explicit time variable model groups all the data for adjacent time periods and then includes discrete time periods as independent variables. Thus, the implicit prices of housing and the coefficients of time-dummy variables are estimated using a single equation. The estimation is done by regressing the natural logarithm of the selling price on a constant, the period (example quarterly) time dummies and a number of independent variables available for the analysis. The model is represented by the equation below.

$$ln P_{nt} = \beta_0 + \sum_{j=1}^{J} \beta_j X_{jnt} + \sum_{t=1}^{T} c_t D_{nt} + e_{nt} \tag{5.2}$$

where

- $ln P_{nt}$ is the log of the transacted price for property n at time t ($n = 1,..., N$);
- c_t is a scaler of estimated coefficients for the time-dummy variables t ($t = 1,...,T$), with values of 1 if the nth house is sold in period t and 0 otherwise;

- β_0 is constant and β_0 is a vector of estimated coefficients for the nth property and its J characteristics $X_{,nt}$ $(j=1,...,J)$. The property characteristics such as the number of bedrooms, the number of public rooms, the number of floors, the number of bathrooms, garden, garage, condition of the property as well as the locational attributes such as the geocodes are all components of $X_{,nt}$; and
- e_{nt} is the transaction specific random error with mean of 0 and variance σ_e^2.

From Equation 5.2, the house price index is derived from the estimated coefficients, c_t of the time-dummy variables. The estimated coefficients, $c_1,...,c_{T_i}$ are ordered chronologically and they represent the log of the cumulative price index over the time period, T. The first-time dummy variable is usually omitted from the regression equation because it serves as the base period and, therefore, there is no estimated coefficient for it. Including it together with β_0 will cause perfect collinearity. The value for the first-time dummy variable is usually represented by zero and so the cumulative price index starts from 100 in the first-time period.

The model assumes that the single regression equation for all observations from all time periods is able to hold the implicit prices of physical and locational attributes constant over time. However, this assumption might not be the case. For example, the presence of two bedrooms may have more influence on house prices in 1994 than it did in 1989 (Costello and Watkins, 2002).

Strictly cross-sectional hedonic index (SCS) model

The strictly cross-sectional hedonic model is an alternative to the explicit time variable hedonic model and helps to deal with the potential biases which are associated with the latter as a result of the potential changes to the implicit house price attributes over time. With this model, the implicit characteristic prices are estimated in a separate hedonic regression for each time period thereby allowing the implicit attribute prices to vary over time (Gatzlaff and Ling, 1994). That is, the same regression equation is used to run a separate regression at each period using each period's cross-sectional data.

This model uses a similar functional form like the one illustrated above. However, the time dummies are excluded from the equation because a new regression is run for each period using the same equation. This equation is presented below:

$$\ln P_{nt} = \beta_0 + \sum_{j=1}^{J} \beta_j X_{jnt} + e_{nt} \tag{5.3}$$

where all the notations are as above.

In order to construct the index from the above equation, a chronologically ordered set of houses is estimated for a given bundle of characteristics using each of the cross-sectional models. Thus, using the same set of housing and locational characteristics for a "hypothetical house", a predicted transaction price (in log) is obtained for each period. Since the regression equation is estimated using the semi-logarithm functional form, we take the exponent of the predicted log prices to be the absolute predicted prices.

The differences between these predicted prices at each period are used to construct the index numbers (Meese and Wallace, 1997). When the initial or base period's set of housing and locational characteristics are used as the weights to estimate the periodic house prices, it is called the Laspeyres price index. The Laspeyres price index (*LI*) for period t is thus:

$$LI_t = \frac{exp\left\{\sum_{j=1}^{J} \beta_{jt} \times X_{jo}\right\}}{exp\left\{\sum_{j=1}^{J} \beta_{jo} \times X_{jo}\right\}} \tag{5.4}$$

However, when the current period characteristics are used, it is called the Paasche price index. The Laspeyres price index (*PI*) for period t is thus:

$$LI_t = \frac{exp\left\{\sum_{j=1}^{J} \beta_{jt} \times X_{jt}\right\}}{exp\left\{\sum_{j=1}^{J} \beta_{jo} \times X_{jt}\right\}} \tag{5.5}$$

Advantages and disadvantages of the hedonic index method

One clear advantage of the hedonic method is that it corrects for the effects of heterogeneity of properties by taking the characteristics of the properties into consideration. The resulting indices are therefore able to monitor price changes in a reliable manner.

One major disadvantage of the hedonic method is omitted variable bias (Meese and Wallace, 1997). This bias occurs when important physical or locational variables are omitted from the analysis. The problem becomes more pronounced when the implicit prices of unobserved attributes change over time. In this case, the estimated hedonic indices will give a misleading impression as to constant-quality house price changes over time (Goetzmann and Spiegel, 1997). Another criticism of the hedonic price index method is the extensive dataset required to implement the method. The implementation of the method requires an extensive dataset of house price observations together with the details on the physical and locational attributes of the properties concerned. It is extremely difficult and expensive, in terms of finance, time and other resources to collect a suitable dataset that will allow sufficiently robust hedonic model estimation suitable for the purpose of constructing house price indices (Leishman and Watkins, 2002; Owusu-Ansah, 2013).

With the single equation or explicit time variable (ETV) hedonic model, another source of bias is concerned with the critical assumption that the implicit physical and locational characteristics prices are constant over time. This assumption is however questionable since demand and supply factors that affect the property market are likely to change over time. To state it differently, the main difference between the two methods is that the single equation restricts the mean and variance of the error term to be identical across all time periods, while the strictly cross-sectional allows the mean and variance of the error term to vary (Bourassa et al., 2006; Owusu-Ansah and Abdulai, 2014). The former model therefore has the potential problem of heteroskedasticity (Goetzmann and Spiegel, 1997).

The repeat-sales method

One of the criticisms of the hedonic method is that it is difficult to collect all the information about the physical and locational characteristics of a transacted house. Omitted variable bias may therefore affect the results. The repeat-sales method avoids this problem by confining the analysis to properties which have been sold at least twice in the sample (Bailey et al., 1963). Each of the observations of the dataset describes the transaction price of the first and the second sale, and the transaction dates, for a given house. Assuming the physical state of the house remains the same between the sales, then the witnessed house price change can be assumed to be due wholly to constant-quality price appreciation or depreciation. The method does not rely on the inclusion of physical and locational attribute variables in the regression equation in estimating the constant-quality price indices.

The repeat-sales method is a variant of the hedonic model with the only difference that the hedonic characteristics are excluded because they are assumed to be the same between the time periods (Costello and Watkins, 2002). There are two basic variations of the repeat-sales method. These are the original repeat-sales (ORS) model proposed by Bailey et al. (1963) and the weighted repeat-sales (WRS) model proposed by Case and Shiller (1987, 1989).

The original repeat-sales (ORS) model

This model regresses the ratio of the logarithm of the second sale price to the first sale price on a set of dummy variables corresponding with the time periods using the ordinary least squares (OLS) regression to get the index. The model uses only properties that have been sold at least twice over the study period. Mathematically, the model is illustrated by Equation 5.6:

$$\ln\left(\frac{P_{nt}}{P_{n\tau}}\right) = \Sigma c_t D_{nt} + e_{n\tau t} \tag{5.6}$$

where

- $\dfrac{P_{nt}}{P_{n\tau}}$ is the price relative to property n sold in t and before that in t;

- D_{nt} is a dummy variable which equals -1 at the time of the initial (first) sale in period, τ, 1 at the time of the subsequent sale in period t and 0 otherwise;
- c_t is the logarithm of the cumulative price index in period t; and
- $e_{n\tau t} = e_{nt} - e_{n\tau}$ is the error term.

Like the ETV hedonic model, the first-time dummy variable is usually omitted from the regression equation because it serves as the base period and also avoids perfect collinearity among the time dummies. Therefore, there is no estimated coefficient for it. The value for the first-time dummy variable is usually represented by zero and so the cumulative price index therefore starts from 100 in the first time period.

Case and Shiller (1987) indicate that the influence of varying holding periods between transactions can cause heteroskedasticity. This is the case because the holding periods are not usually uniformly distributed through the sample period for the repeat-sales data. As Costello and Watkins (2002) note, normally short holding periods are under-represented in the beginning and end periods of the index and this will induce heteroskedasticity by affecting the second moments of the regression disturbances. Case and Shiller (1987, 1989) propose the weighted repeat-sales method as a way of dealing with the heteroskedasticity problem associated with the original repeat-sales model.

The weighted repeat-sales (WRS) model

This weighted repeat-sales method takes into account the fact that house prices will generally increase over time, which induces heteroskedasticity into the model. Following Case and Shiller (1989), assume that the log price of the nth house at time t, P_{nt}, is given by:

$$\ln P_{nt} = I_t + H_{nt} + U_{nt} \tag{5.7}$$

where I_t, is the logarithm of the price level at time t, H_{nt} is a Gaussian random walk, such that

$$E(H_{nt} - H_{n\tau}) = 0 \tag{5.8}$$

$$E(H_{nt} - H_{n\tau})^2 = (t - \tau)\sigma^2 H \tag{5.9}$$

and U_{nt} is white noise, such that

$$E(U_{nt}) = 0 \tag{5.10}$$

$$E(U_{nt})^2 = \sigma_U^2 \tag{5.11}$$

The computation of house price indices by this model involves three steps. The first step of the three-step processes is to exactly follow the ORS procedure as shown above, and the residuals from the regression are estimated for use in the second step. Thus, estimate the regression Equation 5.6. From this equation, the estimated residuals, $(\hat{e}_{nt} - \hat{e}_{n\tau})$ are calculated.

In the second step, the squared residuals from Equation 5.6 $(\hat{e}_{nt} - \hat{e}_{n\tau})^2$ are calculated from the calculated residuals above and these are regressed on a constant and the time interval between sales or the holding periods $(t - t_{-1})$.

$$(\hat{e}_{nt} - \hat{e}_{n\tau})^2 = \alpha_0 + c_t(t - \tau) \tag{5.12}$$

yielding estimates of the variances $\hat{\sigma}_H^2$ and $\hat{\sigma}_U^2$

Lastly, Equation 5.6 is re-estimated by weighted least squares with diagonal elements $\sqrt{\hat{\sigma}_U^2 + (t - \tau)\hat{\sigma}_H^2}$. From this the index numbers are estimated in the same way as done for the ORS above.

Conscious effort must be taken when using properties that involve more than two transactions over the sample period. As Palmquist (1982) notes, when there are more than two transactions for each property and all possible pairs of trans-actions are included in the model, the error covariance matrix is nondiagonal and must be corrected. When there are three transactions for a given property for instance, only two of the three sets of pairs are independent. These are the pairs that involve the first and the second transactions, and the second and third transactions. The pair that consists of the first and the third transactions is not independent of the other two. In the same way, when there are four transactions for a given property, only three out of the possible six pairs are independent. These are the pairs involving the first and the second transactions, the second and the third transactions, and the third and the fourth transactions. The pairs con-sisting of the first and the third transactions, the first and the fourth transactions, and the second and the fourth transactions are not independent of the previous three pairs (Bourassa et al., 2006). To avoid the problem of a nondiagonal matrix of the error covariance therefore, only independent pairs of transactions should be used.

Another variant of the repeat-sales method is the study of Palmquist (1980). Palmquist's method uses the ORS method. However, the ratios of the first and second sales prices are adjusted for the depreciation in the period between the sales using the depreciation estimate from a hedonic result. He employs only the repeat-sales sample of data and so the data requirement is the same as the ORS method.

Another improvement to the original repeat-sales model apart from the weighted repeat-sales method by Case and Shiller (1989) is the hedonic repeated model developed by Shiller (1993). This method makes it possible to account for potential changes in house characteristics between the first and the second sales. In doing this, some hedonic characteristics are included in the traditional repeat-sales model. This method is advocated by Clapp and Giaccotto (1998), who use assessed values at the time of the first and second sales as a way of controlling for the quality of properties.

Advantages and disadvantages of the repeat-sales index method

Given the fact that the physical and locational attributes are not required in the estimation of the repeat-sales method, data is relatively easy and inexpensive to collect when employing the method. Indeed, the only essential data required for each property to be used for the repeat-sales index construction are the ini-tial sale price and sale date, property identity, as well as the subsequent sale price and sale date.

Also, the omitted variable bias problem associated with the hedonic regression method due to the possible exclusion of important hedonic variables is absent in the repeat-sales method when the weighted regression is used since such variables are not needed in the repeat-sales estimation. However, when the implicit prices change over time and the simple or original repeat-sales model is used, then the method will be biased since the ORS does not control for this.

One major problem associated with using the repeat-sales method in the construction of price indices is sample selection bias. The repeat-sales method may be susceptible to the characteristics of the sample of housing repeat-sales transactions used to estimate the index numbers for the population as a whole. According to Clapp and Giaccotto (1992a), datasets comprising only repeat-sale transactions are likely to be over-represented by frequently traded properties. It is normally the case that 'starter homes', which are relatively cheaper, sell more frequently due to the fact that younger homeowners usually upgrade more frequently. Also, the sample normally used to construct repeat-sales indices do not include "brand"-new constructions. This is the case because by its definition, a brand-new building cannot be a repeat sale unless it has probably been on-sold at completion (Costello and Watkins, 2002). Due to the influence of "starter" homes and "brand"-new properties in repeat-sale samples, the sample selection biases in repeat-sales can be either positive or negative.

The repeat-sales indices are also based on relatively small samples as compared to the hedonic regression indices. This is because the fraction of properties that are sold more than once in a sample is very likely to be small. For example, Mark and Goldberg (1984) find 40% of repeats over a 22-year period. Abraham and Schauman (1991) also find 2.5% of repeats over a 19-year interval. The repeat-sales data as a sample of all transactions is also only 8% in Case and Shiller (1989) who use a sample period of over 16 years. Case and Quigley (1991) mention that the sample size of repeats whose characteristics are unchanged is 33% in Palmquist's study, 4% in Case and Shiller's study in Atlanta and Chicago, 3% in Dallas and 7% in San Francisco. Clapp and Giaccotto (1992a) also note that as many as 97% of housing transactions are deleted if only instances of repeat sales are to be considered in their study. These findings clearly show smaller sample sizes with repeat-sales methods.

Furthermore, the repeat-sales method does not explicitly take account of the influence of depreciation on house prices. In using the method, it is assumed that no physical changes have occurred to a house between successive sales. Even if this is the case, the fact is that every house will have aged to some extent between the sales and so indices constructed with the repeat sales may understate house price appreciation (Clapp and Giaccotto, 1992a). Such indices can therefore be thought of as near constant-quality house price indices but not constant-quality due to the age effect between the sales (Leishman and Watkins, 2002).

The hybrid method

The third method often employed to construct house price indices is the hybrid method. The idea of the hybrid method is credited to the study of Case and Quigley (1991). The method works by combining elements of the hedonic and the repeat-sales method to estimate the index. With this method, all the transaction data, both single- and repeat-sales, are used to estimate the indices and so unlike the repeat sales, the sample size of the hybrid method is relatively large. Also, the inclusion of the physical and locational property characteristics in the repeat-sales method to estimate the hybrid method allows for the influence of depreciation on housing transaction prices to be estimated. A lot of improvements have been made to the Case and Quigley's (CQ-hybrid) model. These include the Quigley (Q-hybrid) model, the Hill, Knight and Sirmans (HKS-hybrid) model, and the Englund, Quigley and Redfearn (EQR-hybrid) model.

The Case and Quigley (CQ-hybrid) model

One of the earliest studies of the hybrid approach is the study by Case and Quigley (1991). The authors use three stacked equations that are applied to three different groups of trans- action data. The first equation is a hedonic equation that is applied to all single-sales. Assuming that the price of a property P_{nt}, varies with physical and locational property attributes, X, and assuming that the property values vary over time due to demand and the relative scarcity of X, then the property price of a transaction observed at time t, is

$$\ln P_{nt} = \sum_{n=1}^{J} \beta_{jt} X_{jnt} + e_{nt} \tag{5.13}$$

The second equation is applied to a repeat-sales sample whose characteristics are unchanged. If we observe two sales of a property at times t and τ, $t > \tau$, and the characteristics of the property remain the same during the interval $[t, \tau]$, then the selling price of the property at time t is

$$\ln P_{nt} = \ln P_{n\tau} + \sum_{n=\tau+1}^{J} \beta_{jt} X_{jnt} + e_{nt} \tag{5.14}$$

The third is also applied to a repeat-sales sample whose quality has changed between the first and the second sales. If we observe two sales of a property at time t and, $t > \tau$, and the characteristics of the property have changed from x to x^* at t^*, $\tau < t^* < t$, then the selling price of the property at time t is

$$\ln P_{nt} = \ln P_{n\tau} + \sum_{n=\tau+1}^{J} \beta_j X_{jnt} + \sum_{n=t^*}^{J} \beta_j X_{jnt}^* + e_{nt} \tag{5.15}$$

Case and Quigley (1991) note that the Equations 5.13, 5.14 and 5.15 provide alternative methods for estimating the parameters, and consistent estimates can actually be obtained from any of the three samples as long as the samples are random. However, if information is available for two or more samples, then the relevant equations can be estimated more efficiently by imposing the appropriate cross equation constraints. Mathematically, the three stacked equations are represented by Equation 5.16.

$$\begin{Bmatrix} \log P_{nt} \\ \log P_{nt}/P_{n\tau} \\ \log P_{nt}/P_{n\tau} \end{Bmatrix} = \beta(X_{nt}) + (\epsilon_{nt}) \tag{5.16}$$

where

- P_{nt} is the transaction price of the property n. If the transaction is a repeat-sale, then the transaction price at the time of the second sale;
- P_{nt} is the transaction price of the property at the time of the first sale if any; and
- X_{nt} is a ($1 \times n$) matrix and β is a ($1 \times n$) matrix of estimated coefficient of X.

By estimating Equation 5.16 by ordinary least squares (OLS), all the transaction data is utilised since each transaction will fall into each of the three samples above. Case and Quigley (1991), however, note that more efficient estimates may be obtained by generalised least squares (GLS) instead of OLS.

The Quigley (Q-hybrid) model

One shortcoming of Case and Quigley's methodology is that it does not model the error structure (Quigley, 1995; Hill et al., 1997). Quigley (1995) makes an improvement to the above hybrid method by basing his estimation method upon an explicit error structure that assumes a random walk in housing prices. Quigley (1995) relies upon robust GLS models to achieve asymptotic efficiency. This method combines samples of single- and multiple-sales in a single regression. The first equation for implementing this method is given below:

$$\ln P_{nt} = \beta_t X_{nt} + c_t D_{nt} + \delta_{nt} + u_{nt} \qquad (5.17)$$

where

- P_{nt} is the transaction price of house n at time t;
- β_t is the estimated coefficient associated with the housing and locational • characteristics, X, of property n at time t;
- c_t is the estimated coefficient associated with the time-dummy variables, D_t;
- δ_{nt} is the dwelling-unit-specific factor that represents the unmeasured characteristics of house n at time t; and
- u_{nt} is the random error.

That is, regress the log of sale price on the housing, locational and neighbourhood characteristics, X, a set of dummy variables for time periods, and a set of dummy variables for individual dwellings using only the sample of properties that have been sold more than once. From the above equation, the residuals $\hat{u}$ and its variance $\sigma_{\hat{u}}^2$ are calculated.

Also, a similar equation like the one above is estimated with the multiple-sales sample size, but assume that the individual dwelling-unit-specific, δ_n, is part of the error term. This new equation is illustrated below:

$$\ln P_{nt} = \beta_t X_{nt} + c_t D_{nt} + e_{nt} \qquad (5.18)$$

where e_{nt} is a composite error term representing δ_n and μ_{nt} as above, but all other notations are as before.

After estimating this equation, the residuals $\hat{e}$ and its variance $\sigma_{\hat{e}}^2$ are calculated. After some slight manipulation to $\sigma_{\hat{e}}^2$, we obtain σ_{δ}^2. The next step in the estimation procedure is to assume that housing prices follow a random walk such that:

$$E\,(u_{nt}-u_{n\tau})^2/\sigma_u^2 = A\,(t-\tau)+B\,(t-\tau)^2 \tag{5.19}$$

That is, estimate the above equation using only the transactions that have been sold more than once. This yields the regression coefficients of $\hat{A}$ and $\hat{B}$. All the estimated parameters together identify completely the variance-covariance matrix of the errors in Equation 5.17.

$$E\,(\delta_n+u_n,\delta_j+u_{j\tau}) = \begin{cases} 0 & \text{for } n \neq j \\ \sigma_{\delta}^2+\sigma_u^2[1+\hat{A}\,(t-\tau)+\hat{B}\,(t-\tau)^2] & \text{for } n = j \end{cases} \tag{5.20}$$

Using the entire sample of single- and multiple-sales, Equation 5.17 is estimated by generalised least squares, where the weights are derived from Equation 5.20.

The Hill, Knight and Sirmans (HKS-hybrid) model

Hill et al. (1997) also follow a process similar to Case and Quigley (1991) above. They estimate one hedonic equation and one repeat-sale equation. The hedonic equation is

$$\ln P_{nt} = \alpha X_{nt} + \theta A_{nt} + \beta D_{nt} + v_{nt} \tag{5.21}$$

where

- P_{nt} is the price of property $n(n = 1, \ldots N)$ at time $t(t = 1, \ldots T)$;
- α is a vector of characteristic shadow prices;
- X_{nt} is a vector of asset characteristics;
- θ is a depreciation parameter;
- A_{nt} is the age of the property;
- β is a vector of price index parameters that capture the pure effect of price changes over time;
- D_{nt} $(j = 2,\ldots, T)$ is a dummy variable that is 1 if the asset sold in period j and 0; otherwise
- v_{nt} is a vector of error terms.

If there are repeat-sales samples, then the repeat-sales methodology can also be used to estimate the index. If the asset sales occur S_i periods apart, then for the tth asset,

$$\ln P_{nt+s_n} - \ln P_{nt} = \Delta \ln P_n = \theta S_n + \beta T_n + e_n \tag{5.22}$$

where

- t_n is a vector of dummy variables that take the value 1 if the second sale occurred in period j and the value -1 if the first sale occurred in period j.

They follow the work of Case and Quigley (1991) and jointly estimate Equations 5.21 and 5.22. The stacked equations in matrix form are:

$$\begin{bmatrix} \ln P \\ \Delta \ln P \end{bmatrix} = \begin{bmatrix} X & A & D \\ O & S & T \end{bmatrix} \begin{bmatrix} \alpha \\ \theta \\ \beta \end{bmatrix} + \begin{bmatrix} v \\ e \end{bmatrix} \tag{5.23}$$

Hill et al. (1997) do not however assume a random walk in housing prices as assumed by Quigley (1995). Rather, they assume that market forces are able to eliminate the systematic error over time and so use a first-order autocorrelation scheme:

$$v_{nt} = \rho v_{nt-1} + u_{nt} \tag{5.24}$$

where the autocorrelation parameter is $|\rho| < 1$. They further allow the possibility that the errors u_{nt} are heteroskedastic, with variances σ_n^2. Therefore, the variances of the hedonic equation error terms are:

$$var(v_{nt}) = \frac{\sigma_n^2}{1 - \rho^2} \tag{5.25}$$

and their covariances are:

$$cov(v_{nt}, v_{nt+S_n}) = \frac{\sigma_n^2 \rho^{S_n}}{1 - \rho^2} \tag{5.26}$$

They note that the stochastic properties of the error term e_n in Equation 5.22 follow directly from Equations 5.24 and 5.25. That is, $e_n = v_{n,t+S_n} - v_{nt}$ has variance:

$$var(e_n) = \frac{2\sigma_n^2(1 - \rho^{S_n})}{1 - \rho^2} \tag{5.27}$$

Equation 5.27 allows for the error variance in the repeat-sales model to increase as the time between the repeat-sales increases. If there are no repeat-sales in the dataset, then clearly the autocorrelation parameter ρ is not identified and it cannot be estimated. Using the autocorrelation parameters and the estimates for the error structure, Equation 5.23 is estimated using the maximum likelihood technique. In contrast to Quigley (1995), who uses the robust GLS, Hill et al. (1997) use the complex maximum likelihood techniques to achieve asymptotic efficiency.

The Englund, Quigley and Redfearn (EQR-hybrid) model

Englund et al. (1998) also provide a variation of the above hybrid models by distinguishing between the effects of observable and unobservable aspects of quality and between the effects of "depreciation" and "vintage" on property prices. Depreciation is defined as the decline in quality of houses over some time interval after accounting for normal maintenance. Vintage also refers to the elements of quality and style that are embedded in the dwelling at the time of construction (Englund et al., 1998).

Englund et al. (1998) assume that

$$\ln P_{nt} = \beta X_{nt} + V_t + \delta_n + \varepsilon_{nt} = \beta X_{nt} + V_t + \gamma_{nt} \qquad (5.28)$$

where

- P_{nt}, β and X_{nt} are as above; and
- V_t is the log of the constant-quality housing price index at time t;
- δ_n represents an error term due to the unmeasured, individual-specific characteristics of dwelling i and is distributed with mean of zero and variance σ_δ^2; and
- ε_{nt} is an error term.

They note that components of X_{nt} include the vintage (y_n, year built) and the accumulated depreciation ($t - y_n$, age) of the dwelling. From a sub-sample of repeat-sales at various ages and years, the parameters y_n, $(t - y_n)$ and V_t can be recovered. They therefore estimate Equation 5.28 using the sub-sample of repeat-sales at time t and τ and use the residuals from the regression to estimate jointly the depreciation parameter, β_d:

$$\gamma_{nt} - \gamma_{n\tau} = \beta_d [t - \tau] + \varepsilon_{nt} - \varepsilon_{n\tau} \qquad (5.29)$$

and the error structure, e_{nt}:

$$\varepsilon_{nt} = \rho^{(t-\tau)} \varepsilon_{n,t-\tau} + p_{nt} \qquad (5.30)$$

where

- ρ is the serial correlation coefficient; and
- p_{nt} is the residual and is distributed with zero mean and variance σ_ρ^2.

From Equation 5.30, an estimate of σ_p^2 is obtained. An estimate of σ_δ^2 is constructed from the residuals in the first-step estimation of Equation 5.28, knowing ρ and σ_p^2. Together, these parameters identify completely the variance-covariance matrix of disturbances in Equation 5.28:

$$E(\gamma_{nt} - \gamma_{n\tau}) = \begin{cases} 0 & \text{for } n \neq j \\ \sigma_\delta^2 + \sigma_p^2 \{\rho^{(t-\tau)}/(1-\rho^2)\} + \beta_d^2 AGE_t AGE_\tau & \text{for } n = j \end{cases} \qquad (5.31)$$

Finally, using the entire sample of single-sales and repeat-sales, estimate Equation 5.28 by generalised least squares (GLS), where the GLS matrix is the inverse of the right-hand side of Equation 5.31.

Both Englund et al. (1998) and Hill et al. (1997) reject the random walk assumption introduced by Quigley (1995), and instead assume that the error terms are generated by a first-order autoregressive process. Again, Englund et al. (1998) and Hill et al. (1997) distinguish between vintage and depreciation in their effects upon housing prices. However, in contrast to Hill et al. (1997), Englund et al. (1998) distinguish between the individual-specific components of house values and random errors. The Englund et al. (1998) model is simple to implement as compared to the Hill et al. (1997) model, because the former relies upon a generalised least squares estimator (GLS) rather than a complex maximum likelihood estimator. Other studies that have combined the hedonic and the repeat-sales method include Eichholtz (1997) and Meese and Wallace (1997).

Advantages and disadvantages of the hybrid method

Like the hedonic method, the hybrid method corrects for the effects of heterogeneity of properties by taking the characteristics of the properties into consideration. The method also combines both single- and multiple-sales and not just multiple sales of the same property. The problem of small sample size inherent in the repeat-sales method is therefore reduced.

Again, when only the repeat sample is used, because age and time between sales are perfectly collinear (Hill et al., 1997), it is not possible to isolate the effect of depreciation. When only single transactions of the hedonic model are employed too, serial correlation will be unobservable. Combining the two datasets to construct indices using the hybrid method therefore overcomes these shortcomings.

One clear disadvantage of using the hybrid method, like the case of the hedonic method, is the extensive dataset required to implement the method. The implementation of the method requires an extensive dataset of house price observations together with the details on the physical and locational attributes of the properties concerned. In addition to the extreme difficulty involved in collecting a suitable dataset, the repeat-sale sample will have to be identified and paired before the method can be used, making it more time-consuming.

The hybrid method requires complex econometric models and some technical econometric skills for its implementation. This reduces the confidence level people have in using the method since they cannot be sure if they have followed the right processes.

Comparison of the index methods based on previous empirical findings

There is a vast amount of literature that debates and empirically tests the relative merits and demerits of the various methods of constructing constant-quality house price indices. This section reports some of the findings from these studies and compares the various index methods based on the findings.

Table 5.2 summarises some of the recent studies about house price index construction. Mark and Goldberg (1984) find the repeat-sales indices exhibit

Table 5.2 Recently published studies on house price index construction methods

Authors and year of publication	Data period	Study area	Frequency	Index method(s) used	Result
Case and Quigley (1991)	1980–1987	Kahala, Hawaii, USA	Annual	ETV hedonic, original repeat-sales and hybrid methods	The hybrid method outperforms both the hedonic and repeat-sales methods
Hill, Knight and Sirmans (1997)	1985–1990	Baton Rouge, Louisiana, USA	Annual	Hedonic equations, Repeat-sales equations, and hybrid equations	The hybrid method outperforms the rest of the methods
Meese and Wallace (1997)	1970–1988	Oakland and Fremont, California, USA	Quarterly	repeat sales, hedonic, hybrid and median sales price	The hedonic method outperforms the rest. Repeat sales suffer from sample selection bias
Clapp and Giaccotto (1998)	1981–1991	Fairfax county, Virginia, USA	Quarterly	Original repeat-sales & hedonic repeat model	The hedonic repeat sale is superior to the BMN repeat-sales
Englund, Quigley and Redfearn (1998)	1981–1993	Sweden	Quarterly	Hybrid method	They find their method to be able to investigate price dynamics at the level of individual house sales
Englund, Quigley and Redfearn (1999)	1981–1993	Gothenburg, Malmö, and Stockholm, (all in Sweden)	Monthly, Quarterly Semi-annually, and Annually	WRS and hybrid method	Indices produce by the finest disaggregation of time is better. In terms of accuracy, the hybrid method dominates the WRS method
Costello and Watkins (2002)	1988–2000	Perth, Australia	Quarterly	Hedonic and WRS methods	The hedonic method is slightly superior to the WRS method

Leishman and Watkins (2002)	1983–1999	Aberdeen, Dundee, Edinburgh and Glasgow (all in Scotland, UK)	Quarterly	Original repeat-sales and the WRS methods	Indices estimated with the BMN repeat-sales method are more robust than the WRS method
Bourassa, Hoesli and Sun (2006)	1989–1996	Auckland region, Wellington city and the Christchurch city (all in New Zealand)	Semi-annually	Repeat-sales methods, ETV and SCS hedonic methods and the SPAR method	In terms of constant-quality, the SPAR method outperforms the hedonic methods and produces constant-quality indices similar to the repeat-sales indices
Wilhelmsson (2009)	2000–2007	Stockholm in Sweden	Monthly	The ETV hedonic method	He finds the method to produce constant-quality indices and also finds that seasonality affects house prices in Stockholm

smaller increases as compared to mean and the hedonic indices. Case et al. (1991) also find the repeat-sales indices increase more slowly than those constructed using other methods. They also do not find any clear efficiency gains from using the hybrid method.

Employing data from the Kahala neighbourhood in Hawaii, USA, Case and Quigley (1991) compare their hybrid method with the ETV hedonic and the original repeat-sales methods and find that the hybrid method outperforms the hedonic and the repeat-sales methods. They do this by comparing the confidence interval of the various indices and find their hybrid method to be much narrower than the other methods.

Case et al. (1991) test indices constructed by the hedonic, the repeat-sales and the hybrid methods; and conclude that the hybrid method is sensitive to the inclusion of observations in which there have been physical changes to the house between sales. They find the hedonic method produces more robust indices. Gatzlaff and Ling (1994) also find that house price changes computed from median, hedonic and repeat-sales indices are highly correlated at the annual frequency, but not at the quarterly frequency. The standard repeat-sales index is particularly found to be below the hedonic indices, but a repeat-sales index adjusted for depreciation is not.

One notion about the repeat-sales index is that it does understate house price inflation. Empirically, however, the findings do not provide conclusive results about this notion. Mark and Goldberg (1984) and Case et al. (1991) find that their repeat-sales indices predict lower than expected house price growth. Clapp and Giaccotto (1992a) also find that the prices and assessed values of properties that sell twice are about 15% less than those of properties that sell only once. However, Crone and Voith (1992), Gatzlaff and Ling (1994) and Bourassa et al. (2006) do not find this to be the case.

Hill et al. (1997) also employ data in the USA to compare their hybrid method with that of Case and Quigley (1991), the hedonic method and the repeat-sales method. They find their hybrid model based on maximum likelihood method produces the lowest mean squared error (MSE) of the price index. This is followed by Case and Quigley's hybrid and hedonic methods. Case and Quigley's method, however, outperforms the hedonic method only when the serial correlation is large. The repeat-sales method is found to be the worst estimator of all the methods.

The study by Meese and Wallace (1997) suggests that the hedonic method is better than the repeat-sales and the hybrid methods for the construction of property price indices. They also find the hybrid method overstates house price inflation in respect of their sample. The repeat-sales method is found to be sensitive to small samples and so the repeat-sales indices suffer from sample selection bias.

Englund et al. (1999) also employ very rich transaction data in three regions in Sweden, namely Stockholm, Gothenburg and Malmö, to test the effect of temporal aggregation on house price index methods using the WRS and the EQR-hybrid models. They find the EQR-hybrid method outperforms the WRS in all three regions.

Leishman and Watkins (2002) also compare the ORS and the WRS in four cities in Scotland, UK, namely Aberdeen, Dundee, Edinburgh and Glasgow, at quarterly frequency levels and find that indices estimated with the ORS method are more robust than the WRS method. They define accuracy to be the standard deviation of log index divided by the mean standard error of the regression coefficients of the time-dummy variables, and indicate that the higher the ratio is for a particular index, the more accurate that particular index is. They find the ratio for the ORS indices to be consistently higher than that of the WRS indices. Perhaps, the holding periods between their transactions do not vary much and so heteroskedasticity is not likely to be a problem. Therefore, using the OLS will obviously be the best linear unbiased estimator (BLUE).

In terms of house price index revision, Clapp and Giaccotto (1999) find the revisions in the repeat-sales indices to be large, systematic and insensitive to the sample size. Clapham et al. (2006) find the average revision in the repeat-sales index to be –1.7%. This finding confirms the results of Clapp and Giaccotto (1999) that revisions in repeat-sales indices are downward. Clapham et al. (2006) also note that the hedonic index constructed with time-dummy variables exhibits a downward average revision.

However, the magnitude of the revision is less than that of the repeat-sales, –1.0%. The authors also find the strictly cross-sectional Fisher Ideal hedonic price index, which is a geometric average of the Laspeyres and Paasche indices, exhibits an average upward revision of 0.6%. This is possibly due to the fact that the sample of houses added to the previous dataset is of higher quality.

It is clear from this section that none of the index methods consistently outperform the others in terms of their accuracy. Apart from the fact that differences in characteristics of the different study areas used for these studies can cause this inconsistency, two other possible reasons for this inconsistency are: (i) absence of appropriate proxy for the unobservable "true" house price trend to measure index accuracy; (ii) scarcity and pooling of data together across time (temporal aggregation).

Measuring of index accuracies

The notional "house price trend" is not observed and so there is no specific benchmark against which the relative accuracy of the various price indices can be compared. In the absence of an unobservable "true" price, the average price has often been used by researchers as a proxy for the unobservable "true" house price (see for example Meese and Wallace, 1997; Wang and Zorn, 1997; Leishman and Watkins, 2002). The use of the average price as a proxy for the unobservable "true" house price is contrary to the voluminous literature which argues against the application of the average method since it ignores changes in the mix of houses sold over time (see 5.2). Therefore, using the average price to represent the "true" unobservable house price can cause inconsistencies when comparing the relative accuracy of the various index construction methods.

One other framework that other researchers have adopted which does not require a benchmark index is to directly compare the goodness of fit statistics reported by the various models under investigation (see for example Case and Szymanoski, 1995). However, there is evidence which suggests that the goodness of fit statistics are misleading, especially in cases where price index methods are estimated at high temporal frequencies; and for the repeat-sales method, the criteria overestimate the true reliability of the model (Sommervoll, 2006). Using these criteria to assess the accuracy of the various methods is therefore misleading and questionable and can cause inconsistencies.

The problem of a benchmark or basis of comparing the accuracy of various index methods therefore remains largely unresolved in the literature. This book uses an application of out of sample forecast evaluation to compare the accuracy of the various methods based on their mean squared errors (MSE) in Chapter 7. The MSE technique is not new and is used by Hill et al. (1997) to compare various index methods based on some simulation techniques. However, instead of the complex simulation techniques, this book uses a relatively simpler but effective technique called an out of sample forecast technique. This technique involves setting aside a random subset of the sample during the estimation stage, so that the subset that is set aside can be used to predict the "true" observed sale price. In this case, both the predicted price and the true price are available for the analysis. This analysis is done in Chapter 7.

Temporal aggregation

Apart from the fact that there is no appropriate proxy for the unobservable "true" house price, one other reason is scarcity and pooling of data. Real estate properties are transacted continuously and on daily basis. However, properties that are typically sold in a day are very few and infrequent (Englund et al., 1999), as compared to other financial assets like the stocks. As a result, studies that rely on transaction data often find it necessary to pool data together across time so that the sparse dataset problem could be overcome.

Pooling data together across time to overcome the problem of small sample size, however, involves an implicit assumption that indices generated from broader aggregated samples are statistically the same as those generated from less aggregated constituent sub-samples. For example, when housing transactions are combined to construct a quarterly index, it is assumed that a house transaction in January has occurred at the same time as one in March. Similarly, a house transaction in January is assumed to have occurred at the same time as ones in June and December when constructing semi-annual and annual indices respectively. To estimate a quarterly index therefore, the monthly coefficients are restricted to be equal within the quarter. That is, the quarterly price function is assumed to remain constant through January, February and March and then jumps to a different value for April, May and June. Because demand and supply relationships in the housing markets vary over time, this assumption is questionable. Temporal aggregation may bring about bias in the construction of house price indices and returns (Calhoun et al., 1995). Englund et al. (1999) and Owusu-Ansah et al. (2017) find that indices produced at the finest aggregated levels are better than those produced at broader aggregated levels, and that the estimation of price indices at broader levels of temporal aggregation, such as semi-annual and annual levels is generally unwarranted. From Table 5.2, it seems most empirical studies are conducted using the quarterly frequency interval to compare the various methods.

Even though a broader level of data aggregation is not an effective solution to the small sample size problem, at the finest levels of temporal disaggregation, the sample size may be reduced to the extent that it can no longer be able to support the degrees of freedom required for reliable parameter estimation (Schwann, 1998). The decision to choose the level of aggregation should therefore be considered as a trade-off between the problem of small sample size and bias in the estimation of indices, and the methods used in the index estimation should ultimately make the decision since some methods are more robust when applied to small sample sizes (Schwann, 1998; Sommervoll, 2006). The issue of temporal aggregation is also revisited and empirically examined in Chapter 7.

Conclusion

Due to the importance of house price indices, various studies have been undertaken to examine the accuracy and robustness of the various index construction methods. This chapter has identified and reviewed the various index construction methods, namely the mean or median method, the hedonic methods, the repeat-sales methods and the various hybrid methods. The relative merits and demerits of these methods have also been discussed. It is clear from the preceding discussions that the literature is still inconclusive concerning the most accurate and precise index construction method. The literature suggests that the performance of a particular index method depends on how the accuracy of the various index methods are compared and the level of temporal aggregation used.

6   The study area and the data

Introduction

The previous chapter discussed the various house price index construction methods. The hedonic, repeat-sales and hybrid methods have been discussed and compared based on their performance from previous empirical findings. The chapter has highlighted that previous studies have not provided conclusive evidence about the most accurate index construction method and hence the need for further empirical evidence. In this chapter, the study area is selected and justified and the data for the empirical analysis is also prepared and described. The chapter therefore links the theoretical part of the house price index construction to the empirical part.

The second section presents the geographical areas selected for the empirical illustration. The reasons for the selection of these geographical areas as the case study areas and overview of the Aberdeen housing market are presented in this section. In the third section the major types of economic data, namely the cross-sectional data, time series data, pooled cross-section data and panel data are discussed. The type of data to be used for the empirical analysis is also highlighted and justified in this section. The fourth section describes the data gathering process. The issues to be considered here include identification of the data requirements, investigation of data availability and data quality. In the fifth section, the data is prepared for empirical analysis. The data preparation involves data cleaning and identification of repeat-sales in the dataset. The sixth section presents the final dataset. The descriptive statistics of the data are examined in this section. The aim is to identify the major characteristics of the data and to assess the suitability of the data in constructing house price indices. The seventh section sums up and concludes the chapter.

The study area

This section introduces the different geographical areas used for the various empirical chapters. It begins with explaining why these areas are included in the case study for empirical analysis and is followed by an overview of Aberdeen.

Selection and justification of the geographical area

The North East of Scotland consists of Aberdeen city itself as the main urban centre, with various towns, villages and farmlands further making up Aberdeenshire as shown in Figure 6.1. There are also two main housing market areas (HMAs) and two local council authorities in the North East of Scotland. The HMAs are the Aberdeen HMA and the Rural HMA. The two councils are Aberdeen City Council and Aberdeenshire Council. The Aberdeen HMA incorporates both the Aberdeen City Council (ACC) area and part of the Aberdeenshire Council (ASC) area. The remaining part of the Aberdeenshire council (apart from the areas already incorporated in the Aberdeen HMA) is termed as the Rural HMA. These housing market area definitions are used by the ACC and the ASC for planning purposes and for assessing housing need and demand (ACC, 2015).

ASPC also has its own classification of the housing markets within North East Scotland and this classification is under two broad headings – (a) Aberdeen City and Suburbs and (b) the Country areas (ASPC, 2011a). The first two columns of Table 6.1 show the various areas that fall within each of the ASPC classifications. All the areas under Aberdeen City and Suburbs fall within the Aberdeen HMA identified by the local council areas. The Country areas also comprise the Rural

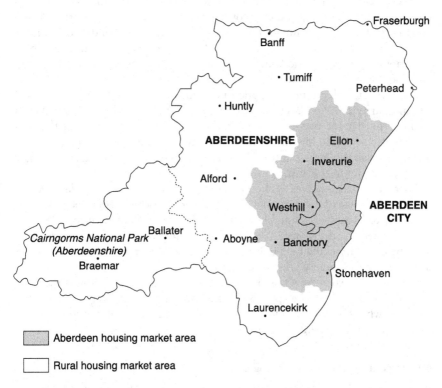

Figure 6.1 Housing Market and Council Areas (Source: Aberdeen City and Shire Strategic Development Planning Authority, 2011)

HMA and the remaining areas within the Aberdeen HMA that do not fall under the Aberdeen City and Suburbs classification. All the country areas are within the jurisdiction of the ASC. The Aberdeen City and Suburbs market area however incorporates both the ACC and part of the ASC. Since the data used for the index construction is sourced from the ASPC, it seems reasonable to use their classification of the housing market rather than using the classification by the councils. Also, since the ASPC comprises the various estate agents within North East Scotland and these agents are experts who are directly involved with activities in the market on a daily basis, it is reasonable to expect that their classification of the housing markets is more functional than that of the local councils.

The Aberdeen City and Suburbs market area defined by the ASPC is used as the case study area for the empirical work in Chapter 6. This geographical area includes all the areas listed in the first column of Table 6.1. As already indicated above, this area covers the Aberdeen City Council area plus some surrounding areas. This market area is seen as a different market from the Country areas and hence the testing of temporal aggregation and accuracy of the different index methods are restricted to this area.

The analyses about the overview of the Aberdeen housing market in this chapter, together with the empirical analyses in Chapters 5 and 6, cover only the Aberdeen City Council area. The third column of Table 6.1 shows the various areas that fall under the jurisdiction of Aberdeen City Council. The reason why the empirical analysis is limited to Aberdeen City Council is that data on building warrants needed to measure the impact of planning regulation on housing supply could not be sourced in time from ASC, and so the other areas controlled by ASC could not be included in the analysis.

The period for which the house price index construction methods are examined is from January 2000 to December 2010, an 11-year period. This period is chosen because the dataset needed to construct indices for the various methods is consistently available for this period. Also, the purpose of the empirical index construction in this book is just for illustration and so how recent the data is does not really matter in this instance.

Aberdeen as a study area is chosen due to the following reasons. First, ASPC has a large volume of transactional data for Aberdeen which can be accessed and so this makes Aberdeen a suitable study area. The second practical consideration that informed the decision to use Aberdeen is the proximity to and familiarity with the city. This could help in gaining personal contact with the data provider and verifying the data (Watkins, 2001).

Even though Aberdeen is used as the case study area, the methods used and analyses undertaken can be applied to other local housing markets as well. After justifying why Aberdeen is selected for the study, the next sub-section provides an overview of the Aberdeen housing market.

An overview of Aberdeen housing market

Aberdeen, also known both as the 'Granite City' and the 'Oil Capital of Europe' (Tiesdell and Allmendinger, 2004), is situated in the north of Scotland, UK, and

Table 6.1 The ASPC housing market areas

Aberdeen city and suburbs	Country areas	Aberdeen City Council area
Aberdeen city centre	Aboyne	Aberdeen city centre
Balmedie	Alford	Bankhead/Bucksburn/ Stoneywood
Banchory-Devenick	Ballater/Braemar	Bieldside
Bankhead/Bucksburn/ Stoneywood	Banchory	Blairs
Bieldside	Banff	Bridge of Don
Blackburn	Brechin/Montrose	Cove Bay/Findon
Blairs	Buckie	Cults/Pitfodels
Bridge of Don	Collieston/Newburgh	Danestone
Cove Bay/Findon	Cruden Bay	Dyce
Cults/Pitfodels	Cullen	Kingswells
Danestone	Drumoak/Durris	Milltimber
Dyce	Ellon	Nigg
Elrick/Skene/Westhill	Fraserburgh	Peterculter
Kingswells	Fyvie/New Deer/Turrif	
Maryculter	Gardenstown/Macduff	
Milltimber	Huntly/Keith	
Muchalls/Newtonhill	Insch	
Nigg	Inverbervie/Johnshaven	
Newmachar	Inverurie	
Peterculter	Kemnay	
Portlethen	Kintore	
Potterton	Laurencekirk	
	Lumphanan	
	Methlick/Tarves	
	Monymusk	
	Oldmeldrum/Pitmedden/ Udny	
	Peterhead	
	Portsoy	
	Stonehaven	
	Torphins	

it is the third largest city in Scotland after Glasgow and Edinburgh. Aberdeen is one of the most northerly cities in the UK as shown in Figure 6.2.

Aberdeen is situated about 205 km and 259 km north of Edinburgh and Glasgow, respectively. Figures 6.3 and 6.4 show the population dynamics in Aberdeen and two other major Scottish cities over the 11-year period, from 2000 to 2010 inclusive. The highest and lowest population growth rates in Aberdeen over the period

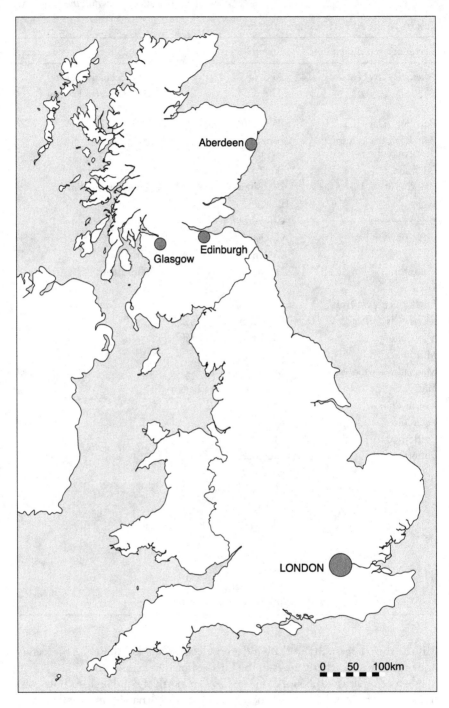

Figure 6.2 A map of the UK showing the location of Aberdeen (Source: Adapted from Tiesdell and Allmendinger, 2004)

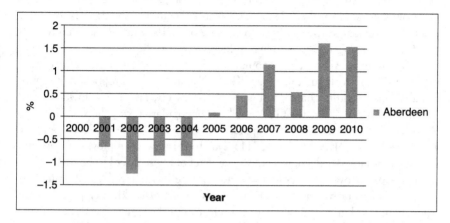

Figure 6.3 Population trend in Aberdeen from 2000 to 2010 (Source: General Office for
Scotland, 2011)

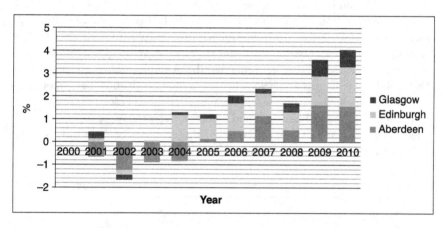

Figure 6.4 Population trend in Aberdeen compared to Edinburgh and Glasgow from
2000 to 2010 (Source: General Office for Scotland, 2011)

are 1.62% and –1.25%, respectively, and these growth rates were recorded in the
years 2010 and 2004, again respectively. The population change over the 11-year
period is approximately 1.8%. This means that the population figure has not
changed much over the period so it is relatively stable. While there was a consistent negative growth rate in population between 2000 and 2004, the later
years have seen a consistent positive growth rate. The population growth rate
reduced slowly on a yearly basis from 2000 until 2004, and thereafter, has been
increasing gently.

The average population figures over the period are 210,100, 461,128 and
581,345 for Aberdeen, Edinburgh and Glasgow, respectively. This means that the

population of Aberdeen is relatively small as compared to the Edinburgh and Glasgow figures. Also, the 0.18% average growth rate in Aberdeen is relatively small as compared to the average growth rate of 0.81% and 0.27% in Edinburgh and Glasgow, respectively, as shown in Figure 6.6.

Even though Aberdeen's population is relatively small, it contributes significantly to Scotland's (and the UK's) GDP, has a higher proportion of economically active adults than Edinburgh and Glasgow, and has a lower rate of unemployment. In 2008, the GVA[1] per head of population was almost £27,400 in Aberdeen and Aberdeenshire, compared to Scotland's average of £20,000 and the UK's average of £21,000 (ACC, 2011). Due to this low unemployment rate and high incomes in Aberdeen, we expect the level of house prices to be high.

Figure 6.5 shows the economic activity rates which reflect the numbers of people of working age that are in employment or seeking employment in Aberdeen, Edinburgh and Glasgow. It is clear from the figure that the economic activity rates for Aberdeen are well above the comparable rate for Edinburgh and Glasgow throughout 2004 to 2010. In the year to December 2010, economic activity rate was about 82.5% for Aberdeen, as compared to 74.9% and 70.9% for Edinburgh and Glasgow, respectively. Figure 6.6 also shows the official unemployment rate in Aberdeen, Edinburgh and Glasgow from 2004 to 2010. These figures refer to people without a job who are available to work, have looked for work in the past four weeks before the survey, or are waiting to start a job they have already secured. The figure shows that the unemployment rates throughout Aberdeen have remained well below the rates in Edinburgh and Glasgow for most periods. The unemployment rate was 6.1% in 2010 for Aberdeen as compared to the 6.3% and 11.7% in Edinburgh and Glasgow, respectively.

Figures 6.5 and 6.6 clearly confirm that the economy of Aberdeen is more resilient to global recession as compared to the other major cities in Scotland.

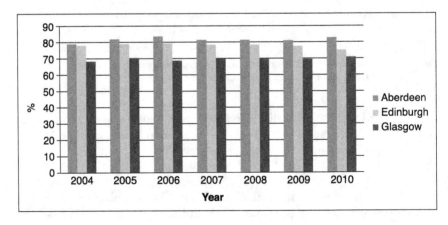

Figure 6.5 Economic activity rate – adults of working age in Aberdeen compared to Edinburgh and Glasgow from 2004 to 2010 (Source: Annual Population Survey, via Nomis, 2011)

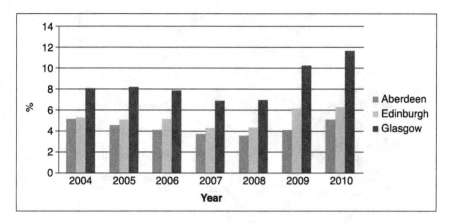

Figure 6.6 Unemployment rate among those of working age in Aberdeen compared to Edinburgh and Glasgow from 2004 to 2010 (Source: Annual Population Survey, via Nomis, 2011)

The reason for this is largely due to the performance of the oil and gas industry (ACC, 2011). The North Sea oil and gas industry has been the main driver of the Aberdeen economy since the late 1960s (Tiesdell and Allmendinger, 2004). The direct employment generated by the industry in Aberdeen is estimated at 23,000 and both direct and indirect employment is estimated at almost 60% of all employment in Aberdeen (ACC, 2011).

Despite the economic boost the North Sea oil and gas industry has given to Aberdeen, the industry has contributed in no small way to the current housing problems facing the city. Aberdeen is a relatively small urban area with a mix of old and established areas as well as newer suburban areas. However, due to the high employment rate provided by the oil industry, there are large demands for residential, retail, hotel and restaurant development and all these have to be accommodated within this historic environment. This has contributed to Aberdeen's high land values and high house prices. The average house prices in Aberdeen are relatively high as compared to the Scottish and the UK average. As at the fourth quarter of 2010, the average house price in Aberdeen was £205,731, compared to the Scottish and the British average of about £140,000 and £170,000, respectively (ASPC, 2011b).

According to the Scottish Household Survey (2007), about 65% of the population in Aberdeen live in owner-occupied properties, 24% live in socially rented properties, 9% in privately rented properties and the remaining 2% live in other properties. From the General Register Office for Scotland (2009), 54% of properties in Aberdeen are classified as flats, 18% are terraced properties, 17% are semi-detached houses, and the remaining 11% are detached houses. The total public sector (social rented) housing stock in Aberdeen as at 2010 was 22,209, which is approximately 7.1% of the total Scottish public sector

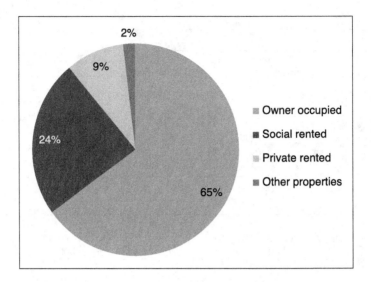

Figure 6.7 Dwellings of the population in Aberdeen

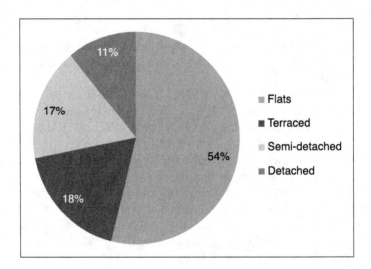

Figure 6.8 Dwelling types in Aberdeen

housing stock figure of 323,138 (Scottish Government Statistics, 2011). Figures 6.7 and 6.8 show the dwellings of the population in Aberdeen as well as the various dwelling types.

Having identified the case study area and examined an overview of the housing market in the area, the next section discusses the type of economic data which will provide the platform to allow for the study to be presented.

Types of economic data

The data used for economic analysis comes in a variety of forms. This section begins with the types of economic data we normally use in empirical studies. These include cross-sectional, time series and panel data.

Cross-sectional data

A cross-sectional data set consists of a sample of units like dwelling units, households, firms, countries etc., taken at a given point in time. The data on all units do not necessarily have to correspond to precisely the same time period. Wooldridge (2009) notes that in a typical cross-sectional analysis, any minor timing differences in data collection can be ignored. For example, if different houses are sold during different dates in the same month, we would still view this as a cross-sectional dataset for the month. Since it is very difficult to obtain a survey for the entire underlying population, cross-sectional data is often obtained by random sampling of the underlying population.

In economics and other social sciences, cross-sectional data are widely used, and is often aligned with the applied microeconomics fields, such as urban economics, local and national public finance, demography, health economics etc. This is because in order to test for microeconomic hypotheses and to evaluate economic policies, data on individuals, households, cities, countries etc. at a given point in time are normally used. The ordering of the dataset is not important in a cross-sectional dataset.

A variant of cross-sectional data is the pooled cross-section dataset. This data has both cross-sectional and time series features. If two cross-sectional surveys are conducted in a particular city for two separate years using the same survey questions, we can combine the two years' cross-sectional data to form a pooled cross-section in order to increase the sample size. When cross-sectional data are pooled from different years, they become an effective way to analyse the effects of a new government policy (Wooldridge, 2009). In this way, cross-sectional data from the year(s) before and after a key policy change is made are collected and analysed to see the effect of the price change.

The analysis of a pooled cross-section is similar to analysing a standard cross-section, with the main difference being that we often have to account for secular differences in the variables across time. Apart from increasing the sample size, one major reason why pooled cross-sectional analysis is useful is that it helps to see how a key relationship changes over time.

Time series data

A time series dataset is made up of observations on a variable or several variables over time. That is, a sequence of observations, which are ordered in time (or space). Such datasets include house price index, stock prices, consumer price index, money supply, gross domestic product, interest rates etc. Greene (2005) notes that past events can influence future events and lags in behaviour are very prevalent in the social sciences, and so time is an important dimension in a time series dataset. Unlike the cross-sectional dataset, the chronological ordering of observations in a time series conveys potentially important information.

One key characteristic of time series dataset is its difficulty during analysis. Time series are normally more difficult to analyse than cross-sectional data because economic observations can rarely be assumed to be independent across time. According to Wooldridge (2009), even though we can use both time series and cross-sectional datasets in most econometric models, more has to be done in specifying econometric models for time series data before the econometric method can be justified.

The frequency at which the data is collected is another key feature of a time series dataset that requires special attention. Time series datasets are normally collected at various frequencies such as daily, weekly, monthly, quarterly and annually. Stock prices, for example, are recorded on a daily basis except on weekends. There are other macroeconomic variables such as interest rates, inflation and unemployment rates that are recorded monthly. Gross domestic product is also an economic variable normally recorded on quarterly basis. Most of these economic time series variables normally display a strong seasonal pattern. Wilhelmsson (2009) for instance finds that house prices in Sweden are very expensive during the spring and summer periods, so house prices can be said to exhibit strong quarterly seasonal trends.

Panel data

A panel or longitudinal dataset consists of a time series for each cross-sectional member in the dataset. For instance, if we collect monthly or quarterly exchange rate data for different countries over a long period of time, for example ten years, or suppose we have employment, health and income history for a set of individuals followed over a five-year period, we call it panel data.

Longitudinal data is distinguished from a pooled cross-section in that for longitudinal data, the same cross-sectional units (for example, cities, firms etc.) are followed over a given time period. For the pooled cross-section data, however, the cross-sectional units are different in the various years to be considered. For the longitudinal data set, each of the cross-sectional units is numbered from i to n, with n being the number of periods under consideration. As with a pure cross-section, the ordering in the cross-section of a panel dataset does not affect the analysis.

Panel datasets have more advantages over cross-sectional data or even pooled cross-sectional since the same units are observed over time. When we have multiple observations on the same units, it allows us to control for certain unobserved characteristics of individuals, firms etc., and can also facilitate causal inference in situations where inferring causality would be very difficult if only a single cross-section were available. Again, panel data allows us to study the importance of lags in behaviour or the result of decision-making. Since many economic policies can be expected to have an impact only after some time has passed, studying lags in behaviour is very important. Panel datasets however require that the same units are replicated over time and so they are more difficult to obtain than pooled cross-sections especially if the data are on individuals, firms etc.

In this book, both cross-sectional and time series data are employed separately for the empirical analysis in Chapters 6 and 7. The cross-sectional data is referred to in this study as the hedonic data and this is used in the construction of the house price indices.

Data gathering

Data identification is the first stage in the data gathering process. Even though the data to be identified may produce a long list, its availability usually determines what should be included in the hedonic model. Therefore, after the data identification stage, the sources and availability of the data will be identified, and this will be followed by an overview of the quality of the data.

Data identification

The first item to be considered in the data gathering process is to identify the data needed to implement the model. In hedonic modelling and house price index construction, three main groups of data are needed as identified in Chapter 3. These are:

i   the transaction prices;
ii   the structural property characteristics; and
iii the locational characteristics.

Apart from these usual data groups, another group of data also identified to play an important role in this study is the property address data, including the post-codes. This data is used to identify properties that are repeatedly sold over the period. All these data groups identified are necessary for the construction of the various house price indices.

Data sources and availability

Data for hedonic modelling can be obtained from primary and/or secondary sources. Primary data are data collected for a specific project in hand by the individual researcher or the research team. Secondary data on the other hand are collected by the same researcher or any other organisation or investigator for a purpose other than the research project in hand. The hedonic data employed for the study is secondary data. The data is mainly provided by the Aberdeen Solicitors Property Centre (ASPC). As part of their normal activities, solicitors buy, sell and lease residential and commercial properties. Because the largest volume of property transaction in Scotland is undertaken by solicitors, the solicitors have grouped together under one umbrella in which details of all properties currently being offered for sale are posted. This gives them market power and ensures efficient marketing of the properties. Even though the Land Registry also keep some data about the Aberdeen housing market, the database does not include the physical characteristics of the properties.

ASPC's database has details of properties transacted in Aberdeen and the North East of Scotland. Their database covers around 95% of all transactions in Aberdeen and the North East of Scotland and so it is a fair representation of transaction activities in the area (White et al., 2009). The data is not publicly available and was obtained on the basis of a non-disclosure agreement between the University of Aberdeen and the ASPC. There is currently an ongoing quality adjusted house price index construction project for the Aberdeen housing market which is a collaboration between the Centre for Real Estate Research in the University of Aberdeen and the ASPC. The Centre for Real Estate Research is responsible for providing the expertise and the ASPC is responsible for providing the data. It is as a result of this collaboration that the data becomes accessible up to the period under consideration.

The ASPC database is able to provide most of the data requirement identified above, namely, the transaction prices; the structural property characteristics, such as the number of rooms (bedrooms, public rooms), number of floors, property type, availability of garages, garden etc.; and the latitudinal and longitudinal coordinates as a measure of location.

Data coverage

A total of 93,431 property data covering the North East Scotland is received in MS Excel format from the ASPC from January 2000 to December 2010. These included properties that were sold, rented or withdrawn from the market. There is also a historical dataset available from the ASPC that date back to 1984. A detailed description of the variables contained in the ASPC raw data is given below:

- **ID:** This is ASPC reference number they use to identify the transactions. The reference numbers consist of a 6-digit number. Each transaction has a reference number different from the reference numbers of other transactions. Examples of such reference numbers in the database are 150823 and 164714.
- **Postcode:** This provides the postcode of the areas where the properties are located. The ASPC obtains the postcodes of the properties from the Royal Mail's postcode database with postcode centres located on a 100m grid. Examples of the postcodes include AB24 4NF, AB54 4JD etc.
- **Areaname:** This is the ASPC's name for the area where the properties are located. There are 130 different area names in the dataset. Examples of the areas are Rosemount, King Street and Ferryhill.
- **Address:** This contains the property number, the street name and in some cases the area name. The area name is not available all the time in the address variable because it is already in the area name variable.

- **Easting and Northing:** These are the locational coordinates of the property. They represent the latitude and longitude, respectively. According to the ASPC, they initially look up the postcode in the Royal Mail's postcode database with postcode centres located on a 100m grid. These locations are the only source available for the properties sold before the year 2000 and it is assumed that the property is at the centre of the postcode. The easting and northing coordinates before the year 2000 cannot therefore be trusted since they are not geocoded. For the properties sold after 1999 however, a map is given to the selling solicitor with a cross at the centre of the postcode, and the solicitors are allowed to move the cross to the location of the property. These coordinates can therefore be taken as correct geocoded locational coordinates. The easting and northing coordinates have 5-digit numbers but about eleven of them have 6-digits. A discussion with the data provider shows that the 6-digit ones are a result of typographical error and so the correct georeference has been provided.
- **Status:** This represents the status of the property, whether it is withdrawn from the market, sold or rented. "W" represents all the properties that were on the market but were not sold, "P" denotes all the properties that were bought and "R" denotes all rented properties. Since this is a transaction database, it is very surprising that rented properties especially are included in the database. A discussion with the data provider however indicates those properties entered the database through an oversight and so could comfortably be dropped.
- **Numsold:** This represents the number of properties sold during a particular transaction. Usually 1, but there are a few housing developments (i.e. one database record covers more than one property). This variable has 15 values ranging from 1 to 36. If the numsold is more than one, it becomes difficult to identify one property from the other since they have all been assigned one address, and, therefore, identifying repeat-sales will be difficult. It is therefore necessary to restrict the numsold to only 1.
- **Saletotal:** This represents the price for all the sold properties involved. In some instances, the number of properties sold (Numsold) is more than one and this saletotal represents the price for all the properties.
- **Prettysolddate:** Coded variable for the date on which the property was taken off the market.
- **Dwellingtype:** This indicates the type of property. "F" represents flats, "D" represents detached houses and "N" represents non-detached houses. The non-detached properties are basically semi-detached and terraced properties.
- **Isnewbuilding:** This indicates whether the property is a new (or recently constructed) or an old one. Values are "True" and "False" to indicate new and old properties respectively. New properties are very few in the database. This is because the new properties are sold directly by the real estate developers and so do not pass through the ASPC system.
- **Asking price:** Price that the sellers request for the property when it is put on the market. The asking price may be different from the actual transaction price because buyer and seller may negotiate over the price.

- **Prettycreationdate:** Coded variable for the date on which the property was put on the market or the date the property was listed on the ASPC web-page.
- **Numfloors:** Number of floors that the property has. This ranges between one and six. The properties with more than three floors are, however, very few in the database.
- **Numpublic:** Number of public rooms that the property has – living room, lounge, kitchen, store room and study room are all considered as public rooms. This ranges between one and eight. Most of the properties transacted have between one and four public rooms.
- **Numbedrooms:** Number of bedrooms that the property has. This ranges between one and ten, with most of the properties having up to five bedrooms.
- **Numbathrooms:** Number of bathrooms that the property has. This ranges between one and four. This variable is missing in most of the observations and this could stem from the fact that the estate agents did not record them or they were simply absent with the property. Most of them have up to two bathrooms.
- **Numshowers:** Total number of showers in the house. This ranges between one and four. More than half of the observations are missing this variable and could be due to the fact that the estate agents did not take note of this variable.
- **NumWCs:** Total number of WCs in the house. This ranges between one and four. Like the numshowers variable, most of the observations are missing this variable.
- **Numgarage:** Number of garages.
- **Hasheating:** Indicates central heating. The value is "True" if the property has a central heating and "False" if not. Most of the observations do not have this variable.
- **Hasglazing:** Indicates windows with double glazing. If it has a double glazing, it is indicated as "True", if double glazing is absent, it is indicated as "False". Most of the observations do not have this variable.
- **Hasgarage:** Indicator for the presence of a garage, contrary to the numgarage variable which shows the actual number of garages. If it has a garage, it is indicated as "True", if a garage is absent, it is indicated as "False".
- **Hasgarden:** Indicator for a garden. "True" and "False" are used to indicate the availability or otherwise of a garden in the property.
- **Bulletintext:** Detailed text description of each property providing additional information.

The dataset presented above has some shortcomings. First of all, there is no variable to accurately measure the effect of the size of the property. From the literature, the size of the property is often included in hedonic analysis. The size is usually represented by one or more of the following: the lot size, floor area, living area and other area, as shown in Table 2.1. However, none of these variables is observed in the dataset. Again, the age of the property is not covered in the dataset. Since this is the perfect way of measuring the effect of depreciation on house prices, it is a major pitfall. While number of rooms may represent size of floor area (Leishman, 2001), there is no variable in the dataset that can be used as a proxy for the age of the property. The age of the property is therefore not included this study.

The dataset presented above requires some adjustments. Some of the properties are rented and withdrawn, some variables are missing values and some are not important to the study. It is therefore necessary for the ASPC dataset to be prepared to suit the study before it can be used. The next section continues the chapter by preparing the data so that it becomes suitable for the price index construction.

Data preparation

The next stage is the data preparation. The process of data preparation used here involves two main stages: data cleaning stage and identification of repeat-sales stage. The data cleaning stage is discussed below.

Data cleaning

The data cleaning stage is the stage where the original dataset is cleaned. This is done by excluding or re-coding the data and variables that are not used in the study or need to be transformed. The purpose of this stage is to ensure that the dataset contains the observations and variables in a format suitable for hedonic regression in the Stata programme. We begin the data cleaning by dropping the observations that are not within the study area, Aberdeen City and Suburbs. Out of the 93,413 property transactions in North East Scotland between January 2000 and December 2010, 26,810, representing approximately 28.7%, are transacted in the Countryside and so outside the study area. These observations are therefore dropped, leaving a total of 66,603. As mentioned in the "numsold" description above, few of the transactions involved more than one property. Out of the 66,603 transactions, only 296 involved more than one property. These 296 transactions are dropped in order to ensure that the property address and locational coordinates relate to a specific property, leaving a total of 66,307 transactions. The next step is by dropping all the variables that do not have a direct use in the construction of house price indices. These variables are the "ID" and the "asking price". The "bulletintext", though they do not have a direct use in the construction of house price indices, is kept until the data cleaning exercise is complete since it is useful here.

Next, we drop the number of properties that were rented and withdrawn from the market. "Rented" are properties that were rented but were mistakenly entered into the transaction database. The withdrawn properties were also not sold and so including such observations to construct house price indices causes bias in the index numbers. Table 6.2 presents the status of the properties in the dataset from which only the sold properties are maintained. That is, about 93.5% of the

Table 6.2 Distribution of property status

Status	Number of observations	Percentage
Sold	61,984	93.5
Withdrawn	4,072	6.1
Rented	251	0.4
Total	66,307	100

observations in the dataset are sold properties and so the dataset is now left with a total of 61,984.

The next step is to drop the variables that are missing most values. Table 6.3 presents the variables, the number of observations they have and the number of missing values. It is clear from the table that the variables "numshowers", "numwcs", "numgarages", "hasheating" and "hasglazing" have about 55% to 83% of the values missing. These variables have missing values possibly because the estate agents failed to take the particulars of those variables. Since it is unethical to assume any values for them, these variables are dropped from the dataset. However, before these variables were dropped, the ETV hedonic model was estimated with only those sales for which all observations exist to ascertain the magnitude and significance or otherwise of the coefficients of these variables.

Table 6.3 Missing values in the dataset

Variables	Number of observations	Number of missing values
Postcode	61,984	0
Areacode	61,984	0
Address	61,984	0
Easting	61,984	0
Northing	61,984	0
Numsold	61,984	0
Saletotal	61,984	0
Prettysolddate	61,984	0
Dwellingtype	61,980	4
Isnewbuilding	61,984	0
Prettycreationdate	61,984	0
Numfloors	61,984	0
Numpublic	61,941	43
Numbedrooms	61,933	51
Numbathrooms	61,773	211
Numshowers	20,495	41,489
Numwcs	10,352	51,632
Numgarages	19,361	42,623
Hasheating	27,456	34,528
Hasglazing	28,182	33,802
Hasgarage	61,984	0
Hasgarden	61,984	0

Table 6.4 shows that by including these variables only 5,956 observations can be used which produces an Adjusted R2 of only 27.34%. The variables "hasheating" and "hasglazing" are omitted because all the sales have heating and glazing and so cannot be included in the model. The "hasgarage" variable is also omitted from the regression output because the "numgarage" is included and captures the same effect. The number of garage variables are also insignificant and surprisingly most of the bedroom variables have negative coefficients, possibly due to the inclusion of the variables that capture the same size effect. Even though showers are significant, the magnitude of the coefficients are relatively small. Thus, in general, it is appropriate to drop "numshowers", "numwcs", "numgarages",

Table 6.4 Magnitude and significance of the dropped variables with the ETV hedonic model with 5,956 observations

Variables	Coefficients	T-values
numfloor2	–0.0010	(–0.05)
numfloor3	0.1672	(5.52)
numpublic2	0.0254	(1.72)
numpublic3	0.1097	(6.79)
numpublic4	0.2023	(9.90)
bedroom2	–0.4733	(–8.37)
bedroom3	–0.3188	(–18.35)
bedroom4	–0.1506	(–10.63)
bathroom2	–0.2040	(–7.95)
shower2	0.1670	13.46
shower3	0.3675	7.36
wc2	0.2252	4.86
numgarage2	0.0749	6.47
numgarage3	0.0861	1.22
garden	–0.0973	(–1.33)
semi-detached	–0.3296	(–3.78)
detached	–0.3487	(–4.02)
X	–457.42	(–6.42)
Y	83.96	(7.35)
X^2	27.92	(2.03)
Y^2	–29.89	(–6.96)
XY	86.80	(5.92)
XY^2	–5.25	(–5.88)
X^3	–2.62	(–2.14)
Y^3	1.99	(6.42)
Constant	347.78	(5.46)
Adjusted R^2	27.34%	

Note: The table shows the coefficient estimates of the property and locational characteristics from the ETV hedonic model using only sales for which all observations exist. Bedroom5, hasheating, hasglazing, hasgarage and east2north are all omitted due to their perfect collinearity with other variables.

"hasheating" and "hasglazing" since they are not significant and also to increase the sample size for the index construction.

The variables "dwellingtype", "numpublic", "numbedrooms" and "numbathrooms" have missing values for only 4, 43, 51, 211 observations respectively. Therefore, instead of dropping those variables, the observations missing the values are dropped. After dropping these observations, the dataset is left with a total of 61,773.

The next step in the data cleaning stage is to undertake frequency distribution of the unique values of the property characteristics. The purpose of this is to drop outliers and the values that have very few observations so that it does not influence the results. The Tables 6.5, 6.6 and 6.7 show the frequency distribution of the structural property variables. The frequency tabulations show that the unique values of "dwellingtype", "hasgarage" and "hasgarden" have enough values and so can be included in the analysis. The values for the "isnewbuilding" variable however suggests that only 591 observations, representing approximately 1%, are newly constructed properties. The variable "isnewbuilding" is therefore dropped since almost all the properties are old properties. Some of the unique values in the number of floors and rooms (public, bedrooms and bathrooms) however need to be deleted since they have relatively few numbers. After simultaneously deleting these observations, the unique values in the number of floors variable are limited to three. With the number of rooms, the unique values are limited to 4, 5 and 2 for "numpublic", "numbedrooms" and "numbathrooms" respectively. After this, the dataset is left with a total of 57,322. The next step in the data cleaning stage is to delete all transactions whose prices do not reflect the market value of the property. Firstly, properties that are likely to have been sold at prices which may not represent open market price. This is done with a clue from the bulletin text in the database. Again, data on any transaction that seems like an outlier is also

Table 6.5 Frequency distribution of isnewbuilding, hasgarage and hasgarden dummy variables

	Isnewbuilding	Hasgarage	Hasgarden
True	591	22,228	42,553
False	61,182	39,545	19,220
Total	61,773	61,773	61,773

Table 6.6 Frequency distribution of the dwellingtype dummy variable

	Dwellingtype
Flat	27,593
Nondetached	17,824
Detached	16,356
Total	61,773

Table 6.7 Frequency distribution of the main variables

	Numfloors	Numpublic	Numbedrooms	Numbathrooms
1	34,512	40,043	16,169	51,149
2	21,986	12,855	21,584	7,017
3	1,964	4,877	14,425	1,020
4	1,348	1,592	5,800	946
5	1,072	1091	2,488	867
6	891	622	523	774
7	0	371	396	0
8	0	322	187	0
9	0	0	124	0
10	0	0	77	0
Total	61,773	61,773	61,773	61,773

deleted. An outlier here is defined as a transaction with log sales prices more or less than three standard deviations away from the mean. Since the outliers are significantly smaller or larger than the other observations, their inclusion could cause bias and inefficiency in the parameter estimates. Thus, the database is left with a total of 57,150 property transactions.

In the next step, some variables are recoded and some new variables are created. The first variable is "saletotal". The "saletotal" variable is renamed as "price" to easily identify it as the transaction price. Apart from this, some dummy variables are also created. The "prettysolddate" variable is used to create the monthly, quarterly, semi-yearly and yearly dummies. In all, there are 132 monthly dummies (month1-month132), 44 quarterly dummies (quarter1-quarter44), 22 semi-yearly dummies (semi1-semi22) and 11 yearly dummies (year1-year11). The "dwelling-type" variable is also used to create three dummy variables, namely detached, flat and semi-detached houses. The "hasgarage" and "hasgarden" variables are used to create the dummies "garage", "nogarage", and "garden", "nogarden", respectively.

Dummy variables are also created from the number of floors and rooms (public, bedrooms, and bathrooms) variables since they are discrete variables. More so, it is not likely that the presence of two bedrooms, for instance, will have exactly twice as much influence on the price as that with one bedroom. The same can be said of the other variables such as the number of public rooms, number of floors and number of bathrooms. These main variables are therefore treated as dummy variables. For any particular property, therefore, the value 1 appears against only one of each of these, and the rest takes the value of 0 (Gallimore et al., 1996b). For example, a two-bedroom house would have the variable bedroom2 coded as 1 and bedroom1, bedroom3, bedroom4 and bedroom5, representing one bedroom, three bedrooms, four bedrooms, and five bedrooms, respectively, coded as 0. The same applies to the number of public rooms, floors and bathrooms variables. As Gallimore et al. (1996b) point out, such dummy variables will allow the regression technique itself to estimate the varying influence of the number of rooms provision, rather than have this imposed by an interval scale of measurement.

Identification of repeat-sales

The data cleaning stage has removed all incomplete information, outliers, unimportant variables, and has created all the dummy variables to be used for the house price index construction. The final stage is the identification of repeat-sales. There are many processes involved in identifying repeat-sales as indicated by Case and Shiller (1987). The processes used here to identify the repeat-sales are similar to those used by Case and Shiller (1987). The first step is to do an exact match on the address and postcodes fields. By doing this, all properties that have the same address are identified.

In the next stage, the property pairs that have been physically altered between the sale periods are dropped from the repeat sample and treated as single-sales. This is done by checking the number of rooms, the number of bedrooms, the dwelling type, whether any room has been "modernised", and the availability or otherwise of a garden and a garage. For example, if a property was semi-detached at the time of the first sale, but has been changed into a detached property, it is excluded. In the same way, if a property had a garage at the time of the first sale but the garage has been converted into a bedroom for instance, this property is dropped. This is to make sure that a change in the house price is not as a result of the changes in the structural attributes. A total of 441 properties are repeat-sales but have been physically altered.

After dropping all the property pairs whose physical characteristics have been altered from the repeat-sales and treated as single-sales, the dataset is still left with a total transaction of 57,150. Out of this, 26,668 are transacted only once. The remaining 30,482 observations involve more than one transaction. Table 6.8 shows the frequency of transactions with 40,971 unique properties. This is the final dataset used for the empirical analysis.

Verification of the final dataset

The previous section, the data preparation stage, has prepared the data and it is now ready to be used. This section now presents an overview of the final dataset. The dependent variable is the transaction price of the properties, which are

Table 6.8 Number of dwellings and sales, 2000:I–2010:IV

Number of sales	Total number of dwellings	Total number of sales
1	26,668	26,668
2	12,861	25,722
3	1,091	3,273
4	286	1,144
5	47	235
6	18	108
7	0	0
Total	40,971	57,150

transformed into their natural logarithms. The independent variables comprise structural variables, absolute locational variables and yearly time dummies, semi-yearly time dummies, quarterly time dummies and monthly time dummies. The distribution of the observations in the dataset and the descriptive statistics are presented below. The aim of this section is to make sure that the data is actually cleaned and suitable for house price index construction.

Distribution of observations

The original data received from ASPC contained a total of 93,431 observations from the period of 2000 to 2010. This dataset has been prepared to finally have a total of 57,150 observations which cover the same period and this dataset is used for the house price index construction. Figure 6.9 shows the yearly distribution of these 57,150 observations by dwelling types. The average number of observations per year is approximately 5,195 with the minimum and maximum observations being 2,931 and 7,212 corresponding to years 2009 and 2002, respectively.

Flat properties dominate the dataset used for the study. About 30,208, representing 52.9% of the observations, are flats. The highest and smallest number of flats occurred in years 2003 and 2009 respectively. Semi-detached properties are the second most transacted property type every year. They constitute about 30.6% of the total observations used for the study. It is however in the years 2002 and 2008 that the maximum and minimum amount of semi-detached properties transacted respectively. Detached properties also constitute 16.5% respectively of the total observations used for the study. This means that detached properties were the least transacted properties over the period with the maximum and minimum amount of detached properties occurring in the years 2001 and 2008, respectively. This gives a good indication that the transacted properties represent the dwelling type distribution of the housing stock as represented by Figure 6.8.

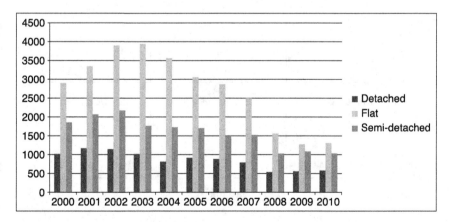

Figure 6.9 Distribution of sales by year and dwelling type

Descriptive statistics

In this sub-section, the descriptive statistics of the basic variables in the dataset are presented. These descriptions are very important since they give an overview of the variables before they are employed in the index construction in the next chapter. Figure 6.10 shows the transformations of the selling prices of the 57,150 observations. It can be observed from the figure that the actual (identity) selling prices have a positively skewed distribution. This means that it is dominated by relatively low-priced properties. Using housing data in the Stafford area between 1992 and 1993, Gallimore et al. (1996b) also find a positively skewed distribution for the transaction prices. These confirm the assertion by Fletcher et al. (2000b) that housing data are not normally distributed.

All the transformations of the actual selling prices, except the natural logarithm, are also not normally distributed. The distribution of the transaction prices is normal only when the log transformation is used as shown in Figure 6.10. Apart from the normal distribution which is achieved when the selling prices are transformed into logs, the specification of the dependent variable in log form and the inclusion of an intercept helps to interpret the coefficient of the time dummies as marginal changes (Wilhelmsson, 2009). Ultimately, the log price is used as the dependent variable.

The distribution of the selling prices and their descriptive statistics are shown in Table 6.9. The table shows that the average nominal house price over the

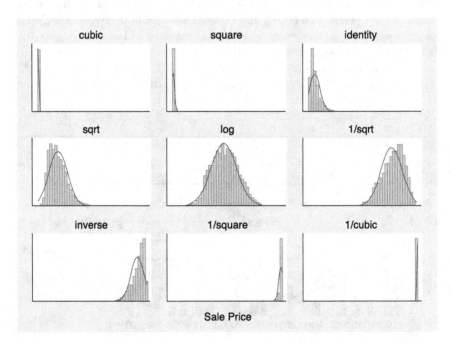

Figure 6.10 Distribution of sale price by various transformations

Table 6.9 Descriptive statistics of selling price over the years

Year	Number of observations	Number of observations (%)	Mean £	Minimum £	Maximum £	Standard deviation £
2000	5,775	10.1	75,959 (75,959)	27,000 (27,000)	501,000 (501,000)	47,749 (47,749)
2001	6,587	11.5	75,999 (74,676)	30,000 (29,478)	495,000 (486,384)	48,010 (47,174)
2002	7,212	12.6	82,045 (79,295)	28,000 (27,061)	805,500 (778,499)	56,513 (54,619)
2003	6,730	11.8	93,760 (88,070)	32,000 (30,058)	907,744 (852,660)	66,451 (62,419)
2004	6,104	10.7	107,255 (97,833)	35,000 (31,925)	1,142,000 (1,041,678)	73,823 (67,338)
2005	5,682	9.9	125,112 (110,987)	35,000 (31,048)	907,500 (805,042)	78,080 (69,265)
2006	5,251	9.2	153,522 (131,972)	47,000 (40,403)	1,595,000 (1,371,108)	93,631 (80,488)
2007	4,812	8.4	199,745 (164,649)	58,000 (47,809)	1,856,789 (1,530,541)	109,731 (90,451)
2008	3,135	5.5	201,059 (159,376)	44,000 (34,878)	2,000,000 (1,585,369)	128,292 (101,695)
2009	2,931	5.1	195,542 (155,831)	60,000 (47,815)	1,120,000 (892,546)	110,130 (87,764)
2010	2,931	5.1	202,570 (154,311)	52,000 (39,612)	925,000 (704,632)	114,348 (87,106)
Total	57,150	100.0	124,095 (108,802)	27,000 (27,000)	2,000,000 (1,585,369)	94,588 (82,931)

Note: The nominal house prices reported are also adjusted with the RPI with year 2000 as base period and these real house prices are reported in parentheses.

period is around £124,000, with the minimum and maximum nominal house prices being £27,000 and £2,000,000, respectively. The average real house price over the period is also £108,800 with the minimum and maximum real house prices being £27,000 and £1,585,369. Even though this produces a very wide range, their natural logarithms reduce the range significantly. The highest mean house prices occurred in the years 2008 and 2010 with mean nominal prices of around £201,000 and £203,000, respectively. The lowest mean was in 2000 and 2001, with a value of around £76,000. Between the years 2000 and 2010, the difference of nominal house price was about £126,611. The difference of real house price between the same period was, however, £78,352. This means that while the average house price has risen about 166.68% in nominal terms, it is only 103.15% in real terms over the same study period.

Table 6.10 Descriptive statistics of selling price over the years

Property type	Number of observations	Number of observations (%)	Mean £	Minimum £	Maximum £	Standard deviation £
Detached	9,452	16.5	219,757 (192,675)	51,000 (44,715)	2,000,000 (1,753,527)	130,704 (114,596)
Semi-detached	17,490	30.6	132,392 (116,076)	35,000 (30,687)	1,226,779 (1,075,595)	85,043 (74,563)
Flat	30,208	52.9	89,360 (78,348)	27,000 (23,673)	957,777 (839,744)	57,315 (50,252)
Total	57,150	100.0	124,095 (108,802)	27,000 (23,673)	2,000,000 (1,753,527)	94,588 (82,931)

Note: The nominal house prices reported are also adjusted with the RPI with year 2000 as base period and these real house prices are reported in parentheses.

Table 6.10 also shows the distribution of house prices by dwelling type. The table shows that detached properties are the most expensive properties in Aberdeen with an average detached nominal and real price being around £220,000 and £193,000, respectively. The minimum and maximum nominal prices of detached properties are £51,000 and £2,000,000, respectively, with a standard deviation of about 59% around the mean value. Semi-detached properties are the next most expensive properties with a mean price of around £132,000. The average price of flats sits at around £89,000. The standard deviation of the semi-detached properties and flats is about 64% around their mean values. This suggests that the price of flats and semi-detached properties is more volatile than the price of detached properties.

The independent variables and their descriptions are presented in Table 6.11. The table shows that with the exception of the absolute location values, all the other variables are used as dummy variables. The independent variables include structural property characteristics, locational characteristics and the various time dummies. The structural property characteristics used for the study are the number of floors, the number of public rooms, the number of bedrooms, the number of bathrooms, the availability of garages, gardens and the dwelling type (flat, semi-detached and detached). The time dummies are the yearly time dummies, the semi-yearly time dummies, the quarterly time dummies and the monthly time dummies.

Table 3.2 shows that neighbourhood and accessibility variables are mostly used in modelling the location effect on house prices. However, these neighbourhood and accessibility variables are not found in the ASPC dataset. An attempt was made to source these variables from the Scottish Neighbourhood Statistics (SNS) and include in the empirical modelling. These variables include the percentage of people who enter into university, percentages of people in the working and pension age, percentage of drug users, unemployment rate, crime rate, air quality, drive times and public transport times to the post office, supermarkets and GP.

Table 6.11 List of the independent variables and their description

Variable	Structural	Location	Time	Type	Description
Numfloor1	*			dummy	Property with one floor
Numfloor2	*			dummy	Property with two floors
Numfloor3	*			dummy	Property with three floors
Numpublic1	*			dummy	Property with one public room
Numpublic2	*			dummy	Property with two public rooms
Numpublic3	*			dummy	Property with three public rooms
Numpublic4	*			dummy	Property with four public rooms
Bedroom1	*			dummy	Property with one bedroom
Bedroom2	*			dummy	Property with two bedrooms
Bedroom3	*			dummy	Property with three bedrooms
Bedroom4	*			dummy	Property with four bedrooms
Bedroom5	*			dummy	Property with five bedrooms
Bathroom1	*			dummy	Property with one bathroom
Bathroom2	*			dummy	Property with two bathroom
Garage	*			dummy	Property with a garage
Nogarage	*			dummy	Property without a garage
Garden	*			dummy	Property with a garden
Nogarden	*			dummy	Property without a garden
Detached	*			dummy	Detached property
Flat	*			dummy	Flat property
Semi-detached	*			dummy	Semi-detached property
X		*		continuous	X-coordinate (latitude)
Y		*		continuous	Y-coordinate (longitude)
X^2		*		continuous	Squared of X- coordinate
Y^2		*		continuous	Squared of Y-coordinate
XY		*		continuous	Interaction of X and Y coordinates
X^2Y		*		continuous	Interaction of X^2 and Y coordinates
XY^2		*		continuous	Interaction of X and Y^2 coordinates
X^3		*		continuous	Cube of X-coordinate
Y^3		*		continuous	Cube of Y-coordinate

(continued)

Table 6.11 List of the independent variables and their description *(continued)*

Variable	Structural	Location	Time	Type	Description
Month1 – Month132			*	dummy	The monthly time dummies
Quarter1 – Quarter44			*	dummy	The quarterly time dummies
Semi1 – Semi22			*	dummy	The semi-yearly time dummies
Year1 – Year11			*	dummy	The yearly time dummies

However, it was recognised that the SNS boundaries have changed over time and the temporal coverage of these variables is relatively short. More so, as shown in Table 6.12, most of these variables are not statistically significant. Only crime rate and number of drug users are statistically significant but the magnitudes of the coefficients are very small. These variables are therefore excluded from empirical modelling. It should also be noted that the use of the location dummies and neighbourhood quality attributes to explain spatial variation is also limited since house prices are averaged over discrete geographic boundaries (Can, 1990). More so, the neighbourhoods and housing submarkets are normally hard to define and also very hard to identify accurately all the locational influences that affect house prices (Orford, 1999).

The absolute location variables, the easting (X) and northing (Y) coordinates are used to control for the locational characteristics of properties. This approach has been used in previous studies like Clapp (2004), Fik et al. (2003) and Pavlov (2000). In all these studies, the linear function is used to model the X and Y coordinates. In this study, the absolute location variables are incorporated into the model to accurately identify and specify locational influences on house prices. The X and Y coordinates are expanded to a third-degree polynomial (X, Y, XY, X^2Y, XY^2, X^2, Y^2, X^3, Y^3) so as to allow the marginal price of the housing attributes to vary in a continuous manner over space (Jones and Casetti, 1992). The use of the absolute location variables through the polynomial expansion is very useful and attractive since it does not require adequate local market knowledge about the division of neighbourhoods or submarkets (Michaels and Smith, 1990). The method is therefore less subjective as compared to the use of location dummies (neighbourhood, submarkets etc.).

The use of the X and Y coordinates is therefore introduced in the hedonic and hybrid methods in the form of polynomial expansion to allow for the influence of location without requiring prior expert knowledge of the geographic markets. One problem with the use of the absolute location variables is that when the polynomial degrees are extremely high, it causes perfect collinearity among them. However, since this study chooses up to the third-degree polynomial, this may not be a serious problem in this study. In cases where collinearity occurs, some of the expanded variables will be dropped. Also, the cubic function can put

Table 6.12 Magnitude and significance of the neighbourhood and accessibility variables sourced from the SNS

Variables	ETV hedonic	SCS hedonic	Q-hybrid
numfloor2	−0.0239 (−4.18)	−0.0275(−1.42)	−0.0243 (−4.24)
numfloor3	0.1406 (10.46)	0.1411 (3.27)	0.1403 (10.44)
numpublic2	0.1821 (41.75)	0.1733 (12.30)	0.1821 (41.76)
numpublic3	0.3086 (46.04)	0.2988 (13.82)	0.3086 (46.05)
numpublic4	0.4048 (40.60)	0.3963 (12.09)	0.4050 (40.62)
bedroom2	0.4353 (106.35)	0.4127 (30.97)	0.4359 (106.17)
bedroom3	0.5726 (101.43)	0.5482 (29.86)	0.5732 (101.39)
bedroom4	0.7713 (96.90)	0.7499 (28.93)	0.7720 (96.93)
bedroom5	0.9307 (79.73)	0.9151 (24.04)	0.9315 (79.77)
bathroom2	−0.0407 (−8.59)	−0.0453 (−3.02)	−0.0407 (−8.60)
garage	0.1272 (27.53)	0.1257 (8.41)	0.1272 (27.52)
garden	0.0710 (15.12)	0.0566 (4.03)	0.0708 (15.08)
nondetached	0.0973 (14.24)	0.1033 (4.49)	0.0977 (14.30)
detached	0.2614 (32.80)	0.2650 (10.05)	0.2622 (32.84)
newbuilding	0.3091 (14.84)	0.3020 (4.81)	0.3090 (14.84)
easting	−0.0001 (−15.13)	−0.0002 (−5.35)	−0.0001 (−15.14)
northing	−0.0001 (−17.92)	−0.0001 (−5.91)	−0.0001 (−17.97)
degree1entrants	0.0084 (5.76)	0.0082 (6.00)	0.0083 (4.97)
S6award5	0.0043 (1.08)	0.0043 (1.52)	0.0043 (0.94)
workingage	0.0148 (0.48)	0.0154 (1.57)	0.0148 (0.42)
pensionage	−0.0099 (−1.35)	−0.0096 (−1.15)	−0.0099 (−1.34)
drugabusepeople	0.0582 (4.23)	0.0156 (1.09)	0.0530 (4.09)
unemploymentrate	−0.0383 (−1.59)	−0.0420 (−1.73)	−0.0384 (−1.62)
crimerate	−0.0059 (−11.05)	−0.0066 (−3.60)	−0.0059 (−11.01)
airquality	0.0131 (1.64)	0.0167 (1.46)	0.0131 (1.68)
podrivetime	−0.0499 (−1.07)	−0.0444 (−1.74)	−0.0485 (−1.88)
smktdrivetime	0.0221 (1.30)	0.0231 (1.61)	0.0220 (1.21)
gpdrivetime	0.0011 (0.32)	0.0092 (0.82)	0.0012 (0.34)
popubtratime	0.0218 (1.00)	0.0207 (1.13)	0.0213 (1.82)
shoppubtratime	−0.0055 (−1.20)	−0.0043 (−1.94)	−0.0056 (−1.26)
gppubtratime	0.0017 (1.00)	0.0006 (0.04)	0.0019 (1.11)
Adjusted R^2	74.32%	73.6%	74.34%

Note: The table shows the coefficient estimates of the property and neighbourhood characteristics from the ETV hedonic, SCS hedonic and the Q-hybrid models. The coefficient estimates from the SCS hedonic model reported is the year 2005 hedonic regression results. The t-values are reported in parentheses and the Adjusted R^2 from each of the models are also reported at the last row of the table.

restrictions on the pattern of spatial variation and peaks from area to area. For example, the method does not take into consideration the fact that presence of water bodies, valleys and mountains can put restrictions on land use. Nevertheless, due to the lack of appropriate accessibility and neighbourhood variables, the inclusion of the expanded absolute location variables seems to be the best way of modelling the location effect.

Analysis of the data shows that most of the transactions took place in the city centre, and all the other areas are fairly represented. Thus, the absolute locational values are finer than the ASPC areas and so it would be more accurate to use the absolute locational values rather than using the areas as dummy variables. For the sake of convenience and easy analysis, the house prices are grouped into (i) very low price – prices under £50,000, (ii) low prices – prices between £50,000 and £100,000, (iii) average prices – prices between £100,000 and £300,000, (iv) high prices – prices between £300,000 and £500,000, (v) very high prices – prices over £500,000. Almost all the transactions involving flats took place in the city centre, suggesting that flats are mostly located in the city centre. Not surprisingly, the prices of the flats are mostly average, low and very low. As many as 99.1% of the flats are within this price range with only 0.90% being high and very high prices.

The semi-detached properties are spread out even though most of them are also in the city centre. Most of the semi-detached properties have average prices. As many as 60.9% of are within the average and high price ranges with about 38.5% having very low and low prices. The detached properties are also spread out evenly but with most of them located outside the city centre. The Newmachar, Kingswells, Maryculter, Dyce, Blackburn and Peterculter areas are among the areas with a lot of detached properties. In the northern part of Aberdeen, around the Newmachar and Balmedie areas, the transactions are dominated by average and high-priced properties. The majority of the high-priced and very high-priced properties are located in the Kingswells, Cults and Pitfodels, Milltimber, Peterculter, Maryculter, Bieldside and Blairs areas. As many as 88.3% of the detached properties transacted are either averagely priced, highly priced or very high prices. Only 11.7% of the transactions have low and very low prices. It should be noted that most of the repeat-sales are flats and are concentrated in the city centre. Not surprisingly, most of them are of very low, low and average prices.

Table 6.13 summarises the descriptive characteristics of the dependent variable and the main independent variables. The description is reported for only the single-sale sample, only the repeat-sale sample and all the sales combined. The purpose for doing this is to find out whether the assertion that the average prices of the repeat-sales sample are usually lower than the average prices of the entire sample is true. The table confirms that the prices of repeat-sale properties are actually lower than the properties that are transacted only once and lower than a combination of both samples. While the average price of the repeat-sale properties is around £87,230, the average price of only single-sales properties and all the properties combined is £145,164 and £124,095, respectively. This means that the price of repeat-sale properties is about 40% and 15% less than the price of only single-sale and all the properties combined respectively. This lends support to previous findings by Meese and Wallace (1997), Clapp and Giaccotto (1992a) and Clapp and Giaccotto (1992b) that repeat-sale houses are generally sold below the average house price. This is not surprising given that about 67% of the repeat sample are flats, with about only 10% and 23% being detached and semi-detached

Table 6.13 List of the independent variables and their description

Variables	Only single-sales				Only repeat-sales				All sales			
	Mean	Minimum	Maximum	Standard deviation	Mean	Minimum	Maximum	Standard deviation	Mean	Minimum	Maximum	Standard deviation
Price (£)	145,164	29,500	2,000,000	103,598	87,230	27,000	1,000,000	60,722	124,095	27,000	2,000,000	94,588
Price (log)	11.682	10.292	14.509	0.637	11.193	10.204	13.816	0.587	11.504	10.204	14.509	0.663
Numfloor	1.514	1	3	0.542	1.320	1	3	0.487	1.444	1	3	0.531
Numpublic	1.532	1	4	0.784	1.307	1	4	0.605	1.450	1	4	0.732
Numbedroom	1.504	1	5	1.012	1.960	1	5	0.946	2.306	1	5	1.022
Numbathroom	1.114	1	2	0.318	1.113	1	2	0.316	1.113	1	2	0.317
Garage	0.355	0	1	0.479	0.212	0	1	0.409	0.303	0	1	0.460
Nogarage	0.645	0	1	0.479	0.788	0	1	0.409	0.697	0	1	0.460
Garden	0.650	0	1	0.477	0.501	0	1	0.500	0.596	0	1	0.491
Nogarden	0.350	0	1	0.477	0.499	0	1	0.500	0.404	0	1	0.491
Detached	0.204	0	1	0.403	0.099	0	1	0.298	0.165	0	1	0.372
Flat	0.449	0	1	0.497	0.668	0	1	0.471	0.529	0	1	0.499
Semi-detached	0.347	0	1	0.476	0.234	0	1	0.423	0.306	0	1	0.461
X	39138.70	28922	41140	360.428	39209.99	37380	39710	284.832	39164.62	28922	41140	336.664
Y	80647.73	73912	85000	435.870	80631.19	79210	82360	367.381	80641.72	73912	85000	412.353

properties respectively, as shown in Table 6.13. Since flats are the least expensive properties and detached properties are the most expensive properties in Aberdeen, it is not surprising that the prices of the repeat-sales sample are very low. Even though the dependent variable is described well above, it is worthy to highlight the minimum and maximum values of the actual selling prices and its logarithm transformation. The figures suggest that with the actual selling price, the price distribution is not positively skewed. However, with the logarithm transformations, the price distribution seems to be positively skewed.

Apart from the dependent variable, Table 6.13 also shows that the average characteristics of the repeat-sale properties are lower than the average character-istics of only the single-sale properties and all the properties combined. For example, while the average value of the number of bedrooms is 2.50 for single-sale properties, it is only 1.96 for repeat-sale properties. Also, the descriptive charac-teristics show that while about 36% of single-sale properties have a garage, only 21% of repeat-sales properties have a garage. These are not surprising given the fact that flats dominate the repeat sample and the average prices of repeat-sales are lower than the single-sale properties.

The last column of Table 6.13 shows the descriptive statistics of all sales combined. From the table, the average values of the number of floors, number of public rooms, number of bedrooms, and number of bathrooms are 1.44, 1.45, 2.31 and 1.11, respectively. It also shows that about 30.3% of the properties have a garage and about 59.6% have a garden.

Conclusion

This chapter has described the study area, Aberdeen City and the Suburbs market area classified by ASPC, and the data that has been gathered, verified and prepared for the empirical part of the house price index construction. This data includes various structural property characteristics and absolute locational values. The chapter therefore serves as a link between the theoretical part of the house price index construction and the empirical part.

In this chapter also, the housing transaction data used to construct house price indices has been described. The processes of data gathering and data preparation are undertaken in this chapter. The data groups that are gathered are transaction prices, structural property characteristics and absolute locational values. Even though in the literature a lot of structural and locational attributes are identified, it has been highlighted in this chapter that the availability of the variables in the dataset determines the variables to be included in the model. The quality of the data gathered from ASPC are discussed in this chapter. The conclusion is that even though the dataset misses some important hedonic variables like floor size and age of property, the available housing characteristics are enough for house price index construction.

It has been highlighted in the chapter that the original data received from ASPC do not constitute a workable dataset for house price index construction. The data is therefore verified and cleaned in this chapter. The necessary dummy variables needed to construct the house price indices are created and the repeat-sales are identified. In all, a total of 57,150 observations with different independent variables are used for the index construction. Out of this about 36.4% are repeat-sales.

Finally, the final dataset is presented in this chapter. The distribution of the variables shows that the dwelling type that dominates the dataset is flats. Flats make up about 53% of the entire dataset and are mostly located in the city centre. This is followed by semi-detached and detached properties, and this is in line with the stock data. The descriptive statistics of the variables show that detached properties are the most expensive properties, followed by semi-detached and flats. Also, the average price of repeat-sales properties is found to be lower than that of single-sales and all the dataset combined. The log of transaction price is found to be normally distributed. Having prepared the data, the next step is to empirically examine the alternative index construction methods by employing this dataset. This is the aim of the next chapter.

Note

1 Gross Value Added (GVA) is a measure of the value of the goods and services produced in the economy and it is the Office for National Statistics' (ONS) preferred measure for monitoring economic performance and overall economic well-being (ACC, 2011).

7 Empirical demonstration of property price index construction

Introduction

The previous chapter dealt with the data used for house price index construction. This chapter provides the results from estimating house price indices. Chapter 5 provides evidence that none of the index construction methods consistently outperform the others in terms of their accuracies. Apart from the fact that the empirical studies examined in the chapter are from different study areas and so can cause this inconsistency, two other possible reasons for this inconsistency as noted in the chapter are

i   absence of appropriate proxy for the unobservable "true" house price trend to measure index accuracy;
ii scarcity and pooling of data. This chapter employs the out of sample technique to measure the mean squared error (MSE) of the various index construction models to examine the accuracy of the different index models.

The effect of temporal aggregation on house price indices is also examined in this chapter. Five different house price index construction models are implemented for the analysis: two are based on the hedonic method; two are based on the repeat-sales method; and one is based on the hybrid method. These models are:

i   the explicit time variable (ETV) hedonic model;
ii the strictly cross-sectional (SCS) hedonic model;
iii the ordinary repeat-sales (ORS) model;
iv the weighted repeat-sales (WRS) model; and
v   the Quigley's hybrid (Q-hybrid) model.

These models and their strengths and weaknesses have already been discussed in Chapter 5. The reason for implementing both the ETV and SCS hedonic models is to test the assumption that the implicit prices of the housing attributes are constant over time. Implementing the two repeat-sales models will also help to find out if there is any efficiency gain in using weighted least squares (WLS) instead of ordinary least squares (OLS) in implementing the method. The Q-hybrid model is the only hybrid method implemented because the age of the property, which is a cardinal variable in the implementation of the other hybrid models (like the ones proposed by Englund et al., 1998 and Hill et al., 1997), is absent in the dataset as mentioned in Chapter 6. As discussed in Chapter 5, the age variable makes it possible for Englund et al. (1998) and Hill et al. (1997) to distinguish between depreciation and vintage in implementing the hybrid method. The rest of the chapter is organised as follows.

The second section presents and examines the results obtained from the estimates of the hedonic characteristics. The hedonic characteristics results estimated by the ETV hedonic, the SCS hedonic and the Q-hybrid models are presented and analysed. The aim here is to find out if the estimated implicit prices of the hedonic characteristics are different with each of the models, and to find out which model fits the data best according to their Adjusted R-squares. More importantly, the section identifies whether the housing characteristics differ over time and, if so, whether the assumption holds that the implicit prices of the hedonic characteristics are constant over time. In the third section, the house price indices constructed by the various models are compared. Monthly, quarterly, semi-annual and annual indices are constructed with each of the models and these indices are presented. Presenting the various indices will reveal if the pattern of price change is the same for each model. The overall accuracy of the various indices across time is also examined based on the mean squared error (MSE) criteria. Finally, the section looks at whether the differences between the various models as given by the MSE are statistically significant. The fourth section looks at the influence of temporal aggregation on house prices. The aim here is to find out if pooling data together across time is warranted in constructing house price indices. Housing transactions are executed on a daily basis but are often pooled together across time since the daily transactions are typically few and infrequent. It is therefore necessary to examine how aggregated the data pooling should be in the construction of indices. Even though only Aberdeen is used as the case study area to undertake this test, the findings and conclusions to be drawn may be applicable to other markets. The last section concludes the chapter.

Presentation and analysis of the hedonic characteristics results

This section presents and discusses the empirical results estimates relating to the hedonic characteristics. In particular, the influence of the hedonic characteristics on price as estimated from the ETV hedonic, SCS hedonic and the Q-hybrid models is presented and discussed. In this section, also, the assumption that the implicit prices of the housing attributes are constant over time is tested using the Chow test.

Hedonic characteristics estimates

Table 7.1 shows the estimated coefficients from implementing the ETV hedonic model (Equation 5.2), the SCS hedonic model (Equation 5.3) and the Q-hybrid model (Equations 5.17 through 5.20). As indicated in Chapter 5

Table 7.1 A comparison of the ETV, SCS and Q-hybrid hedonic estimates

Variables	ETV hedonic	SCS hedonic	Q-hybrid
numfloor2	−0.0239 (−4.18)	−0.0035(−0.19)	−0.0243 (−4.24)
numfloor3	0.1406 (10.46)	0.2030 (4.62)	0.1403 (10.44)
numpublic2	0.1821 (41.75)	0.1752 (13.08)	0.1821 (41.76)
numpublic3	0.3086 (46.04)	0.3292 (15.33)	0.3086 (46.05)
numpublic4	0.4048 (40.60)	0.4273 (11.49)	0.4050 (40.62)
bedroom2	0.4353 (106.35)	0.4651 (36.98)	0.4359 (106.17)
bedroom3	0.5726 (101.43)	0.6155 (34.63)	0.5732 (101.39)
bedroom4	0.7713 (96.90)	0.8175 (32.90)	0.7720 (96.93)
bedroom5	0.9307 (79.73)	0.9571 (25.69)	0.9315 (79.77)
bathroom2	−0.0407 (−8.59)	−0.0474 (−3.09)	−0.0407 (−8.60)
garage	0.1272 (27.53)	0.1290 (8.71)	0.1272 (27.52)
garden	0.0710 (15.12)	0.0756 (5.09)	0.0708 (15.08)
nondetached	0.0973 (14.24)	0.0643 (2.91)	0.0977 (14.30)
detached	0.2614 (32.80)	0.2144 (8.19)	0.2622 (32.84)
X	−2182.45 (−5.72)	−16141.95 (−3.70)	−2150.23 (−4.37)
Y	14501.15 (20.50)	31176.12 (9.34)	13385.4 (18.20)
X^2	386.39 (7.30)	2862.40 (3.58)	46.29 (0.72)
Y^2	−1827.69 (−24.66)	−4155.11 (−9.55)	−1767.52 (−23.56)
XY	175.70 (1.29)	1246.07 (3.89)	494.62 (2.88)
X^2Y	10.64 (3.06)	−158.15 (−3.86)	103.88 (12.43)
XY^2	−15.14 (−1.99)	−	−79.71 (−7.91)
X^3	−42.38 (−7.44)	−137.76 (−3.26)	−77.81 (−9.92)
Y^3	77.30 (26.53)	171.11 (9.52)	85.22 (27.21)
Adjusted R^2	80.8%	72.0%	81.2%

Note: The table shows the coefficient estimates of the property and neighbourhood characteristics from the ETV hedonic, SCS hedonic and the Q-hybrid models. The coefficient estimates from the SCS hedonic model reported in the third column of the table is the yearly regression of year 2005. The t-values are reported in parentheses and the Adjusted R^2 from each of the models are also reported at the last row of the table. "−" means that the variable is dropped due to its perfect collinearity with other variables.

the dependent variable is the natural logarithm of the transaction price and the independent variables include both physical property characteristics and locational variables. The physical property characteristics used are the number of floors, the number of rooms (public rooms, bedrooms and bathrooms), the availability or otherwise of a garage and a garden and the dwelling type (whether detached, semi-detached or flat).

The locational variables used are the absolute location variables, the easting (X) and northing (Y) coordinates. The absolute location variables are incorporated into the model to accurately identify and specify locational influences on house prices. The X and Y coordinates are expanded to a third-degree polynomial (X, Y, XY, X^2Y, XY^2, X^2, Y^2, X^3, Y^3) so as to allow the marginal price of the location to vary in a continuous manner over space (Jones and Casetti, 1992). The use of the absolute location variables through the polynomial expansion is very useful and attractive since it does not require adequate local market knowledge about the division of neighbourhoods or submarkets (Michaels and Smith, 1990). The method is therefore less subjective as compared to the use of location dummies (neighbourhood, submarkets etc.). The usefulness of the location dummies and neighbourhood quality attributes to explain spatial variation is limited since house prices are averaged over discrete geographic boundaries (Can, 1990). Further, the neighbourhoods and housing submarkets are normally hard to define and it is also very hard to identify accurately all the locational influences that affect house prices (Orford, 1999). X and Y coordinates are therefore introduced to the hedonic and hybrid methods in the form of polynomial expansion to accurately estimate the influence of location in an absolute sense without having prior expert knowledge of the geographic markets. The five-digit easting and northing coordinates are divided by 10,000 before they are incorporated into the models. This rescale is necessary to prevent the reporting of insignificant zero numbers.

The yearly time dummies are included in the ETV and the Q-hybrid models and are not reported here, but rather are used to construct the index numbers to be discussed in the next section. The coefficient estimates from the SCS hedonic model reported in the third column of the table is the year 2005 regression estimates. The year 2005 regression estimates are presented here for the purpose of comparison because it is the median year over the period. The results from the different separate monthly regressions, quarterly regressions, semi-annual regressions and annual regressions from the SCS hedonic model are presented at Appendices 1, 2, 3 and 4, respectively. Appendices 5 and 6 show also the hedonic characteristics results from the monthly, quarterly, and semi-annual ETV hedonic and the Q-hybrid models respectively.

As shown in Table 7.1, the Q-hybrid model and the ETV hedonic model exhibit approximately the same Adjusted R-squared. Each of the two models explains approximately 81% of the variation in house prices. With each of the models, therefore, only about 19% of the variation is left unexplained. This means that even by incorporating the individual-specific error variance and the random walk in housing prices, the explanatory power of the hedonic model could not be improved significantly. The explanatory power (Adjusted R-squared) of the ETV hedonic model is higher than the 72% Adjusted R-squared produced by the SCS hedonic model. This is not surprising because, by pooling the data together, the dataset becomes larger and so the explanatory power is expected to increase.

With the exception of XY (interaction of the easting and northing coordinates), all the other variables are statistically significant at a 5% significance level in the ETV hedonic model. In the Q-hybrid model, only the X^2 (easting coordinate squared) is insignificant. Also, all the explanatory variables, except XY^2 (interaction of the easting and northing squared coordinates) and numfloor2, in the SCS model are also statistically significant at a 5% significance level. Indeed, the XY^2 is dropped due to its perfect collinearity with the other absolute locational variables. It can be observed from the table that most of the estimated parameters have the expected signs and this is consistent across all the models. For example, semi-detached, detached, garage and gardens have positive signs. This means that the price of a semi-detached or detached house is higher than the price of a flat, all other things being equal. Also, the price of a property which has a garage is higher than the price of property without a garage, and similarly, the price of a property which has a garden is higher than the price of a property without a garden.

Again, the number of rooms (bedrooms, public rooms and bathrooms) increase as an additional room is added. For example, the coefficient of three bedrooms (bedroom3) is more than that of two bedrooms (bedroom2). Similarly, the coefficient of four bedrooms (bedroom4) is more than that of three bedrooms (bedroom3). The same thing can be said of the other room variables and this is consistent for all the models. However, it is clear that the magnitude of increment changes as more and more rooms are added. For example, the price of two public rooms (numpublic2) in the ETV hedonic model is about 18% higher than that of one public room, but the price of three public rooms (numpublic3) is only almost 12% (0.3086-0.1821) higher than the price of two public rooms. The price diminishes further as additional public room is added. This clearly confirms the fact highlighted in Chapter 3 that housing as an economic good is affected by the law of diminishing returns (see Gallimore et al., 1996b).

Also, the price of houses with a garage is higher than that of houses without a garage, all other things being equal. Detached houses are the most expensive houses in Aberdeen. For example, from the Q-hybrid model, the price of detached houses in the city is about 26% higher than the price of flats and are about 16% (0.2622-0.0977) higher than price of semi-detached houses. The price of semi-detached houses is also about 10% higher than the price of flats. These findings are very consistent in all the methods. The significance of the absolute locational variables and their polynomial expansion suggests that distinct geographical and spatial differences exist in the housing market, and the inclusion of these variables thus controls for the differences. Figures 7.1, 7.2 and 7.3 show a 3-dimensional plot of the absolute locational values estimated by the ETV hedonic yearly model, SCS hedonic model for year 2005 and Q-hybrid yearly model, respectively. The SCS hedonic model for the other years are shown at Appendix 7. The figures show that the absolute locational values are not linear. That is, an increase in the easting and/or northing coordinates does not necessarily increase or decrease the property values in a linear way. Instead, the plots have irregular shapes meaning that property values vary across space.

It should be mentioned here that the coefficient estimate of the variables from the SCS hedonic model changes from period to period (results shown at the appendix). For example, the coefficient estimates of bedroom4 is about 78% higher than the coefficient estimate of bedroom1 in the year 2000, but, in the following year (2001), the coefficient of bedroom4 is only 73% higher than that of bedroom1. This finding is similar across all the periods.

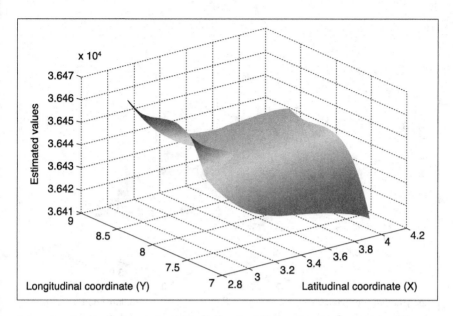

Figure 7.1 A 3-dimensional plot showing the absolute locational values estimated by the ETV hedonic yearly model

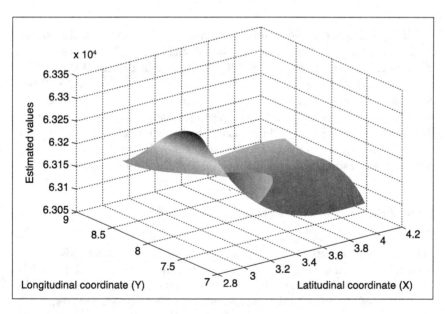

Figure 7.2 A 3-dimensional plot showing the absolute locational values estimated by the SCS hedonic model for year 2005

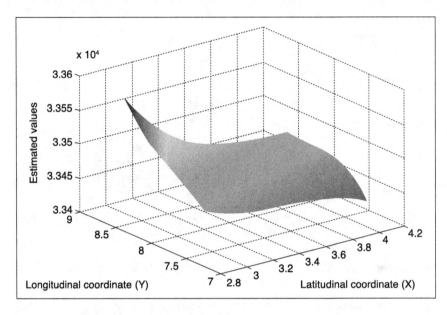

Figure 7.3 A 3-dimensional plot showing the absolute locational values estimated by the Q-hybrid yearly model

This suggests that the value of utility consumers place on housing and locational attributes varies over time as found in Gatzlaff and Haurin (1997), Costello and Watkins (2002) and Bourassa et al. (2006). The implicit prices of the housing and locational attributes depend both on demand and supply factors. While consumer preference is the main demand factor, new housing supply through technology development is the main supply factor. Developers will develop where they will make most profits and this affects the implicit price. However, it is not known if the changes in the coefficient estimates of the housing attributes over time are statistically significant, and this is the aim of the next subsection.

A test of the constancy of the hedonic characteristics prices over time

In the previous subsection, the implicit prices of the hedonic characteristics have been estimated using the ETV hedonic, SCS hedonic and the Q-hybrid models. The key difference between the ETV hedonic and the SCS hedonic models is the assumption of constancy of the implicit prices of the housing attributes. While the ETV hedonic model assumes that the implicit prices are constant over time and so pools the data together over the entire period in implementing the model, the SCS hedonic model allows the implicit prices to change over time and so a separate regression is run for each time period. In this sub-section, this assumption of constancy of the implicit prices is empirically tested using the Chow test (Chow, 1960).

The Chow test is a statistical test of whether the coefficients of the parameters in two different datasets are equal. Even though Chow (1960) restricts this test to only two sub-samples, the test can be applied to more than two sub-samples. Assume that we have an equation:

$$\ln P = \alpha + \beta_1 X_1 + \beta_2 X_2 + \cdots + \beta_J X_N + e \tag{7.1}$$

where

- P is the transaction price;
- a is the constant;
- $\hat{\beta}_J$ is the estimate of the assumed, but unknown, coefficient of the hedonic characteristics, X_n, with; $j = 1,2,...J$ and $n = 1,2,...N$; and
- e is the error term.

If we assume that the coefficients change from year to year, the dataset can be split into 11 sub-samples since the dataset covers a period of 11 years. If we represent the number of sub-samples by S, and hence $S = 11$, we can write

$$\begin{bmatrix} P_1 \\ P_2 \\ \vdots \\ P_S \end{bmatrix} = \begin{bmatrix} \alpha_1 + \beta_{1,1}X_1 + \beta_{2,1}X_2 + \cdots + \beta_{J,1}X_N + e_1 \\ \alpha_2 + \beta_{1,2}X_1 + \beta_{2,2}X_2 + \cdots + \beta_{J,2}X_N + e_2 \\ \vdots \\ \alpha_S + \beta_{1,S}X_1 + \beta_{2,2}X_2 + \cdots + \beta_{1,S}X_N + e_S \end{bmatrix} \tag{7.2}$$

From Equation 7.2, we can test the null hypothesis that all the coefficients (including the intercept) are the same in all the 11 groups. That is, we test:

$$H_0: \alpha_1 = \alpha_2 = \cdots = \alpha_S, \beta_{1,1} = \beta_{1,2} = \cdots = \beta_{1,S}, \beta_{2,1} = \beta_{2,2}$$
$$= \cdots = \beta_{2,S}, \cdots, \beta_{J1} = \beta_{J2} = \cdots = \beta_{JS} \tag{7.3}$$

The alternative hypothesis is that all the coefficients (including the intercept) are not the same in the 11 groups. That is,

$$H_1: \alpha_1 \neq \alpha_2 \neq \cdots \neq \alpha_S, \beta_{1,1} \neq \beta_{1,2} \neq \cdots \neq \beta_{1,S}, \beta_{2,1} \neq \beta_{2,2}$$
$$\neq \cdots \neq \beta_{2,S}, \cdots, \beta_{J1} \neq \beta_{J2} \neq \cdots \neq \beta_{JS} \tag{7.4}$$

These two hypotheses in Equations 7.3 and 7.4 can be tested by two main ways: (i) by using the sum of squares test and (ii) by using the dummy variable test. The use of the sum of squares test requires that 11 different regressions be run using Equation 7.2, where each regression is run using one of the 11 sub-samples. Let

$\hat{e}_1, \hat{e}_2, ..., \hat{e}_s$ be a vector of residuals from the 11 separate regressions, and sum of squares $RSS_1 = \hat{e}'_1\hat{e}_1$, $RSS_2 = \hat{e}'_2\hat{e}_2$, ..., $RSS_s = \hat{e}'_s\hat{e}_s$. The unrestricted sum of squares for the whole dataset which has $n - Tk$ degree of freedom will be

$$URSS = \sum_{t=S}^{T} RSS_t \qquad (7.5)$$

where

- n is the sum of the total number of observations in each of the sub-samples and k is the total number of parameters. In addition, another regression is run using Equation 7.1 and the entire dataset. Let the residuals from this equation be $\hat{e}$, and the restricted sum of squares $\hat{e}'_1\hat{e}_1$ be RSS with $n-k$ degrees of freedom. The Chow test using this sum of squares test is performed by calculating the F-statistic under H_0:

$$F = \frac{(RRSS - URSS)/k}{URSS/(n - Tk)} \sim F_{k,n-Tk} \qquad (7.6)$$

The alternative way of performing the test is by using the dummy variable test procedure. By this we interact each of the parameters or variables in Equation 7.1 with each of the T sub-samples. The model therefore becomes

$$P = \sum_{t=1}^{T} \alpha_t d_{t,n} + \sum_{t=1}^{T} \beta_{1t} X_1 d_{t,n} \sum_{t=1}^{T} \beta_{2t} X_2 d_{t,n}$$
$$+ \cdots + \sum_{t=1}^{T} \beta_{Vt} X_i d_{t,n} + \sum_{t=1}^{T} e_t d_{t,n} \qquad (7.7)$$

where

$$d_{t,n} = \begin{cases} 1 \text{ if property } n \text{ is sold in } t \\ 0 \text{ if property } n \text{ is sold in } t \end{cases}$$

The null hypothesis we test is the same as in Equation 7.3 and this can be tested with the usual F-statistics. Even though both the dummy variable test and the sum of squares test lead to numerically identical F-statistics, the dummy variable test is used here because it has an added advantage in that we can use it to test if some of the parameters are the same in two or more periods. This test is very necessary because it can be the case that the coefficient estimates of the number of bedrooms variable are statistically the same for each of the periods but that of the number of public rooms may be different.

Table 7.2 presents the results from Equation 7.7 which is the same as the yearly regressions from implementing the SCS hedonic model. The last column of the table also shows the results of the Chow test that is performed with the asterisks, ***,**and * representing significance at a 1%, 5% and 10% levels. It is clear from the table that with the exception of "bathroom2" variable, the F-statistic rejects the null hypothesis that the implicit prices of the other property physical characteristics are the same. The implicit prices of the property physical characteristics therefore change from period to period.

Table 7.2 A test of the assumption of constancy of implicit prices of the housing attributes

Variables	Estimated coefficients within each year group											Chow test
	Y2000	Y2001	Y2002	Y2003	Y2004	Y2005	Y2006	Y2007	Y2008	Y2009	Y2010	
numfloor2	-0.022	-0.025	-0.013	-0.015	-0.032	-0.004	-0.012	-0.040	-0.039	-0.070	-0.030	1.76*
numfloor3	0.179	0.219	0.122	0.192	0.109	0.203	0.112	0.093	0.097	0.067	0.160	2.67***
numpublic2	0.182	0.186	0.220	0.202	0.190	0.175	0.166	0.138	0.177	0.145	0.125	3.68***
numpublic3	0.350	0.323	0.357	0.329	0.314	0.329	0.274	0.236	0.281	0.266	0.228	3.42***
numpublic4	0.547	0.527	0.490	0.437	0.443	0.427	0.445	0.320	0.415	0.423	0.435	2.57***
bedroom2	0.383	0.405	0.451	0.519	0.484	0.465	0.375	0.371	0.368	0.351	0.368	14.05***
bedroom3	0.534	0.529	0.614	0.676	0.627	0.616	0.493	0.492	0.469	0.488	0.493	9.34***
bedroom4	0.775	0.733	0.817	0.877	0.810	0.817	0.707	0.669	0.674	0.712	0.659	5.47***
bedroom5	0.935	0.890	0.963	1.067	1.045	0.957	0.869	0.833	0.805	0.869	0.833	4.21***
bathroom2	-0.026	-0.052	-0.067	-0.047	-0.051	-0.047	-0.059	-0.046	-0.001	-0.021	-0.080	1.47
garage	0.111	0.147	0.110	0.126	0.125	0.129	0.155	0.156	0.093	0.087	0.145	2.32***
garden	0.117	0.083	0.087	0.117	0.083	0.076	0.026	0.024	0.011	-0.013	0.011	6.26***
nondetached	0.062	0.089	0.104	0.069	0.093	0.064	0.117	0.102	0.132	0.177	0.128	3.18***
detached	0.225	0.246	0.303	0.260	0.268	0.214	0.235	0.254	0.297	0.322	0.291	3.51***
X	8029.20	-25220.37	5745.28	-19722.50	44478.1	-16141.95	-12462.44	-10032.90	-5610.13	24264.14	-1012.90	4.32***
Y	17571.04	25966.61	39377.12	36620.69	45428.41	31176.12	38284.02	26642.56	33666.60	31310.09	20638.74	7.93***
X^2	877.66	5470.40	-1453.34	3625.64	-11398.43	2862.40	2264.81	1760.74	849.74	-6246.40	303.68	5.04***
Y^2	-1481.18	-3449.35	-4872.65	-4868.14	-5625.68	-4155.11	-4958.66	-3484.51	-4304.18	-3883.78	-2536.73	5.77***
XY	-2810.00	981.59	–	1400.66	–	1246.07	900.68	782.52	561.62	–	-60.96	4.91***
X^2Y	362.7603	-209.52	778.92	-176.61	1408.05	-158.15	-112.34	-97.93	-69.66	809.73	11.51	3.45***
XY^2	–	42.02	-374.15	–	-678.72	–	–	–	–	-388.88	–	5.02***
Y^2	60.27	135.21	260.87	200.50	341.24	171.11	204.44	143.48	177.45	222.81	104.23	5.27***
All												6.41***

Note: The table shows the coefficient estimates of the property and locational characteristics and the F-statistics from implementing the Chow test. The ***, ** and * by the F-statistics represent significance on 1%, 5% and 10% levels. "–" means that the variable is dropped due to its perfect collinearity with other variables. Clearly, the test rejects the null hypothesis that all the implicit prices of the housing attributes are the same over the whole period.

The F-statistic also rejects the null hypothesis that the implicit prices for the absolute location variables and their polynomial expansion on a 1% level are the same. This suggests that preferences of homeowners have changed over time. The last row on the table presents an F-statistic that tests the null hypothesis that all the parameters (including the intercepts) in all the groups are the same. On a 1% significance level, the null is rejected, meaning that the 11 sub-samples are statistically different. This finding confirms the evidence of the significant parameter inconstancy find by Berndt and Rappaport (2001) and Pakes (2003) when constructing price indices for desktop and mobile personal computers.

The results from the Chow test presented in Table 7.3 show that the assumption of the constancy of the implicit prices of housing attributes made by the ETV hedonic model is not true. The 11 different yearly groups are actually different from each other. However, even if the implicit prices change over time, it does not necessarily bias the overall price appreciation or index numbers (Wilhelmsson, 2009). This is because when the implicit price of one property attribute increases between the period $t-1$ and t, the implicit price of another property attribute may decrease over the same period. These positive and negative price changes among the variables may cancel each other and so the overall price appreciation may not necessarily be biased.

The decision to use either the ETV hedonic model or the SCS hedonic model should not be based on the constancy of the implicit prices assumption alone. The SCS hedonic model is more general than the ETV hedonic model since it allows for the implicit prices to change over time. Therefore, one could think that the SCS hedonic model should always be used. However, imposing restrictions in the case of the ETV hedonic model could lead to a better estimator especially where the sample size per period is small. When the sample size per period is relatively small, then using the SCS hedonic model may produce large variance.

The decision to use either the SCS hedonic or the ETV hedonic model should therefore be seen as a possible trade-off between unbiasedness and small variance. Unbiasedness because of the assumption of the constancy of the implicit prices over time and small variance because of the problem of small sample size, a common problem in many real estate studies that involve the use of real estate transaction data. A comparison and examination of the accuracy of the various indices are therefore necessary to ascertain the most accurate model, and that is the aim of the next section.

Empirical results and analysis of the various indices

The previous section has presented the results of the coefficient estimates of the ETV hedonic, SCS hedonic and the Q-hybrid models. The section has also tested and rejected the assumption that the implicit prices of the housing attributes are constant over time. In this section, the house price indices constructed from the two hedonic models, the two repeat-sales models and the Q-hybrid model are also presented. The five indices are compared and the accuracy of the various models are measured and discussed using the mean squared error (MSE) technique.

Finally, the differences between the accuracy of the various models are tested. The aim is to find out if the differences between the models in terms of their accuracy are significant.

Comparison of the various index models

Figure 7.4 compares the indices constructed from the various models – the ETV hedonic model, the SCS hedonic model, the ordinary repeat-sales (ORS) model, the weighted repeat-sales (WRS) model and the Quigley's hybrid (Q-hybrid) model. The ETV hedonic and the Q-hybrid indices are constructed from the time dummy (yearly) coefficients obtained from implementing Equation 5.2 (ETV hedonic model) and Equations 5.17 through 5.20 (Q-hybrid model), respectively. The ORS and WRS indices are also constructed from the time dummy (yearly) coefficients obtained from implementing Equations 5.6 (ORS model) and the WRS model. The first dummy variable (the year 2000 in this case) in each of the methods is omitted from the regression equations because they serve as the base period on which the other periods' time dummies are measured. The value for the first-time dummy variable is usually represented by zero and the coefficient estimates of the other time dummies are interpreted as the price change from the base period to that period. The indices constructed at the semi-annual level, quarterly level and the monthly level are also reported in Figures 7.5, 7.6 and 7.7 for comparison purposes.

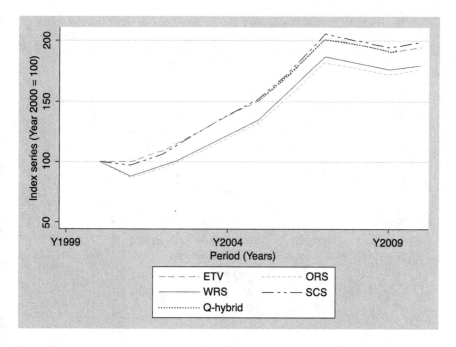

Figure 7.4 A graph showing the annual indices of the various models

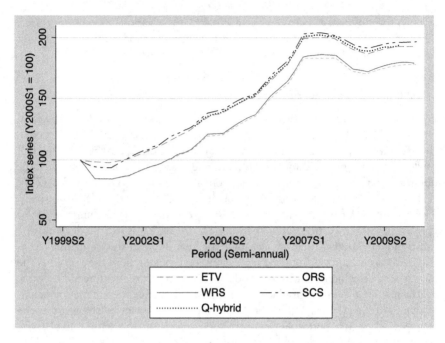

Figure 7.5 A graph showing the semi-annual indices of the various models

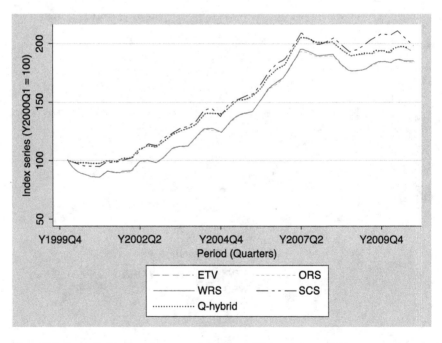

Figure 7.6 A graph showing the quarterly indices of the various models

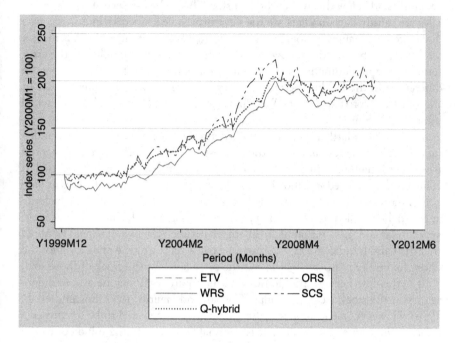

Figure 7.7 A graph showing the monthly indices of the various models

For the SCS index, however, no time dummies are included in the regression equation since separate regressions are run for each period (yearly period in this case). Using the same set of median housing and locational characteristics of a "hypothetical house" in the initial period, a predicted transaction price (in log) is obtained for each period. The differences between these predicted prices at each period are used to construct the index numbers. All these indices are estimated using a random sample of 75% from the dataset. The remaining 25% sub-sample is used to assess the accuracy of the various indices.

From Figure 7.4, it can be seen that, in general, the house price pattern in Aberdeen is similar even though different estimators are used. Over the study period, house prices decreased between years 2000 and 2001 and increased thereafter until it reaching its peak in the year 2007. Beyond this point, house prices began to fall until the year 2009. Between the year 2009 and 2010, there was another increase in house prices. This pattern of house prices is expected given the fact that there was a housing boom in the UK in 2007 and housing crises thereafter until 2009. Clearly from Figures 7.5, 7.6 and 7.7, the behaviour of the indices of all the methods is similar across all the levels of time.

It is also clear from all the figures that the repeat-sales indices tend to track the house prices below the hedonic and the hybrid indices in almost every period. This finding lends support to a previous findings document by Meese and Wallace (1997), and Clapp and Giaccotto (1992a, 1992b) that repeat-sale houses are generally sold below the average house price. This is the case because the repeat-sales are mostly flats and flats are the least expensive properties in Aberdeen as discovered in Chapter 6. Comparing the two repeat-sales indices, the WRS index tends to track house prices above the ORS index. That is, by including the error terms in the modelling process to control for heteroskedasticity caused by the differences in the holding periods, house prices are growing at a greater rate in the long run as predicted by the WRS index than implied by the indices estimated using the ORS model.

In terms of volatility of price changes, the SCS or multiple hedonic index immediately stands out as having the greatest volatility of price changes over the period. This high volatility could stem from the fact that the sample size used to compute the SCS hedonic indices for each period is relatively small. This finding confirms the previous results obtained by Bourassa et al. (2006). The ETV hedonic and Q-hybrid indices track housing prices at the same level. The two indices are very similar and there is not much difference between the two. It should be noted that the various indices computed do not exactly represent the price level for the entire inventory of houses, but rather the price level for the stock of those sold. This is the case because the houses sold in any interval may be a nonrandom sample of the stock (see for example Gatzlaff and Haurin, 1997; Englund et al., 1998). However, the sample used for the analysis is assumed to be a representation of the entire stock and so it is reasonable to impute these indices to the entire inventory.

Overall accuracy and precision of the index methods

As at this stage, the index type that is most accurate has not been established. As already indicated, the dataset is split into two so that the accuracy of the various methods to predict the unobservable true price pattern for housing can be addressed. The first sub-sample consists of 75% of all observations and this sample is used to compute the indices reported above. The remaining 25%, the second sub-sample, is used to predict or forecast house prices for each observation. For each index model, therefore, sub-sample 2 will have two sets of house prices for each observation. The first one is a forecast sale price, $\hat{P}_{nt}$, and the second one is an actual sale price P_{nt}. Standard forecast analysis statistics is used to evaluate the relative accuracy of the different index models according to the overall MSE for each index model. MSE is used, not other measures like the mean absolute error (MAE), because MSE is a second moment of the error and thus incorporates both the variance of the estimator and its bias (Shaul et al., 1999). This makes it more appropriate to compare the alternative index models. The MSE is calculated by dividing the sum of the squared predicted price error by the total number of observations used to predict the price. This is represented by:

$$\frac{1}{N}\sum_{n=1}^{N} (P_{nt} - \hat{P}_{nt})^2 \tag{7.8}$$

where

- n is the number of predicted prices;
- P_{nt} is the actual price of observation n at time t; and
- $\hat{P}_{nt}$ is the predicted price of observation n at time t.

The idea is that the model with the smallest MSE for individual price predictions should be used to measure the house price trend. One can rewrite Equation 7.8 as sum of estimated bias and estimated variance of predictor. The error, $\hat{e}_n \equiv P_n - \hat{P}_n$. If an index model is unbiased, then $\bar{e} \approx 0$ because $E[\hat{e}_n] = 0$. Equation 7.8 can thus be rewritten as

$$\frac{1}{N}\sum_{n=1}^{N}(\hat{e}_n)^2 \tag{7.9}$$

Equation 7.9 is expanded and simplified as follows:

$$= \frac{1}{N}\sum_{n=1}^{N}[(\hat{e}_n - \bar{e}) - (0 - \bar{e})]^2 \tag{7.10}$$

$$= \frac{1}{N}\sum_{n=1}^{N}[(\hat{e}_n - \bar{e})^2 - 2(\hat{e}_n - \bar{e})(0 - \bar{e}) + (0 - \bar{e})^2] \tag{7.11}$$

$$= \frac{1}{N}\sum_{n=1}^{N}[(\hat{e}_n - \bar{e})^2 + (0 - \bar{e})^2] \tag{7.12}$$

$$= Var[\hat{e}_n] + Bias(\hat{e}_n)^2 \tag{7.13}$$

That is, the MSE is a combination of bias and variance in the estimated price index. Unbiasedness alone is not necessarily the best criterion. Parsimonious models may perform better even though they are simplifications. According to this criterion, the lower the MSE, the better the index model is.

Table 7.3 presents the MSE for the five house price index models. As illustrated above, if the MSE value is relatively small for a particular index model, then that index model indicates a better accuracy and precision. The objective here is therefore to minimise the MSE. The MSEs of the various models are compared at the various levels of time aggregation. However, since the sample size used for estimating the MSE values of the hedonic and hybrid models are different from that of the repeat-sales models, the MSE values of the hedonic and the hybrid models and that of the repeat-sales models may be very different. More so, the repeat-sales models predict the price trend, but do not account for house characteristics as the other house characteristics do. Therefore, a comparison of the MSE values of the hedonic and hybrid models are separated from a comparison of the repeat-sales models.

It is clear from the table that at the broader level of time aggregation (yearly and semi-yearly levels), the SCS hedonic model stands out as the most accurate

Table 7.3 Accuracy of the house price index construction models using the MSE

Index models	Index frequency			
	Yearly	Semi-yearly	Quarterly	Monthly
ORS	0.1721	0.1708	0.1701	0.1693
WRS	0.1715	0.1708	0.1704	0.1696
SCS	0.0605	0.0619	0.0668	0.0741
ETV	0.0652	0.0648	0.0642	0.0639
Q-hybrid	0.0649	0.0646	0.0642	0.0640

Note: The table shows the Mean Squared Error (MSE) statistics for the five index models estimated at four different levels of temporal aggregation. An index model that produces the lowest MSE at a certain level of temporal aggregation is considered as the most accurate model at that level of temporal aggregation.

index model. This finding is not surprising because at the broader levels of aggregation, the sample used to construct the SCS hedonic index is relatively large and since the implicit prices of the housing attributes change from time to time, it is reasonable for the SCS hedonic model to perform better than the rest of the models, particularly the ETV hedonic model. This confirms the finding by Diewert et al. (2007) and Costello and Watkins (2002) that the SCS hedonic model outperforms the ETV hedonic model.

At the lower level of time aggregation, however, the SCS hedonic model is clearly outperformed by the Q-hybrid and the ETV hedonic models. The possible reason for this finding is that at the lower level of time aggregation, the sample for each of the periods is relatively small and so the degree of freedom reduces and this problem might have over-shadowed the advantage inherent in running separate regression for each period.

The second best ranked model at the broader level of aggregation is the Quigley's hybrid model. This is also not surprising because the model combines both the single- and multiple-sales and incorporates an explicit error structure as part of the modelling process. Like the ETV hedonic model, the hybrid model pools all the data together. However, unlike the ETV hedonic model, the Q-hybrid model incorporates the error structure in its implementation and so increases the accuracy level. The ETV hedonic model follows closely as the third best ranked model at the broader level of aggregation.

However, even though at the broader level of temporal aggregation, the Q-hybrid model outperforms the ETV hedonic model, at the lower level of temporal aggregation, the accuracy of both models are the same. Both models stand out as the best models when constructing house price indices at the quarterly and monthly levels of frequency. They perform better than the SCS hedonic model even though the implicit prices of the housing attributes vary over time. This suggests that at the lower level of aggregation, the problem of small sample size becomes more pronounced with using the SCS hedonic model and so pooling the data together to increase the sample size by using the Q-hybrid or the ETV hedonic model improves the estimates. Because the SCS hedonic model allows for the implicit prices to change over time and pooling the data over a year or over a six-month period makes the dataset large enough for hedonic analysis, the model does better at the broader of aggregation. However, as we move from annual and semi-annual indices to quarterly and monthly indices, since the dataset over such a single quarter or month is relatively small, using the SCS hedonic model causes bias in the estimates due to loss in degree of freedom. It is therefore better to pool the data together over the sample period by using the ETV hedonic or probably the Q-hybrid model. This confirms the assertion of Wilhelmsson (2009) that even if the implicit prices change over time, the index numbers may not necessarily be inaccurate. Clearly, this is a trade-off between unbiasedness and small variance and that trade-off depends on the level of temporal aggregation used in the construction of the house price indices.

A comparison of the two repeat-sales models shows that at the broader level of temporal aggregation, the WRS model outperforms the ORS model. Even though the sample size utilised to implement the ORS and the WRS are the same, the WRS model is improved since it employs the residuals from the former model in the estimating process. That is, the problem of heteroskedasticity usually caused by the ORS model as a result of the influence of varying holding periods between the transactions is dealt with by the WRS model which utilises the generalised least squared (GLS) model in the estimation process. This finding is similar to the finding by Case and Shiller (1989) and Costello and Watkins (2002) that the WRS is superior to the ORS.

However, even though at the broader level of temporal aggregation the WRS outperforms the ORS, at the lower level of aggregation the latter model is superior to the former. That is, as the level of temporal aggregation reduces, the influence of varying holding periods reduces and so there is no efficiency gain in using the GLS instead of OLS. In this case, the OLS will be the best linear unbiased estimator (BLUE). This finding is consistent with the finding of Leishman and Watkins (2002) who constructed quarterly indices and find that in terms of accuracy, the ORS model is better than the WRS when estimating house price indices for British cities.

Statistical significance of the differences between models

The previous subsection has demonstrated that the MSE values are substantially different across most of the different index methods. However, it has not been established whether the differences in MSE values across the different models are statistically significant. In this subsection the differences among the MSE values of the different methods are tested to find out if they are statistically significant. Finding this will lend more support to the analysis undertaken above.

The Morgan-Granger-Newbold test is used for this purpose. This test is proposed by Granger and Newbold (1977) and they use an orthogonalizing transformation devised by Morgan (1939). The test procedure requires the correlation ρ_{ij} between the sequences of errors i and j from the models a and b to be calculated.

That is, we calculate $i_n = (e_{na} + e_{nb})$, and $j_n = (e_{na} + e_{nb})$ and then find the correlation between them. e_n is the forecast error of each observation, n. The null hypothesis of interest is that there is no difference in forecast accuracy between models a and b. If this null hypothesis of equal forecast accuracy holds, then i and j will not be correlated. That is, $H_0 : \rho_{ij} = 0$ and $H_1 : \rho_{ij} \neq 0$.

The test statistic that is used to test the null hypothesis, H_0, is:

$$MGN = \frac{\hat{\rho}_{ij}}{\sqrt{\dfrac{1 - \hat{\rho}_{ij}^2}{T - 1}}} \tag{7.14}$$

which is distributed as Student's t with $T - 1$ degrees of freedom, and where

$$\hat{\rho}_{ij} = \frac{i'j}{\sqrt{(i'i)(j'j)}} \tag{7.15}$$

If the null hypothesis is rejected, then a positive correlation between a and b indicates that model a has a larger forecast error than model b. This test is conducted for all the models at the lowest level (monthly) of aggregation. The reason why the lowest level of aggregation is chosen is that from the previous subsection, we find two of the models, namely the ETV hedonic and the Q-hybrid models to have similar MSE values at the lower level of aggregation so it will be interesting to test if these two models actually give the same forecast accuracy at the lower level of aggregation.

Table 7.4 provides the results for these tests. Each of the elements in the table provides the Morgan-Granger-Newbold sample correlation coefficient for two different models, a and b, with $a \neq b$. a represents a model on the vertical left-hand column and b represents a model on the horizontal row. The results from Table 7.4 provide convincing evidence that the prediction errors from most of the models are actually statistically different. With the exception of the prediction errors between the ORS and the WRS models, and that between the ETV hedonic and the Q-hybrid models, the t-statistics allow the rejection of the null hypothesis of an equal MSE across models, mostly at a 1% significance level.

The positive significant correlations between models a and b shown in Table 7.4 suggests that models a (those at the vertical left column) produce larger prediction errors than models b (those at the horizontal top row). This means that the SCS hedonic, ETV hedonic and the Q-hybrid models are more accurate than the ORS and the WRS models. Also, the ETV hedonic and the Q-hybrid models are more accurate than the SCS hedonic model at the lower level of temporal aggregation. Between the ETV hedonic and the Q- hybrid models, however, there is no significant difference in terms of prediction accuracy. These findings lend support to what was established in the previous subsection

The message from this section is that at the broader level of temporal aggregation (annual or semi-annual), the SCS hedonic model is the most accurate model to construct house price indices. At the lower level of temporal aggregation

Table 7.4 The Morgan-Granger-Newbold Correlation Tests

Index models	Morgan-Granger-Newbold Correlations			
	WRS	SCS	ETV	Q-hybrid
ORS WRS	−0.0021	−0.0319**	0.0434***	0.0463***
SCS		−0.0299*	0.0452***	0.0480***
			0.0806***	0.0832***
ETV				0.0036

Note: The table shows the Morgan-Granger-Newbold Correlations. The correlations are calculated at the lowest (monthly) level of temporal aggregation. The asterisks ***, ** and * denote significance of the correlation between models a (vertical left-hand column) and b (horizontal top row) at a 1%, 5% and 10% significance level. If the correlation between a and b, ρ_{ab} is found to be statistically significant, then a positive ρ_{ab} indicates that model b produces more accurate forecast than model a.

(quarterly or monthly) also, either the ETV hedonic model or the Q-hybrid model is superior. However, given the technical and cumbersome nature of implementing the latter model, the ETV hedonic is ultimately more suitable in constructing house price indices at the lower level of temporal aggregation. Having established that different index models perform better at different levels of temporal aggregation, the question that arises is which level of temporal aggregation is better in constructing house price indices? Finding an answer to this question will naturally lead to the model to be employed and that is the aim of the next section.

Test of temporal aggregation

The issue of temporal aggregation is very important in the construction of house price indices. Housing transactions are typically executed on a daily basis but the daily transactions are very few and infrequent as compared to transactions on the stock market for instance. Therefore, in most studies that employ housing transaction data, researchers have often found it necessary to pool the data together across time so as to overcome the problem of small sample size and preserve degree of freedom. For example, when housing transactions are combined to construct a quarterly index, it is assumed that a house transaction in January has occurred at the same time as one in March. Similarly, a house transaction in January is assumed to have occurred at the same time as ones in June and December when constructing semi-annual and annual indices respectively. The aggregation of time, however, involves an implicit assumption that indices generated from broader aggregated samples are statistically the same as those generated from less aggregated constituent sub-samples. Because the demand and supply relationship in the housing markets varies over time, this assumption is questionable.

In this section, the issue of temporal aggregation is empirically examined. More formally, the null hypothesis that house price indices generated at different levels of temporal aggregation are the same is tested. The testing is achieved by restricting the house price index coefficients to be equal within the aggregation period. For example, to estimate a quarterly index, the monthly coefficients are restricted to be equal within the quarter. That is, the quarterly price function is assumed to remain constant through January, February and March and then jumps to a different value for April, May and June. We test this hypothesis using four of the index construction models discussed. These are the ETV hedonic, Q-hybrid, ORS and the WRS models. The SCS hedonic model is excluded here because the time dummies which are excluded in using the SCS hedonic model are needed for the test. The analysis is done by using different levels of temporal aggregation, namely, monthly, quarterly, semi-yearly and yearly.

Following the work of Englund et al. (1999), we test six joint null hypotheses for each of the four methods. The six null hypotheses take the following form:

$$H_0^{m,q}: \emptyset_{m1} = \emptyset_{m2} = \emptyset_{m3} = \emptyset^{q1}; \emptyset_{m4} = \emptyset_{m5} = \emptyset_{m6} = \emptyset^{q2}; \tag{7.16}$$
$$\emptyset_{m7} = \emptyset_{m8} = \emptyset_{m9} = \emptyset^{q3}; \emptyset_{m10} = \emptyset_{m11} = \emptyset_{m12} = \emptyset^{q4}$$

$$H_0^{m,s}: \emptyset_{m1} = \emptyset_{m2} = \emptyset_{m3} = \emptyset_{m4} = \emptyset_{m5} = \emptyset_{m6} = \emptyset^{s1}; \tag{7.17}$$
$$\emptyset_{m7} = \emptyset_{m8} = \emptyset_{m9} = \emptyset_{m10} = \emptyset_{m11} = \emptyset_{m12} = \emptyset^{s2}.$$

$$H_0^{m,y}: \emptyset_{m1} = \emptyset_{m2} = \emptyset_{m3} = \emptyset_{m4} = \emptyset_{m5} = \emptyset_{m6} = \emptyset_{m7} = \tag{7.18}$$
$$\emptyset_{m8} = \emptyset_{m9} = \emptyset_{m10} = \emptyset_{m11} = \emptyset_{m12} = \emptyset^{y1}$$

$$H_0^{q,s}: \emptyset_{q1} = \emptyset_{q2} = \emptyset^{s1}; \emptyset_{q3} = \emptyset_{q4} = \emptyset^{s2} \tag{7.19}$$

$$H_0^{q,y}: \emptyset_{q1} = \emptyset_{q2} = \emptyset_{q3} = \emptyset_{q4} = \emptyset^{y1} \tag{7.20}$$

$$H_0^{s,y}: \emptyset_{s1} = \emptyset_{s2} = \emptyset^{y1} \tag{7.21}$$

where m, q, s and y represent monthly, quarterly, semi-yearly and yearly dummies respectively. According to the first null hypothesis, $H_0^{m,q}$, the coefficients on monthly prices within quarters are identical. That is, if monthly data are grouped into quarters, the temporal aggregation condition requires the coefficients for January, February and March within the first quarter to be equal to justify the pooling of data together to construct the first quarter index (Calhoun et al., 1995). $H_0^{m,s}$ also tests the null hypothesis that the coefficients on monthly prices within half years are identical. The third null hypothesis is represented by $H_0^{m,y}$ which tests if the coefficients on monthly prices within years are identical. From $H_0^{q,s}$, we test the null hypothesis that the coefficients on quarterly prices within half years are identical. $H_0^{q,y}$ also tests the null hypothesis that the coefficients on quarterly prices within years are identical. Finally, the last null hypothesis represented by $H_0^{s,y}$ tests if the coefficients on semi-yearly prices within years are identical. That is, with each of the six null hypotheses, we test if house price indices generated at different levels of temporal aggregation are equal. If house prices are constant over the entire period of aggregation being considered, then any temporal aggregation structure leads to the same result and so the estimation of one price level for the particular temporal aggregation is justified.

Table 7.5 presents the statistical comparison of price indices computed at the four different levels of temporal aggregation, namely, monthly, quarterly, semi-yearly and yearly. The same comparison is made for each of the four models – the ETV hedonic, the Q-hybrid, the WRS and the ORS models. In the table, the F-statistics of the restrictions that are inherent in representing time in the computation of price indices by aggregate measures are reported.

The F-statistics compare more restricted models (rows) to less restricted models (columns) for all four aggregations of time initially measured in days and for each of the four models. The six joint null hypotheses are tested and presented in the table. For example, the F-ratio presented in the first row and column provides a test of the first null hypothesis, $H_0^{m,q}$ (Equation 7.16). That is, for the ORS model, the coefficients on monthly prices within quarters are identical and so it is enough to pool monthly data together to construct quarterly price levels. The

Table 7.5 Tests of disaggregation of price trends over time

Index models		Time period		
		Months	Quarters	Half years
ORS				
	Quarters	2.72(0.000)		
	Half years	5.30(0.000)	15.92(0.000)	
	Years	8.33(0.000)	23.78(0.000)	186.17(0.000)
WRS				
	Quarters	3.55(0.000)		
	Half years	8.56(0.000)	19.02(0.000)	
	Years	12.12(0.000)	26.19(0.000)	226.65(0.000)
ETV				
	Quarters	2.02(0.000)		
	Half years	4.13(0.000)	12.20(0.000)	
	Years	6.92(0.000)	20.35(0.000)	34.26(0.000)
Q-hybrid				
	Quarters	2.11(0.000)		
	Half years	4.94(0.000)	14.26(0.000)	
	Years	7.93(0.000)	21.85(0.000)	40.74(0.000)

Note: The table reports F-statistics with their P-values in parentheses of the restrictions inherent in representing time in the computation of price indexes by aggregate measures. The F-statistics compares more restricted models (rows) to less restricted models (columns) for all four aggregations of time initially measured in days and for each of the methods. For example, the F-ratio presented in the first row and column provides a test of the null hypothesis that for the ORS model, the coefficients on monthly prices within quarters are identical.

table shows that at one percent significant level, the more aggregated models are consistently rejected against the less aggregated alternatives. This is because the F-ratios of the more aggregated models are consistently higher than that of the less aggregated levels. For example, the F-ratio of equating the monthly indices to a yearly one using the ORS model is 8.33, as compared to the F-ratios of equating the quarterly and the semi-yearly indices into yearly ones, which are 23.78 and 186.17 respectively.

The above finding is consistent across all the four models. The F-ratios at the lower levels of temporal aggregation are smaller than at the broader levels. In terms of comparing the index models, the F-ratios of the two repeat-sales models are relatively larger at the different levels of temporal aggregation as compared to the other ETV hedonic and the Q-hybrid models, especially at the broader level of temporal aggregation. At the different levels of temporal aggregation also, the ETV hedonic model produces the lowest F-ratios. This also confirms the previous finding that the accuracy levels of the ETV hedonic and the Q-hybrid models are different from the repeat-sales models possibly due to the smaller sample size associated with the repeat-sales models.

The table clearly provides the convincing conclusion that time should be represented using the lower levels of aggregation as much as possible when constructing house price indices. These results and findings are consistent with those reported by Englund et al. (1999) and Calhoun et al. (1995). The results also confirm the superiority of the ETV hedonic and the Q-hybrid models as established in the preceding section. Having established that lower levels of temporal aggregation is better, the next question to ask is what are the consequences of constructing house price indices at the yearly or semi-yearly level instead of at the lower levels of temporal aggregation like the monthly or the quarterly? This question is answered in this section by analysing the calculated average values of the price indices constructed at the four different levels of temporal aggregation and for each of the models. The SCS hedonic model is also included in this analysis. In addition to the calculated average values of the price indices, the annualised returns of each of the indices together with their volatilities are calculated. Analysing such estimates will give a clue as to the implications of aggregating time in the construction of house price indices. Perhaps, even though statistically temporal aggregation is important, economically it may not matter.

Table 7.6 presents the results of the calculated average index numbers, their annualised returns as well as their volatilities, as a way of indicating some of the implications of aggregating data over time. There is no particular pattern of the calculated mean values of the price indices for most of the models. For the ORS and the WRS models, the quarterly level of temporal aggregation has the highest mean values and the semi-annual has the lowest mean values. For the ETV hedonic and the Q-hybrid models also, the annual and the monthly levels of temporal aggregation have the highest and lowest calculated mean index values respectively. There is however a downward trend for the SCS hedonic as the level of temporal aggregation increases.

Table 7.6 Estimates of house prices, returns and volatilities across time aggregation and the various methods

		ORS	WRS	SCS	ETV	Q-hybrid
Calculated mean value of price index						
	Monthly	139.61	139.99	155.44	150.82	151.57
	Quarterly	140.58	141.22	155.21	152.25	152.79
	Semi-annual	138.00	137.38	154.51	151.30	152.04
	Annual	138.37	139.30	153.69	152.44	152.79
Calculated mean returns (Annualised percent change)						
	Monthly	7.63	7.64	7.54	7.18	7.17
	Quarterly	7.61	7.63	7.56	7.21	7.19
	Semi-annual	7.60	7.61	7.57	7.22	7.20
	Annual	7.59	7.60	7.59	7.24	7.22
Calculated volatility (Standard deviation in annualised percent change)						
	Monthly	8.65	8.65	8.81	7.30	7.31
	Quarterly	8.67	8.68	8.79	7.27	7.28
	Semi-annual	8.68	8.70	8.76	7.26	7.26
	Annual	8.71	8.72	8.74	7.24	7.24

Note: The table presents the average index values, annualised returns and volatilities for each of the methods and for each time disaggregation. The results indicate some of the implications of the aggregation of time in the construction of indexes. The estimates are based on all the five index construction models for different representations of time.

The calculated annualised returns measure the calculated mean returns to investment in owneroccupied housing for a one-year holding period. There seems to be an upward trend for the two hedonic models and the hybrid model as the level of temporal aggregation increases. This suggests there is some tendency for returns estimates to be larger for broader aggregation of time. Even though this confirms the conclusion by Calhoun et al. (1995) that aggregation bias is positively correlated with the rate of change of house prices, the differences are very small and at one decimal places, there are no differences. This finding however is in contrast to the results by Englund et al. (1999) who report returns estimates to be smaller for a larger aggregation of time. The returns estimates based on the SCS hedonic model are generally higher than the rest of the models. The two repeat-sales models generally yield lower estimated rates of return as compared to the ETV hedonic and the Q-hybrid models.

The volatilities of the annual returns computed at the various levels of temporal aggregation by the various models are also reported in the table. For the two hedonic and the Q-hybrid models, the volatilities seem to have a downward trend as the level of aggregation increases. The volatilities of the two repeat-sales models however do have upward trends as the level of temporal aggregation increases. The SCS hedonic model always gives the highest standard deviation which lends support to the previous analysis that the SCS hedonic has the greatest volatility of price changes over the period. This finding is similar to the previous results obtained by Bourassa et al. (2006). Like the calculated returns, the differences between the calculated volatilities across time aggregation are very small and insignificant and so could be ignored. Thus, statistically, the level of temporal aggregation matters in the construction of indices and the lower level of temporal aggregation is better but, economically, temporal aggregation does not matter because the calculated returns and volatilities are similar among the different levels of temporal aggregation.

Conclusion

This chapter has conducted empirical analysis for five different house price index models based on the hedonic, repeat-sales and the hybrid methods. The models used here are the explicit time variable (ETV) hedonic, the strictly cross-section (SCS) hedonic, the ordinary repeat-sales (ORS), the weighted repeat-sales (WRS) and the Quigley's hybrid (Q-hybrid) model. Several empirical tests and analyses relating to house price index construction have been conducted. The first test conducted relates to the assumption that the implicit prices of the housing attributes are constant over time. This is the main assumption that distinguishes the ETV hedonic model from the SCS hedonic model. Using the Chow test, the null hypothesis that the implicit prices are the same over the various years is rejected at a 1% level. Thus, the implicit prices of the housing attributes differ from year to year.

In examining the indices constructed from the various models, the SCS hedonic model is found to produce the most volatile index. This confirms the finding by Bourassa et al. (2006) that the volatility of the SCS hedonic model is much greater on average. Again, the chapter confirms the finding by Clapp and Giaccotto (1992b) and Meese and Wallace (1997) that the repeat-sales indices track house prices below the other index types. The accuracy of the various models is also examined by using the MSE technique based on out of quasample forecast evaluation. The SCS hedonic model is found to be the most accurate model to construct house price indices at the broader level of temporal aggregation (annual or semi-annual). At the lower level of temporal aggregation (quarterly or monthly), however, either the ETV hedonic model or the Q-hybrid model is superior. The ETV hedonic model is however suitable in constructing house price indices at the lower level of temporal aggregation given the technical and cumbersome nature of implementing the Q-hybrid model. The MSE differences among most of these models are found to be statistically significant on a 1% level.

The next test conducted relates to the issue of temporal aggregation in constructing house price indices. The F-test is employed to test the null hypothesis that house price indices generated at different levels of temporal aggregation are the same. At a 1% level, the tests conducted consistently reject the null hypothesis that the indices are the same. The F-ratios at the lower levels (like the monthly and quarterly levels) of temporal aggregation are smaller than at the broader levels (like the yearly and semi-yearly levels), suggesting that time should be represented using the lower levels of aggregation as much as possible when constructing house price indices. This finding is very consistent across all the models and confirms the results by Englund et al. (1999) and Calhoun et al. (1995). The aggregation bias is positively correlated with the calculated rate of change of house prices when the hedonic and the Q-hybrid models are used. That is, as the level of temporal aggregation increases, the calculated annualised returns also increase. However, the differences among the calculated returns at the various levels of temporal aggregation are really small and insignificant. Thus, even though temporal aggregation is statistically important and so the lower level of temporal aggregation should be used, economically, the level of temporal aggregation does not really matter.

The message from this chapter is clear – the lower levels of temporal aggregation are more desirable than the broader levels, and the ETV hedonic model produces the lowest mean squared error (MSE) at this level of temporal aggregation.

8 Applications of property price indices

Introduction

The previous chapter employed five different models to construct quality adjusted house price indices using data from the Aberdeen City and Suburbs. Several diagnostic tests and significant points are made in the chapter. Notably, the chapter showed that the implicit prices of the housing attributes differ over time. Also, the explicit time-variable hedonic model is found to be most accurate model when constructing indices at the lower level of temporal aggregation, that is, at the quarterly and the monthly levels. The strictly cross-sectional hedonic model is found to be the most accurate model at the higher level of temporal aggregation, that is, the annual and the semi-annual. Statistically, the indices constructed at the lower level of temporal aggregation (quarterly and monthly levels) are found to be better indices than indices constructed at the broader levels (annual and semi-annual levels).

This chapter provides an academic application of property price indices. In the academic literature, property price indices have been applied differently in many areas. They are used to test the efficiency of the housing market (Linneman, 1986; Case and Shiller, 1988; Pollakowski and Ray, 1997; Meen, 2002); to understand the role of housing in a mixed asset portfolio (Hoesli and Hamelink, 1997; Cocco, 2004; Yao and Zhang, 2004; Sousa 2014); to examine the hedging mechanism for house price volatility (Kearl, 1979; England et al., 2002; Iacoviello and Ortalo-Magne, 2003; De Jong et al., 2008; Han, 2008, 2010); to estimate real estate derivatives and home equity insurance (Case et al., 1993; Shiller and Weiss, 1999, 2000; Clapham et al., 2006; Shiller, 2008; Englund, 2010); to estimate the relationship between house price and housing demand (Follain and Jimenez, 1985; Goodman, 1988; Rapaport, 1997; Bajari and Khan, 2005; Ioannides and Zabel, 2008); and to model the supply of housing (DiPasquale, 1999; Mayer and Somerville, 2000; Malpezzi and Maclennan, 2001; Ball et al., 2010; Owusu-Ansah, 2014).

This chapter demonstrates one of the applications of the property price index. The property price index numbers together with other variables are used to examine the determinants of new housing supply and to estimate the price elasticity of supply for the Aberdeen housing market using different model specifications. The rest of the chapter is organised as follows:

The next section provides the motivation and justifies why housing supply studies are important and needed at the local housing market level. This provides the basis for the other sections in the chapter to be undertaken. In the third section, the determinants of new residential construction (housing supply) are discussed. Notably, house prices, construction costs, interest rates and planning regulations are identified as the main factors that affect new housing invest- ments. The expected signs associated with the various factors are identified and highlighted based on previous empirical findings.

The fourth section reviews previous empirical housing supply studies. The methodologies that have been employed over time, the data used and elasticities estimated are discussed. This is done with regards to the UK and other countries. In the fifth section, the methodology and models used for the empirical analysis in the chapter are developed. This section draws inspiration from the preceding section to identify the various models to be tested in order to compare the various elasticities estimated from the various models. The data needed for the study are identified in this section and the econometric issues associated with time series data (including stationarity) are discussed to set the platform for the data to be presented and pretested.

The sixth section identifies the sources of the data employed for the study. The data is also formally presented and pretested and stationarity is examined using the ADF and the KPSS stationary tests. This will help to identify how the data should be transformed during the empirical modelling. The seventh section presents the empirical results and discusses them while the final section summarises and concludes the chapter.

Determinants of new residential construction and price elasticity of supply

The housing market, like any other market, comprises demand and supply sides. The actors on the supply side of the housing market include the central government, various regional and local authority councils, real estate developers, housing associations and individuals. The actors on the demand side of the housing market also include corporate bodies, individuals etc. House prices are determined by the equilibrium of the total quantity of housing (housing stock) and the total demand for residential space.

The demand side of the housing market is a more researched area than the supply side (DiPasquale, 1999). DiPasquale also notes that the empirical evidence on the demand side of the housing market is much more convincing than the small evidence we have on the supply side. Simple questions about the price elasticity of housing supply can even produce a wide range of estimates (Ball et al., 2010). The reasons for these divergent estimates may be down to a number of factors. First, the studies are conducted at the different levels of the housing market, ranging from national, regional, local and even at the micro level examining house building firms. Second, different datasets and variables are used for the empirical modelling depending on the available data and the housing market level under study. Finally, different methodological and analytical app-roaches are adopted, ranging from reduced form equations where demand and supply housing functions are combined into a single equation, just modelling con-struction starts as a function of house prices and various cost shifters, to combining both approaches.

Most of the housing supply studies, particularly in the UK, are conducted at the national and in some limited cases regional levels (see for example Malpezzi and Maclennan, 2001; Tsoukis and Westaway, 1994; Bartlett, 1988) as compared to local housing market studies. Using aggregated data is a problem because it hides interesting variation in the timing of real cycles across regions and also shrouds inter-metropolitan area movements in population (Goodman, J.L., 1998). However, even though disaggregated level study is more desirable, it seems very difficult for such local level studies to be conducted. The reason why it seems difficult to conduct such disaggregated level study is attributed to lack of consistent time series data at the local levels. As a result of this, the studies conducted at the local or district levels in the UK mostly employ cross-sectional data (see for example Pryce, 1999; Monk and Whitehead, 1999; Bramley, 1993a, 1993b; DeLeeuw and Ekanem, 1971; Ball et al., 2010). The problem of employing cross-sectional data to estimate housing price elasticities is that when cross-sectional data is used to simulate outcomes over time, the reliability of the results will be questionable since the cross-sectional data usually cover a very short period of time (Evans, 1996; Pryce, 1999) and so cannot be applied to other points in time or cannot be used to measure long-run values (Bartlett, 1988). Clearly, using time series data has an advantage in that it helps to examine elasticities over long periods of time.

This chapter provides further evidence about the determinants of housing construction and housing price elasticity of supply in the local housing markets in the UK. Unlike the many local housing market studies in the UK, this study employs quarterly time series data for a twenty-five-year period. Several models are employed and both housing starts and housing stock elasticities are estimated for the various models.

Determinants of housing construction

The supply of housing at any period in time comes from two main sources. The first source is new housing construction that arises as a result of the production decisions of builders of new units. New construction, whether from private developers or the public sector, contributes to the already existing housing stock. The second source of housing supply comes from the decisions made by housing owners and/or their agents concerning the conversion of existing stock of hous-ing. Housing owners can, for example, convert two or more units into one to reduce the supply of housing. A very large single-family home can also be con-verted into several small apartments. Again, owners may decide to renovate an existing unit to increase the flow of housing services that are being provided by that unit or decrease the flow of housing services being delivered by an existing unit by decreasing maintenance (DiPasquale, 1999). Even though improvements to existing stock also contribute to the actual stock, in the USA for instance, new construction is the main source of additions to the existing stock (Baer, 1986).

In modelling housing supply, several variables have been used in the literature to represent housing supply. These include new construction starts, stock or changes in stock, completed houses etc. Table 8.1 summarises some of the recent studies about housing supply. The table reveals that housing supply studies usually employ either total housing stock (i.e. total housing supply) or new construction starts (new units) as the dependent variable to measure housing supply, with housing construction or starts dominating. New residential construction or housing starts are the main means of moving the housing stock from one equilibrium to another following a shock in demand for housing (Baer, 1986; Mayer and Somerville, 2000). The use of housing starts is therefore more appealing in analysing the factors that determine housing supply. It is also clear from Table 6.28 that several factors affect the supply of housing. These factors can be grouped into house prices, cost of construction, interest rate, planning regulations and market conditions.

House prices

The price of a house is considered as the main determinant of new residential construction. The price of a house is of great concern to private real estate developers, especially those in the private sector. This is because the aim of public housing providers is not profit maximisation but rather to provide the housing needs of people in society who do not have housing. The aim of private developers is to maximise profit and this to a large extent depends on the price of houses. Since housing starts are only a small percentage of the existing stock, the price of existing properties ultimately determines the decision to construct new houses or not, all other things being equal. If house prices increase and all other factors remain the same, profitability increases and so new houses are developed. On the other hand, if house prices decrease and all other factors remain the same, then profitability reduces and there will be no new construction. Thus, the price of houses has a positive impact on new residential construction and this is confirmed in the studies by Ball et al. (2010), Wigren and Wilhelmsson (2007), Neto (2005), and all the other studies reported in Table 8.1.

The price of a house is determined by the interaction of demand and supply factors. While the supply factors are the main factors under examination in this chapter, the demand factors are also important and are briefly discussed in this subsection. The demand factors that influence house prices include gross domestic product (GDP) or income, population, employment rate and interest rate.

Gross domestic product (GDP)/Income

The gross domestic product (GDP) or GDP per head affects the price paid for a property. When GDP or GDP per head increases, all other things being equal, the income of people increase and so demand for durable goods like housing increases.

Table 8.1 Recently published studies on housing supply

Authors and year of publication	Period	Explained variable	Explanatory variables	Estimated sign
Ball, Meen and Nygaard (2010)	1969–2007	Changes in log of new construction	Log of housing stock	+
			Lagged changes in log of real house price	+
			Changes in short term interest rate	–
			Changes in log of construction cost	–
Wigren and Wilhelmsson (2007)	1976–1999	Log housing stock	Log of GDP	+
			Log of construction price index	–
			Log of property price index	+
			Log of interest rate	–
			Log of consumer price index	+
			Log of price level	+
Neto (2005)	1989–2005	Housing starts	House price	+
			Real interest rate	–
			Cost of construction	–
			Urban land	+
			Rural land	+
Riddel (2004)	1967–1998	Log of residential unit stock	Price index	+
			Rate on 3-month treasury bills	–
			GDP	+
			Apartment vacancy	+
			Construction cost index	+
Harter-Dreiman (2004)	1980–1998	Log price	Log investment	+
Kenny (2003)	1975–1998	Private new homes completed	Real price of new housing	+
			Real cost of construction	–
			Real interest rate	–
			Time trend	+
Malpezzi and Maclennan (2001)	1850–1995 1889–994	Log price of new residential construction	Log GDP per capita	+
			Log population	–
			Log stock$(t-1)$	+
			AR(1)	+
Mayer and Somerville (2000)	1975–1994	Construction starts	Change and lagged changes in price	+
			Change in real prime rate	–
			Lagged stock	+
			Change in real material cost index	+
			Median month on the market	–

Authors and year of publication	Period	Explained variable	Explanatory variables	Estimated sign
Blackley (1999)	1950–1994	Real residential construction	Real price of houses	+
			Real price of construction materials	–
			Real wage	+
			Real short-term interest rate $(t-1)$	–
			Real price of agricultural land	+
			Real price of non-residential construction	+
Lee (1999)	1963–1991	Housing investments	House price	+
			Inflation rate	–
			Real interest rate	–
			AR(1)	+
Pryce (1999)	1988, 1992	Private house starts	House price	+
			Unemployment rate	–
			Land supply	+
			Percentage of residential development on land in former urban uses	–

People who could not afford to buy a house may now be able to purchase one and those who occupied smaller units of housing or were hitherto enjoying smaller housing services can now afford to enjoy more services due to the increase in income. All these increases the demand for housing and hence the price to pay for housing.

Employment rate

Closely related to the gross domestic product is the employment rate in the nation, region or local area. As more and more people are employed in society, all things being equal, they will earn some income and hence demand for goods including housing services also increases. With the increase in demand, housing prices will increase, all other things being equal. However, if employment rate decreases, the people who are out of a job will not be able to purchase the housing services they were hitherto enjoying, and so this reduces demand and hence price.

Population

The population level or its growth in an area also determines the price of existing housing units. When there is an increase in population, the demand for housing will also increase so that the increased number of people can be accommodated.

When demand increases with supply remaining the same, the price of the existing stock will increase. On the other hand, when population decreases, demand for housing units will decrease and some existing units which were occupied will be left vacant. This will therefore decrease the price of the existing stock, all other things being equal.

Interest rate

The last demand factor examined is the interest rate. Interest rate affects both housing demand and housing supply. In housing demand models, interest rate can be used as a measure of both the costs of borrowing and the opportunity cost of investing (Ball et al., 2010). When interest rates or the cost of borrowing increases, the number of people who could afford mortgages and hence demand for housing will decrease. When demand decreases and supply remains the same, then house prices will fall. On the other hand, a decrease in interest rate will increase demand and hence the price of houses. The effect of interest rates on house prices may be greater particularly in countries where people do not self-finance their housing purchases but rather rely mainly on mortgages (Abdulai, 2010). Using interest rates to measure the opportunity cost of investing also has a negative impact on housing demand. When interest rates and, for that matter, the opportunity cost of investing in housing increases, rational investors may find it profitable to channel their money to other forms of investment than investing in housing.

Cost of construction

The cost of construction also influences developers' decisions to start new residential construction or not. The costs of construction can be many and diverse. They include the cost of raw building materials, cost of labour in the construction sector, cost of capital and cost of land. Table 8.1 shows the estimated signs of the cost of construction that have resulted in some recent empirical studies. Even though most housing supply studies do not find housing construction cost to have a significant effect on housing supply (see for example Mayer and Somerville, 2000; DiPasquale and Wheaton, 1994; Topel and Rosen, 1988; Poterba, 1984), the estimated sign has mostly been negative (Ball et al., 2010; Wigren and Wilhelmsson, 2007; Neto, 2005; Kenny, 2003; Blackley, 1999).

The negative estimated sign of the cost of housing construction on housing supply is not surprising. When the cost of construction increases and house prices remain the same, then the profitability level will decrease and rational developers will reduce or will not initiate new residential construction. On the other hand, when the cost of raw building materials, labour and land decrease, and house prices remain the same, then it will be more profitable for developers to initiate new residential construction. Studies such as Riddel's (2004) and Mayer and Somerville's (2000), however, find no relationship between construction costs and housing supply.

Interest rates

Interest rates, apart from its impact on housing demand as discussed above, also influence housing supply. The inclusion of interest rates in housing supply models can be seen as either a measure of the opportunity cost of investment for private real estate developers or a measure of the cost of capital in financing housing supply investments. Either of them is however consistent and is left to the interpretation of the researcher. When it is included as either opportunity cost of capital or cost of borrowing, the impact it has on housing supply is negative as can be seen in Table 8.1.

Table 8.1 shows that in all the recent supply studies listed, there is a negative relationship between housing supply and interest rate. This negative relationship is not surprising whether interest rate is used as the opportunity cost of capital or the cost of borrowing. When it is used as the opportunity cost of capital and interest increases and all other things remain the same, rational investors will reduce investment in housing and channel their resources to other investment avenues that will give them higher returns. Also, when it is used to measure the cost of borrowing and it increases and all other things remain the same, the cost of construction to investors will increase and hence housing supply will be reduced.

Planning regulations and other governmental policies

Government policies and planning regulations have a profound impact on housing supply. Government policy can affect housing supply directly through the construction of public housing and tax policies and other incentives designed to encourage private construction of new housing. When the government or local authority decide to increase public housing supply, then the overall housing stock will be increased. Also, when taxes are reduced and the cost of borrowing to private developers is reduced and all other factors remain the same, then the cost of building will be cheaper for private developers and so housing supply will be expected to increase.

Planning regulations can also increase or restrict the supply of land available for development and hence housing supply. As a result of the need to protect the natural environment and to avoid uncontrolled development, new housing can only occur subject to planning approval. Due to industrial restructuring, vacant and deserted land in many urban cities has made urban regeneration an important part in planning policies which attract new housing development to 'brownfield' land, but subject to approval from the appropriate local authority.

In the UK, even though planning remains a largely centralised and uniform activity in all parts of the country, local planning authorities have the autonomy to interpret the policy framework in the light of local circumstances when making decisions on individual development applications (White and Allmendinger, 2003). It is therefore the case that some areas in the UK have tighter planning systems than other areas (see for example Bramley, 1993a, 1993b; Cheshire and

Sheppard, 1995; Pryce, 1999). Cheshire and Sheppard (1995) particularly note that the planning system in Reading is very tight and as result has restricted land supply and housing supply. House prices in Reading are therefore high as compared to Darlington which does not have a tight planning system. Land-use planning system in the UK imposes major supply constraints, particularly in the southern regions (Bramley, 1993a).

In countries like the USA, land-use planning is largely localised and so while some areas have virtually no planning regulation, other areas have extremely complex planning regulations (Cullingworth, 1997). Greater volatility of house prices in the coastal states in the USA has been attributed to the stronger zoning regulations (Glaeser et al., 2008). Thus, the nature of planning regulations clearly has an impact on land supply and hence housing supply and there are differences in different local areas and so examining it as a national variable may not be appropriate.

Time on the market

New residential construction is also dependent on the time properties stay on the market to be sold at the current market prices. If the time properties stay on the market increases and all other things remain the same, then it provides a signal to builders that demand has decreased and so the builders being rational will reduce new housing construction. On the other hand, when time on the market decreases and all other factors remain the same, then it means there has been an increase in demand and so supply will increase. Thus, time on the market has a negative relationship with new residential construction. This negative relationship is confirmed by Mayer and Somerville (2000), reported in Table 8.1, and also confirmed by Topel and Rosen (1988).

Other factors suggested in the literature to influence housing construction include volume of transactions (Ball et al., 2010), credit availability (Ambrose and Peek, 2008) and weather conditions (Goodman, 1987; Fergus, 1999). Even though the supply factors are many, no study has empirically included all of them. In principle, if all variables are included in the housing supply equation, the variables will be linearly dependent (Ball et al., 2010). For example, time on the market and volume of transaction virtually measure the same thing – the condition of the market. If time on the market increases then it is reasonable to expect the volume of transactions to decrease. This is because the more time that properties stay on the market, the less will be the volume of properties to be transacted at the period. The next section shows how housing supply has been modelled in the literature and also presents some results about price elasticity of supply.

Review of empirical modelling and price elasticity of housing supply

Housing supply comes from private investors and the government (social housing) and both are driven by different aims. From the perspective of the private investors or developers, the aim of investing in housing is profit maximisation. The profit maximisation aim is influenced by demand (price for completed houses), cost (construction and land), opportunity cost (interest rate) and expectations. There are basically two main approaches that are used to estimate the relationship between housing supply (starts) and the various determinants. In the first approach, housing supply and demand functions are combined into a single reduced form equation. In this case, the price elasticity of starts is derived from the coefficients on supply and demand shifters in the reduced form regression (Muth, 1960; Follain, 1979; Stover, 1986; Malpezzi and Maclennan, 1994). In the second approach, an aggregate supply curve is directly estimated for new residences by modelling construction starts as a function of the level of house prices and various cost shifters (Poterba, 1984, 1991; Topel and Rosen, 1988; DiPasquale and Wheaton, 1994). Mayer and Somerville (2000) also use the second approach to model housing starts but use changes in house prices instead of price levels, a technique consistent with the urban growth model. This model and the use of price changes instead of price level will be discussed in detail in this section. This section discusses how the supply of housing has been modelled by previous studies using one or both of the approaches outlined. The section first discusses the previous empirical studies from some international markets at the national and local levels and then narrows it down to look at the studies that have been conducted with UK data, also at the national and local levels.

Modelling and price elasticities from some international markets

National studies

Extensive literature has been developed outside the UK to examine housing supply and to estimate the price elasticities of supply, with most of these studies coming from the USA. One of the earlier studies that empirically examine the supply side of the housing market in the USA is the study by Muth (1960). Muth regresses the rate of housing construction on the relative price of housing, income and mortgage interest rate using 8-year time series data from 1922–1929, inclusive. The equation he estimates is:

$$I_t = \beta_0 + \beta_1 P_t + \beta_2 Y_t + \beta_3 R_t \tag{8.1}$$

where I_t is the rate of housing construction, P_t is the long-run equilibrium price, Y_t is the per capita income and R_t is the long-run equilibrium interest rate on mortgages. He finds no significant relationship between output and price. He then reverses the model with house price as the dependent variable and the rate of housing construction and the other factors as the dependent variables. Again, Muth finds no significant relationship between price and quantity in this model and so concludes that housing supply is highly elastic. The annual time series data for the only 8-year period and the use of national data may give rise to this perfectly elastic evidence (Stover, 1986).

Follain (1979) also estimates two equations, a supply equation and a demand equation, and combines them into a single reduced form equation so as to examine the factors that influence the housing market. The supply equation is:

$$I_t = \alpha_0 + \alpha_1 P_t + \alpha_2 C_t + \alpha_3 L_t + \alpha_4 R_t \tag{8.2}$$

where I_t is housing starts, P is the long-run price of unit housing, C is a price index of construction materials, L is a labour wage rate and R is the interest rate. The equation for demand for new residential construction in period t is:

$$I_t = \delta_0 + \delta_1 P_t + \delta_2 Y_t + \delta_3 PO_t + \delta_4 R_t + dS_{t-1} \tag{8.3}$$

where Y is the income of the households, PO is the price of other goods and S_{t-1} is the actual number of stock in the previous period, and the other variables are as before.

He obtains a reduced form equation for P_t by relating the price to the exogenous variables in Equations 8.2 and 8.3:

$$P_t = \beta_0 + \beta_1 C_t + \beta_2 L_t + \beta_3 R_t + \beta_4 Y_t + \beta_5 PO_t + \beta_6 S_{t-1} \tag{8.4}$$

He estimates Equations 8.2 and 8.4 to estimate the supply of housing. In Equation 8.4, he includes population as one of the independent variables in a specification. He finds the estimates of the coefficient of price not to be significantly greater than 0, and so, like Muth (1960), concludes that the supply curve is perfectly elastic. The reason for the elastic supply curve conclusion has been attributed to the use of national data and the reduced form equation used instead of modelling only the supply side (see Topel and Rosen, 1988). In their widely cited paper, Topel and Rosen (1988) formalise the house building firms' decision of how many new residential units to start so as to maximise their profits in the presence of adjustment costs. They hypothesise that marginal costs rise with both level of and changes in new construction activity. As a result of this, when there is a positive demand shock, the building firms lower costs by smoothing their increase in output over a period rather than building all units at one time. They estimate the model

$$I_t = \beta_0 + \beta_1 I_{t-1} + \alpha\beta_1 E_t I_{t-1} + \beta_2 P_t + \beta_3 R_t + u_t \tag{8.5}$$

where I_t is housing starts, P is the long-run price of unit housing, R_t is the long-run equilibrium interest rate on mortgages, E_t is expectation formed at time t and α is a discount factor. β_1 reflects adjustment costs whose absence ($\beta_1 = 0$) reduces the model down to the simply supply model relating quantity to price.

Topel and Rosen employ the instrumental variable approach to estimate Equation 8.5 because of the possible endogeneity of P_t, even though they indicated that endogeneity is unlikely to be a serious problem because investment is such a small fraction of existing stock. The instruments used include current and lagged values of interest rate, current and lagged values of income and current and lagged values of energy price index. Using quarterly data from 1963 to 1983, they find empirical evidence to support the introduction of dynamic adjustment cost aspects in housing supply models with both lagged and future starts being correlated with current period starts. They also estimate a long-run flow elasticity of 3. This approach is able to place new construction in a dynamic framework and the assumption that builders smooth production in response to shocks in demand is very intuitive. Their model is completely supply side, with all relevant demand-side information being captured in the price level of houses.

The major criticisms levelled against Muth, Follain and Topel and Rosen's models has to do with econometric concern of misspecification because of non-stationary time series. House price levels are used instead of price changes. When starts are estimated as a function of price level, it would predict a permanent increase in the number of new construction starts that result from a one-time shock in demand (Mayer and Somerville, 2000). New residential construction starts increase only as needed to accommodate new residents, a one-time event. More so, estimating starts as a function of price levels has an econometric problem because house price levels are generally found to be non-stationary (see Holland, 1991; Meese and Wallace, 1994; Rosenthal, 1999; Mayer and Somerville, 2000).

Another widely cited paper is that of DiPasquale and Wheaton (1994). The authors present a stock-adjustment model that incorporates a simple model of urban form and in which they allow for the possibility that it takes several years for the housing market to be in equilibrium. Their stock-flow model estimates current starts as a function of the difference between desired stock and the stock in the previous period adjusted for removals. They estimate housing starts, I_t, as a function of current house prices, P_t, an array of cost shifters, and the previous period's housing stock, S_{t-1}. The cost shifters include the real short-term interest rate, R_t, cost indices for construction, C, and land, F_t.

$$I_t = \alpha_1 + \alpha_2 P_t + \alpha_3 R + \alpha_4 F + \alpha_5 C - \alpha S_{t-1} \tag{8.6}$$

In another model, they included the current change in employment and the number of months on the market for new homes recently sold. They estimated these models with simple linear OLS equations. Using data series from 1963 to 1990, they estimate housing supply elasticity to be in the range of 1.0 and 1.4. Like the previous studies, the DiPasquale and Wheaton's model use house price levels instead of changes in house prices.

Mayer and Somerville (2000) also estimate an alternative stock-adjustment model which is in spirit similar to that of DiPasquale and Wheaton's. However, they use price changes instead of price levels and argue that the nature and supply of land makes housing construction different from other forms of investment. According to them, land is inelastically supplied but its prices and, for that matter, housing prices must ensure a spatial equilibrium in a metropolitan area. When there is an increase in the demand for properties and more residential construction has to take place, it normally takes place at the fringes so the city expands so as to accommodate these additional households. This causes a permanent increase in house prices. This permanent increase in prices is necessary to ensure an equilibrium for the now larger city. This is because when the city expands, the new construction will take place at the fringes. The house prices at the urban fringe remain the same, but the fringe is now further from the city centre. To ensure that households are indifferent between living in houses at the newer, more distant locations and existing units, the price of houses at developed locations must rise relative to their level prior to the demand shock. In this new equilibrium, population is stable and there are no expectations of further growth, so starts are again equal to zero.

New residential construction starts therefore increase only as needed to accommodate the new residents, a one-time event. They estimate the following equation where construction starts are a function of current and lagged changes in house prices, real interest rates and construction costs:

$$I_t = g[\Delta P_t, ..., \Delta P_{t-j}, \Delta R_t, \Delta R_{t-1}, \Delta C_t]$$

where I is housing start, P is house price change, R is real interest rate and C is the construction cost.

They estimate the above equation using an instrumental variable approach due to the possible endogeneity between starts and both current period house prices and construction costs. The instruments they used include lagged changes in construction costs, current and lagged changes population, the user cost of capital, nonconstruction employment, real energy prices and current and lagged exogenous variables. In another specification, they excluded the cost of construction since it was insignificant in the first model. In their third specification they included the median months on the market until new properties are sold and in their fourth model, they included the previous period's stock. They employ quarterly American aggregate data from 1975 to 1994 to estimate the various specifications and obtain a stock elasticity of 0.08 (that is, a 1% increase in price yields a 0.08% increase in the total housing stock) and a flow elasticity of 6.3 (that is, starts increase 6.3% when price increases by 1%).

Harter-Dreiman (2004) investigates the price elasticity of supply of housing in the USA for the period 1980–1998. He estimates supply price elasticity to be in the range of 1.8 and 3.2. Blackley (1999) also compares the reduced form equation to a flow equation and estimates the long-term price elasticity to be in the range of 1.6–3.7, thereby concluding that the housing supply is price elastic. Other housing supply studies in the USA include Kearl (1979), Huang (1973), Poterba (1991).

Malpezzi and Mayo (1987) estimate the price elasticity of supply for Malaysia and Korea and find the elasticity to be in the range of 0 and 1. Employing a model similar to the adjustment cost model by Topel and Rosen (1988) on Irish data spanning the period 1975Q4–1998Q3, Kenny (2003) estimates a unit elastic equilibrium housing supply curve, suggesting that the Irish housing market is significantly less elastic as compared to some of the US studies reviewed above. Hakfoort and Matysiak (1997) also employ two different equations to estimate the supply elasticity for the Dutch housing market over the period 1977Q1–1994Q4. The first model is based on the assumption that building firms do not face adjustment costs when altering their output schedule and the second model distinguishes between short-run and long-run elasticities of supply where building firms are assumed to face adjustment costs. Using an instrumental variable approach, the first model yields a supply elasticity of 1.6 and the second model produces short-run and long-run elasticities of 2.3 and 6, respectively.

Local studies

Housing supply studies from international markets are mostly conducted at the national level. Local level studies are relatively few. Even though the models used are quite similar, the variables that are used in the local housing models are quite different from the national models. This is because national housing supply is an aggregation of local supply and the various local areas can be different. The local characteristics like local planning regulations or land supply can therefore be incorporated into the local models but cannot easily be incorporated into national models. This explains why in the national studies reviewed above, such variables are absent and the focus is more on macroeconomic indicators.

In the USA for instance, land-use planning is largely a local matter. There is therefore great variance in the way planning is carried out (Cullingworth, 1997). This suggests that there may be areas where there are virtually no planning regulations and other areas where planning may be tight and complex. Thus, there is an absence of national land-use planning policy. Clearly, this will make it difficult to incorporate planning variables in national models. Planning variables are however important in determining housing supply. DeLeeuw and Ekanem (1971) examine the supply of rental housing services across thirty-nine metropolitan areas. They employ a reduced form equation to explain the variation in rent index with the price of capital inputs, price of operating inputs, income and the stock of households as the dependent variables. They estimate the elasticity of the supply of housing services with respect to price per unit of services to be in the range of 0.3 to 0.7. Stover (1986) also estimates a translog cost function using cross-section data from sixty-one metropolitan areas. He finds results which suggest an infinite supply elasticity. He argues that the finding of perfectly elastic supply by Muth (1960) and Follain (1979) might be due to aggregation bias which arises as a result of the use of national data.

Modelling and price elasticities from the UK

The literature on housing supply and price elasticity of supply in the UK is less than that of the USA. Some of the housing supply studies at the national (and regional) and local housing markets in the UK are examined below.

National studies

One of the earlier studies in the UK is that by Whitehead (1974). She explicitly estimates the price elasticity of supply using quarterly time series data from 1955 to 1972. Using a series of related stock-adjustment models, she estimates elasticities ranging from 0.5 to 2. Nellis and Longbottom (1981) also estimate reduced form models of UK housing prices but do not focus particularly on behavioural elasticities. Stern (1992) also uses time series data from 1971–1989 to estimate a two-stage least squares model. He finds that prices adjust to an increase supply only after a lag of several periods.

Tsoukis and Westaway (1994) estimate a dynamic flow model and make allowance for adjustment cost. Their model is similar to that of Topel and Rosen (1988), Equation 8.5. However, unlike Topel and Rosen, they recognise the fact that construction takes time to complete and so use both current and future house price levels. Using quarterly UK data, they include the current house price levels, future house price levels up to four leads, lagged housing starts and various cost shifters to analyse the UK housing starts. They find only lagged starts and interest rates to influence current housing starts in the UK. They compare their model to that of Topel and Rosen and find that there is no autocorrelation with their model, an advantage they find over Topel and Rosen's model. They do not attempt, however, to estimate price elasticity of supply.

Malpezzi and Maclennan (2001) also estimate a long-term price elasticity of the supply of housing construction in the UK and USA, employing the reduced price equation. Their work employs a relatively long series of data. The available data they utilise in the UK covers the period 1850–1995, more than 150 years. For the USA also, the data covers a period of more than a century, 1889–1994. They regress the price of new residential construction on gross domestic product (GDP) per capita, population, housing stock and an autoregressive representation. They estimate the price elasticity of supply to be approximately between 0 and 4 in the UK, and 4 and 13 in the USA. This means that the supply elasticity in the UK is far lower than that of the USA.

Another supply study that compares the UK with other international markets, namely the USA and Australia, is the study by Ball et al. (2010). They estimate several models with changes in logstart as a function of current and lagged changes in house prices, log of the ratio of volume of transactions to the actual stock, current and lagged changes in short-term interest rate, as well as the log of construction cost. They estimate the short-run price elasticity of starts to be 1.01 and long-run elasticity to be 2.07 using an OLS model. Using the same model, they estimate the price elasticities to be in the range of 3.0 and 3.5 for the USA. Due to the possibility of house prices being endogenous, they employ the Seemingly Unrelated Regression (SUR) model and estimate the short-run and long-run price elasticities to be 1.68 and 3.27 respectively for the UK, and 2.98 and 12.74 for Australia. The results confirm the those found by Malpezzi and Maclennan (2001) above that the price elasticity of supply in the UK is much lower than that of the USA, and it is also lower than elasticities in Australia. One commonly suggested explanation for the lower price elasticity of supply in the UK is that housing supply in the UK is constrained by land availability problems due to a sluggish planning system (Ball et al., 2010; White and Allmendinger, 2003; Pryce, 1999).

Ball et al. (2010) also test if using price changes instead of price levels have an effect on price elasticity of housing supply. They find a much larger difference between price elasticity estimated from a model that uses price changes and a model that uses price levels. While the long-run price elasticity from the model that uses price changes is estimated to be 3.27, it is only 0.16 for the model that uses price levels. The use of price changes instead of levels is more consistent with the stock-adjustment model (Mayer and Somerville, 2000; Ball et al., 2010).

Local studies

The housing supply studies that have been conducted in the UK have mainly used cross-sectional data instead of time series data. Bramley (1993a, 1993b) examines the impact of planning regulations on housing output and prices. He constructs a cross-sectional dataset at a disaggregated level. These datasets are constructed for 90 local authorities in England, most of which are located in the West Midlands. The dataset includes house price, housing supply, demographic, economic and geographical variables. The dataset covers the time period 1986– 1988. He employs a modelling framework which assumes that the market can clear within one year while output is a function of current and expected prices and profitability and expected land supply, which is defined as land with planning permission. Instead of using the flow of housing services which is common in the literature, he employs housing units to model the housing market.

Bramley's methodology is clearly different from macroeconomic analyses of regional and national housing markets in the UK which use time series data, and the incorporation of the planning variables clearly distinguish it from the regional and national housing market models. They find the planning policy variables to have a negative impact on supply. Thus, when the planning policies are tight, housing supply decreases. He also finds the response of supply to price to vary across different local areas. The average house price elasticity of supply over all the areas covered is 0.99 with the lowest and highest price elasticity of supply being 0.29 and 2.11 in Birmingham and Worcester, respectively.

Cheshire and Sheppard (1995) adopt a hedonic methodology to examine the impact of planning systems on housing construction in two British cities, namely, Darlington and Reading. They find open-access land to have a positive effect on new housing construction in Darlington but a negative one in Reading. They attribute these different findings to the nature of planning systems in the two cities, with Reading having relatively tight planning. Pryce (1999) also employs a cross-sectional dataset for two different years – 1988, a booming period, and 1992, a period of slump conditions – to analyse the effect of land availability on housing supply and also to estimate supply elasticities. They define land supply as land with outstanding planning permission. Even though he employs a dataset provided by

Bramley, his methodology is different in that he uses private housing starts rather than completions. He estimates structural supply and demand relationships as follows:

$$Q^S = \alpha_1 + \alpha_2 P + \alpha_3 P^2 + \alpha_4 L + \alpha_5 D + \alpha_6 U + \alpha_7 U^2 + \epsilon_S \qquad (8.7)$$

$$Q^D = \beta_1 + \beta_2 P + \beta_3 U + \beta_4 Z + \epsilon_D \qquad (8.8)$$

where Q^S and Q^D are quantities supplied and demanded respectively, P is house price, U is unemployment, L is land supply, D is the percentage of residential development on land in former urban uses and Z is the percentage economically active in social classes I and II. He finds that there is the presence of the backward bending supply curve in the 1988 boom period but not in the 1992 slump conditions. His estimates of the price elasticity of supply are 0.58 in 1988 and 1.03 in 1992, even though the same dataset is used.

Ball et al. (2010) examine housing supply elasticities in the 210 Medium Level Super Output Areas (MSOA) in the Thames Gateway located to the east of Central London. They use the percentage net change in the total housing stock in each of the 210 areas between 2004 and 2007 as the dependent variable. The key explanatory variables they employ are the level of and expected change in house prices. Other variables include proportion of land devoted to paths, domestic gardens, green space and water. They find the responses to changes in prices to be greater than the price levels. Similar findings are also reported for their national models as mentioned above. Although there is no explicit estimation of price elasticities, their results suggest that housing construction on land currently given over to water, gardens, green space and paths have a lower price elasticity of supply than new construction on brownfield land that is currently devoted to domestic and non-domestic building.

Hilber and Vermeulen (2010) also used annual panel data for 353 local planning authorities between 1974 and 2008 to explore the causal effects of regulatory and physical supply constraints on house prices in England. Using the reduced form equation, they found regulatory constraints to have a very substantive positive long-run impact on house prices. They found that the effect of constraints due to scarcity of developable land is confined to highly urbanised areas and that uneven topography has a quantitatively less meaningful impact. They also established that the effect of supply constraints on the price-earnings elasticity is greater during the boom than bust periods. Thus, planning and regulatory factors play a crucial role in examining housing supply at local levels.

Several important conclusions are drawn from the review above. First, local housing supply studies are relatively few as compared to the national and regional levels and since national supply elasticities are an aggregation of local elasticities, more and less responsive areas cannot be detected when national elasticities are estimated. This study provides further evidence about price elasticities for a local housing market.

Second, most of the local supply studies employ cross-sectional data because of the difficulty involved in gathering appropriate time series data. Cross-sectional data, however, do not provide the opportunity to examine the long-run elasticities of housing supply. This study mitigates such a problem by employing time series data over a twenty-five-year period.

The third issue has to do with whether house price levels or house price changes should be used in empirical modelling. The magnitude of the price elasticity of housing supply are dependent on whether changes in the variables are used or their levels are used. The price elasticities are found to be greater when changes are used than when levels are used. Even though it is possible to make a case for either or both (Ball et al., 2010), the use of changes in house prices seems to be more consistent (Mayer and Somerville, 2000).

Finally, most of the studies using the time series data employ an instrumental variable (IV) approach instead of OLS. This is due to the possible endogeneity between starts and both current period house prices and construction costs. This endogeneity problem is discussed further in the subsequent sections.

In the next section, the methodology employed for this study is discussed and the models for the various estimations are also developed, which will form the basis for the empirical analyses to be undertaken.

Methodology

The econometric model

The econometric model is based on the empirical papers examined above. Theory suggests that the profit maximisation aim of private real estate developers is influenced by demand (price for completed houses) and cost of construction, including the cost of land, building materials and borrowing. The basic model employed is similar to that of Mayer and Somerville (2000):

$$I_t = f(\Delta P_t, ..., \Delta P_{t-j}, \Delta R_t, \Delta C_t) \qquad (8.9)$$

That is, current housing investment or starts (It) is expressed as a function of current and lagged changes in prices of houses and various cost shifters. Even though in most of the housing supply literature house price levels are used (see for example Muth, 1960; Follain, 1979; DiPasquale and Wheaton, 1994), the use of changes in house prices rather than levels is more intuitive (see for example Blackley, 1999; Mayer and Somerville, 2000; Hwang and Quigley, 2006). This is because changes in the scale of the home building industry may entail changes in price and so housing starts may be viewed as a one-time event needed to accommodate a demand shock caused by an increase (a change) in house prices. Also, starts are usually generally stationary while house price levels are not. Changes in house prices are however stationary and so it is econometrically justified and intuitive for changes in house prices to be used. This model is completely supply side with all the relevant demand-side information summarised in the house price change. All the demand factors are assumed to determine the price change. This modelling approach is used due to the difficulty involved in identifying the underlying price elasticity of supply in a reduced form and structural equations like VAR (Ball et al., 2010; Tsoukis and Westaway, 1994).

Using Equation 8.9 as the basic model, several specifications are estimated by including or excluding some additional housing supply variables to analyse the impact on the price elasticity. These specifications are presented and discussed below:

Specification 1

The first model to be estimated is exactly as we have in Equation 8.9. From the literature, we expect the sign on the change in house prices to be positive and negative for cost of construction and interest rate. This model is similar to the basic model of Mayer and Somerville.

Specification 2

In Specification 2, the cost of construction is excluded from the basic model in order to analyse if the cost of construction has an effect on price elasticities. The reason is that most studies have found the cost of construction to have no effect on housing supply (see for example Mayer and Somerville, 2000; Topel and Rosen, 1988; Poterba, 1984). The model is also similar to the second model of Mayer and Somerville. That is,

$$I_t = f(\Delta P_t, ..., \Delta P_{t-j}, \Delta R_t) \tag{8.10}$$

Specification 3

In the Specification 3, the average number of days properties stay on the market until they are sold is included to the basic model. This variable has been found to have a large negative impact on housing supply (see for example Mayer and Somerville, 2000; Topel and Rosen, 1988). Thus, an increase in the number of days suggests to suppliers that the market is slow and so starts will be reduced. In the same way, when the number of days decreases, the signal is that the condition of the market is good and so suppliers being rational will increase starts to supply more. The specification is thus,

$$I_t = f(\Delta P_t, ..., \Delta P_{t-j}, \Delta R_t, \Delta C_t + \Delta T_t) \tag{8.11}$$

where T_t is the time on the market and all the other variables are defined above.

Specification 4

The impact of planning regulation on housing supply is also examined in Specification 4. In doing this, the ratio of building warrants approved to the total building warrant applications made is included in the basic model. An increase in the ratio suggests that more land has been made available for development and so with all other things being equal, supply will also increase. We therefore expect a positive sign on the ratio of building warrants approved to the total building warrant applications made. The model is presented by Equation 6.69:

$$I_t = f(\Delta P_t, ..., \Delta P_{t-j}, \Delta R_t, \Delta C_t + \Delta(BWG_t/BWA_t)) \tag{8.12}$$

where BWG/BWA_t is the ratio of building warrants granted to the total number of building warrant applications in Aberdeen City District Council. Planning variables have not been found in any of the national and regional models reviewed above. In the local models that use planning variables also, the dataset employed has been mainly cross-sectional, covering just a few years. Employing the ratio of building warrants approved to the total building warrant applications in such a local model with about twenty-five-year quarterly data is clearly a major contribution to the literature and the results will help to analyse the true impact of planning regulation in the long run.

Specification 5

In Specification 5, the lagged stock is introduced into the basic model to control for the role of depreciation in explaining new housing construction. If we assume a constant depreciation rate as almost all supply studies do, then starts should increase with the stock as more units depreciate and need to be replaced. We therefore expect a positive relationship between starts and lagged stock as evidenced in much of the housing supply literature (DiPasquale and Wheaton, 1994; Mayer and Somerville, 2000). The specification is thus,

$$I_t = f(\Delta P_t, ..., \Delta P_{t-j}, \Delta R_t, \Delta C_t + \Delta S_{t-1}) \tag{8.13}$$

where S_{t-1} is the lagged of the total dwelling stock.

Specification 6

In Specification 6, the lagged of the dependent variable, housing starts, is introduced into the basic model to find out if the past construction starts affect the current construction starts. Like the inclusion of the stock, we expect a positive relationship between starts and lagged stock:

$$I_t = f(\Delta P_t, ..., \Delta P_{t-j}, \Delta R_t, \Delta C_t + I_{t-1}) \tag{8.14}$$

Specification 7

In Specification 7, the adjustment cost hypothesis by Topel and Rosen (1988) is incorporated into the basic model. The assumption that marginal costs rise with both level of and changes in new construction and so building firms lower costs by smoothing their increase in output over a period is very intuitive and evidence of this has been found by Topel and Rosen (1988), Tsoukis and Westaway (1994), and Kenny (2003). We therefore introduce both lagged of housing start (I_{t-1}) and expected future housing start ($E_t I_{t+1}$) into the model. The model is presented by Equation 8.14:

$$I_t = f(\Delta P_t, \dots, \Delta P_{t-j}, \Delta R_t, \Delta C_t + (\alpha E I_{t-1} + I_{t-1})) \tag{8.15}$$

where EI_{t+1} and I_{t-1} are the future and lagged starts respectively and a is the discount factor which constraints the coefficients of EI_{t+1} and I_{t-1} to differ. Following Topel and Rosen (1988), the discount factor, a, is taken to be 0.98.

Specification 8

In Specification 8, all the variables with the exception of the lagged stock are included in the basic model to analyse their impact on both new construction and price elasticity of supply. The lagged stock is dropped in this model so that multicollinearity problem likely to arise as a result of the inclusion of both lagged stock and lagged starts will be avoided. This model is presented by Equation 8.15:

$$\begin{aligned} I_t = f(\Delta P_t, \dots, \Delta P_{t-j}, \Delta R_t, \Delta C_t + \Delta T_t \\ + \Delta(BWG_t/BWA_t), (\alpha E I_{t-1} + I_{t-1})) \end{aligned} \tag{8.16}$$

Following Mayer and Somerville (2000), Tsoukis and Westaway (1994) and Topel and Rosen (1988), we estimate all these models using the instrumental variables (IV) approach. The reason for using the IV approach is due to the possible endogeneity between housing starts and both current period changes in house prices and construction costs.

The endogeneity problem arises because while price and cost influence new residential construction, the price of a property and construction costs are also influenced by property supply. If more properties are supplied and demand remains the same, then prices will fall. In the same way, as more construction takes place as a result of the desire to supply more properties then there will be more demand for land, construction materials and labour; hence construction cost will increase. Therefore, when house prices and construction enter into Equation 8.9 using OLS, then one of the OLS classical assumptions that the variables should be linearly independent is violated and hence the results will be biased. More so, the error term will not be uncorrelated with the independent variables (Wooldridge, 2009).

Endogeneity is however not likely to be a serious problem because housing start is just a small fraction of existing stock. The variables used as instruments to represent house price include current and lagged values of one-year LIBOR rate (London Interbank Offered Rate) to represent the user cost of capital, current and lagged changes in GDP to represent changes in income, current and lagged changes in the ratio of the volume of transactions to actual housing stock, changes in population as well as the exogenous variables. All these are demand factors and hence including them together into the model serve as instrument for price. These instruments are chosen to be consistent with previous published studies (Mayer and Somerville, 2000; Tsoukis and Westaway, 1994; Topel and Rosen, 1988). Since there is no appropriate instrument that is not correlated with housing demand to correct for the endogeneity between starts and cost of building materials, we use lagged changes in the real building materials (Mayer and Somerville, 2000).

Following Mayer and Somerville (2000) and DiPasquale and Wheaton (1994), we also include seasonal dummies to control for the possible seasonality of the variables and trend variables in all the regressions. The AR(1) term is also included to analyse if the disturbance terms are serially correlated.

Stationarity

Stationarity is a situation where the unconditional mean, variance and auto-covariance are constant over time, that is, the movement of the variable does revert to the mean (Wooldridge, 2009). When a variable is integrated of order zero, that variable is stationary. A variable that has to be differentiated once to become stationary is integrated of order one. When non-stationary variables are used to perform regressions, the results become spurious (Wooldridge, 2009). The stationary assumption of individual variable plays a crucial role in our modelling strategy and hence the tests.

The variables are tested for stationarity using two different unit root tests, namely, the Augmented Dickey-Fuller (ADF) test and the Kwiatkowski-Phillips-Schmidt-Shin (KPSS) test. These two stationarity tests are employed because they have different null hypotheses which can lead to conflicting outcomes. The ADF test is a form of unit root test that has been utilised over the years to analyse whether series are stationary. This is done by testing the hypothesis that the lagged level of a variable can explain the change. We test the null hypothesis that the series are unit root. That is, $H_0 : q = 0$. If the null hypothesis can be rejected, that is, $H_1 : q \neq 0$, then the variable is stationary. The null hypothesis of a unit root is rejected in favour of stationarity if the test statistic is more negative than the critical value (Wooldridge, 2009). The KPSS test has the null hypothesis that an observable time series is stationary and do not have a unit root. That is, $H_0 : q \neq 0$. When we test both the unit root hypothesis (ADF) and the stationarity hypothesis (KPSS), we can distinguish series that appear to be stationary and series that appear to be non-stationary so as to be sure whether the series are stationary or integrated.

The data is presented in the next section and stationary tests discussed above are empirically conducted on the dataset.

Data

Definition and sources of data

The variables that are used for the empirical part of this chapter are described in this section. The variables are housing starts (I), actual housing stock (S), house prices (P), cost of raw building materials (C), the interest rate (R), real gross domestic product (Y), time on the market (T), volume of housing transactions (V), the number of building warrant applications (BWA), the number of building warrants granted (BWG) and population (POP). These variables are gathered from different sources and are defined in Table 8.2. The housing starts variable is defined as the number of new private single-family housing starts in Aberdeen City District Council. The housing starts information is sourced from Scottish Government Statistics. According to Scottish Government Statistics, a dwelling is considered as started on the date that work begins on the foundations of the block of which the dwelling will form a part, and not on the date when site preparations begin.

The house price series is measured as an index (constant-quality). The house prices are sourced from Aberdeen Solicitors' Property Centre (ASPC). The variables in this dataset are already described in Chapter 6. Using the ASPC dataset, we are able to construct constant-quality house price indices for the period under study using the explicit time variable hedonic model. The base period for the index is the first quarter of 1986 (1986Q1=100). The raw building material cost index is also sourced from the Building and Construction Information Service (BCIS) department of the Royal Institution of Chartered Surveyors (RICS). Even though this is published at the national level, we expect the material costs to be similar throughout the entire UK. Both the housing price index series and the raw building material cost index series are transformed from nominal to real values based on the retail price index (RPI). The RPI is sourced from the Office of National Statistics (ONS).

The next variable we describe is the interest rate. This is defined as the nominal three-month Treasury Bill rate and it is sourced from the Office of National Statistics. The real gross domestic product variable is defined as the real gross domestic product in Scotland. Since GDP is not consistently available at the

Table 8.2 Definition of data variables

Variables	Definition
Starts	Number of private housing starts
Stock	Number of total housing stock
House prices	Property price index
Cost of raw building materials	Material cost index
Interest rate	Nominal 3-month T-bill rate
Gross domestic product	Gross domestic product in Scotland
Population	Number of people in Aberdeen
Time on the market	Average number of days property stay on market
Volume of transactions	Number of properties that are sold
BWA	Number of building warrant applications made in Aberdeen
BWG	Number of building warrant granted in Aberdeen

local level for the time period employed for this analysis, the regional values are used to represent the local area. Since this variable does not enter Equation 8.9 directly but rather as an instrument together with other variables, it is not likely to bias the results. The GDP information is also sourced from the Office of National Statistics. The GDP variable is measured in pounds sterling and in nominal terms but it is transformed to real values using the RPI. Population is defined as the number of people within Aberdeen City District Council. The population figures are sourced from the General Register Office for Scotland.

The time on the market is the average number of days properties in Aberdeen stay on the market per quarter before they are eventually sold. This variable is calculated as the difference between the date the properties are advertised and the date they are actually sold. Both the advertisement and sold dates are sourced from the ASPC dataset. The volume of transactions is also sourced from the ASPC dataset and it is defined as the number of properties that are sold every quarter in Aberdeen. The ratio of the volume of transactions to the actual building stock is used as an instrument since it gives the signal of demand and hence house price. The building warrant applications are the number of building applications made by private developers to start new housing development in Aberdeen. The building warrants granted, on the other hand, are the number of building warrants approved by the city council to private developers. This information is sourced from Aberdeen City Council (ACC). The ratio of BWG to BWA is used to analyse the impact of planning regulation on housing supply.

Presentation of data

Table 8.3 presents the summary statistics of the variables. The dataset comprises the quarterly data of these variables and covers the period from the first quarter of 1986 to the fourth quarter of 2010 (1986Q1–2010Q4), that is, a 25-year period or a total of 100 quarters. The table shows the average starts in Aberdeen are 173 every quarter with the minimum and maximum starts being 11 and 590 respectively. The standard deviation is about 124, which is almost 72% around the mean value, meaning a very high volatility. The average volume of housing stock in Aberdeen stands around 96,056. That is, housing starts are only about 0.18% of the existing stock, far less than the approximate 2% reported from other studies. The reason for this small percentage of starts in Aberdeen may be attributed to the fact that most of the new developments take place at the outskirts of Aberdeen where land is more readily available and these areas are governed by Aberdeenshire Council and so are excluded from the study.

From the table it can be seen that the average percentage rate of change in house prices in Aberdeen is about 0.95% per quarter with the minimum and maximum rate of change being −6.64% and 6.27% respectively. The rate of change in building material cost is about 1.09% every quarter. The minimum and maximum rates of change are −1.03% and 4.41% respectively. The rate of change of PPI seems more volatile than the MCI with their standard deviations being

Table 8.3 Summary statistics of data

Variables	Unit	Average	Min.	Max.	Std. Dev.
Starts	Number	172.89	11	590	124.35
Stock	Number	96055.87	89093	102570	4078.229
Property price index rate of change	Percentage	0.95	–6.64	6.27	2.38
Material cost index rate of change	Percentage	1.09	–1.03	4.41	1.16
Retail price index	Percentage	3.52	–1.38	10.43	2.09
Interest rate	Percentage	6.40	0.39	14.50	3.40
Gross domestic product growth rate	Percentage	1.36	–2.55	3.74	0.90
Population growth rate	Percentage	0.01	–0.36	0.47	0.22
Time on the market	Number of days	108.54	36.11	215.41	44.40
Volume of transactions	Number	1115.73	567	1712	243.02
BWA	Number	580.05	1	1244	349.91
BWG	Number	537.33	0	1220	334.54

Note: Data are quarterly time series from 1986Q1–2010Q4.

2.38% and 1.16% around their means respectively. The average inflation rate is also 3.52% with a standard deviation of 2.09%.

The average interest rate is about 6.4% per quarter, with the minimum and maximum interest rates being 0.39% and 14.50% respectively. The average GDP growth is 0.07% with a volatility of 0.03%. The average number of days properties stay on the market before they are eventually sold is 109 every quarter, which is approximately 3.5 months, with the minimum and maximum number of days being 36 and 215 respectively. This is considered relatively small as compared to the 6.5 months reported by Mayer and Somerville (2000) for the American market. Every quarter, an average of 1,116 properties are transacted in Aberdeen. Thus, the percentage of the volume of transactions to the actual stock in Aberdeen is approximately 1.16%. The average number of building warrant applications (BWA) and building warrants granted (BWG) are 580 and 537 respectively. This means the average number of building warrants approved by the city council every quarter is about 92.64% of the total building warrant applications made every quarter. This figure is relatively high and suggests that planning regulations are not very tight in Aberdeen.

Figures 8.1 to 8.10 graphically present the variables employed for the basic model. Examination of Figures 8.1 and 8.9 clearly shows that the new construction starts and GDP variables are stationary. The other variables – property price index, material cost index, interest rate etc. – seem non-stationary as depicted in Figures 8.2, 8.3 and 8.4. Despite the graphical examination of these variables, an

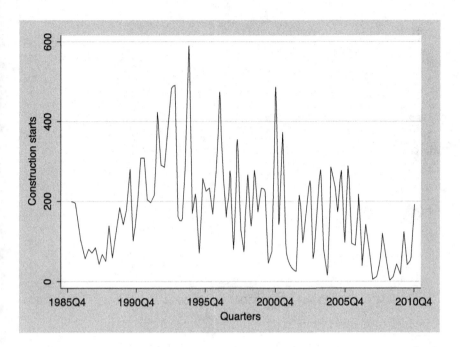

Figure 8.1 A graphical presentation of the housing starts variable

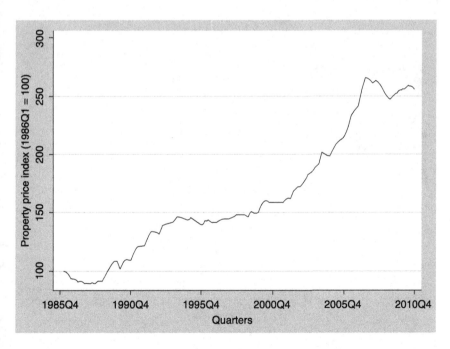

Figure 8.2 A graphical presentation of the property price index variable

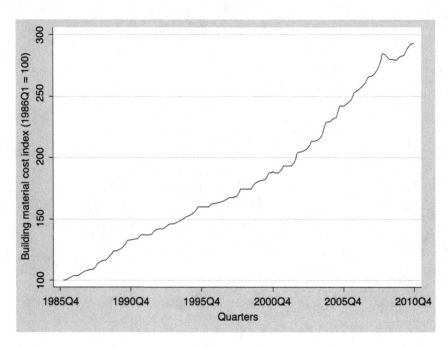

Figure 8.3 A graphical presentation of the material cost index variable

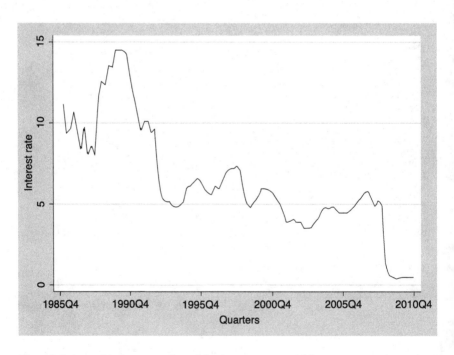

Figure 8.4 A graphical presentation of the interest rate variable

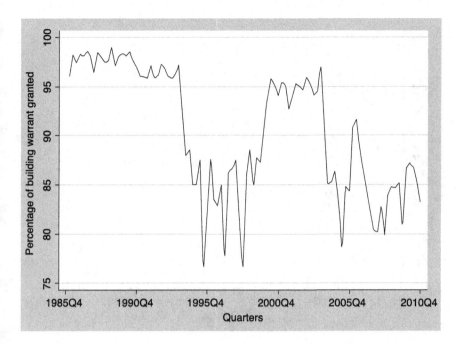

Figure 8.5 A graphical presentation of the percentage of building warrants granted

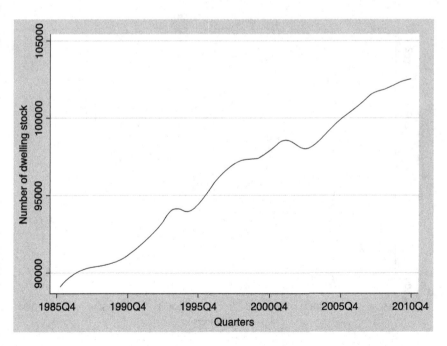

Figure 8.6 A graphical presentation of the number of dwelling stock

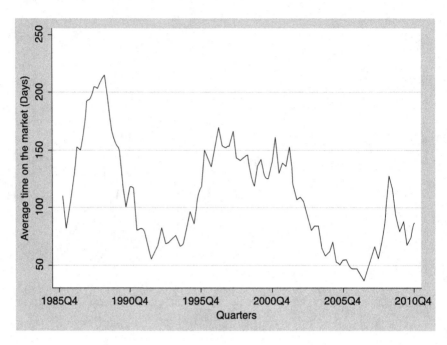

Figure 8.7 A graphical presentation of the average number of days properties stay on market

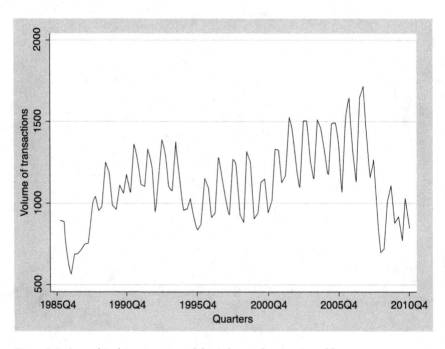

Figure 8.8 A graphical presentation of the volume of properties sold

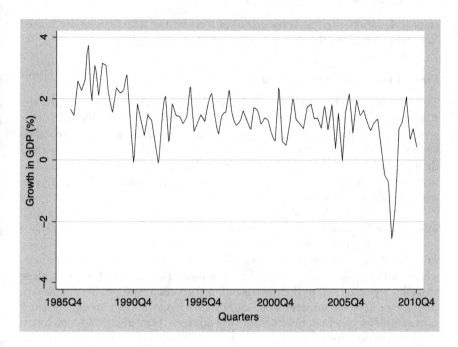

Figure 8.9 A graphical presentation of the growth in GDP

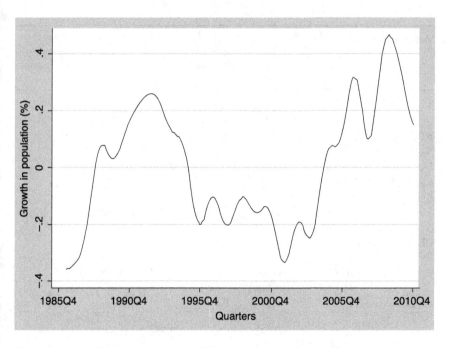

Figure 8.10 A graphical presentation of the growth in population

empirical stationarity test is needed to prove whether the variables are indeed stationary or not and this is conducted in the next sub-section.

Pre-test (stationary test) of the data

Table 8.4 presents the results obtained from the two stationarity tests, namely the Augmented Dickey-Fuller (ADF) test and the KPSS test. The table shows that generally most of the variables are not stationary when they are in levels. The variables that are stationary in levels according to both tests are housing starts and the ratio of volume of transactions to the stock. The real gross domestic product is also stationary in levels using the ADF test but it is integrated in order one when the KPSS test is used.

The variables – real property price index, real material cost index, nominal interest rate, population, time on the market and the ratio of building warrants granted to building warrant applications – are integrated in order of one according to both the ADF and the KPSS tests. That is, these variables are only stationary when their changes rather than levels are used. This means that when these variables are employed in their levels rather than changes to do the regressions, then they will be inconsistent since starts are stationary in their levels. The stock is integrated in order of one according to both tests, but only with the inclusion of a deterministic trend. In general, both the ADF and the KPSS produce similar results except these two variables.

Table 8.4 Unit root tests for stationarity

Variables		T-statistics	ADF Integration order	P-value	T-statistics	KPSS Integration order
STARTS			I(0)			I(0)
	Level	−5.867***		0.000	0.390	
STOCK			I(1)			I(1)
	Level	−1.323		0.618	0.869***	
	Change	−2.100		0.244	0.372*	
REAL PROPERTY PRICE INDEX			I(1)			I(1)
	Level	−0.028		0.956	0.832***	
	Change	−8.299***		0.000	0.077	
REAL MATERIAL COST INDEX			I(1)			I(1)
	Level	−0.818		0.814	0.876***	
	Change	−10.369***		0.000	0.127	
NOMINAL INTEREST RATE			I(1)			I(1)
	Level	−0.992		0.756	0.709**	
	Change	−8.815***		0.000	0.051	

Variables	T-statistics	ADF	P-value	T-statistics	KPSS
		Integration order			Integration order
REAL GROSS DOMESTIC PRODUCT		I(0)			I(1)
Level	−5.823***		0.000	0.877	
Change				0.561*	
POPULATION		I(1)			I(1)
Level	−0.258		0.931	0.816***	
Change	−3.109		0.479	0.485*	
TIME ON THE MARKET	−1.697	I(1)			I(1)
Level	−9.048***		0.433	0.775***	
Change			0.000	0.079	
RATIO OF VOLUME TO STOCK		I(0)			I(0)
Level	−4.336***		0.000	0.204	
RATIO OF BWG TO BWA	−2.332	I(1)			I(1)
Level	−15.683***		0.162	0.528**	
Change			0.000	0.108	

Note: We reject the null hypothesis of a unit root using the ADF test, and reject the null hypothesis of stationarity using the KPSS test at the following levels of significance: *, **, *** representing 10%, 5% and 1% level respectively.

Estimation results and discussions

This section presents the empirical results obtained from the chapter. The results presented are based on Equation 8.9 and as indicated in the methodology section, eight different models are estimated based on the IV approach. The empirical regression results from these estimations are presented and discussed below.

Instrumental variable regression results

Table 8.5 presents the results obtained from the empirical modelling. The first column in the table shows the variables included in the specifications. The lags are chosen to be sufficient to remove any autocorrelation in the specifications. The table shows that serial correlation is absent in all the models as the coefficient of AR(1) is not significant on a 5% level for any of the models. Columns two to nine also show the estimated coefficients from the eight specifications.

The first specification is a direct estimate of Equation 8.9. The model produces an R-squared of approximately 24% with the current changes in house prices, changes in house prices in the fourth lag and the constant term being statistically significant on a 5% level. The changes in house prices however have the greatest impact on house prices with a coefficient of 3.7% in the current period and 3.6% in the last four quarters. Changes in interest rate also have a negative but insignificant effect on housing starts in the current period. Even though it is not significant, the negative sign is expected and consistent with the previous literature as discussed above. It should be noted here that interest rate not only affects housing supply but housing demand as well. The impact of changes in interest rate on housing demand is captured in the price change variable since current changes and lagged changes in the one-year libor rate are used as instruments for price changes. Thus, the direct effect of interest rate on housing starts suggests that much of the effect of interest rate on the housing market occurs through demand rather than supply. Like the changes in interest rate variable, the changes in the real cost of building materials is also not significant. The insignificancy of the real cost of building materials is evidenced in a number of empirical studies (see Topel and Rosen, 1988; DiPasquale and Wheaton, 1994; Mayer and Somerville, 2000).

Because changes in the real cost of building materials are not significant in the first model, we exclude it in the second model to see if that will have any impact on the results. The results from Specification 2 (Equation 8.10) indicate that even though the changes in raw building material cost do not have any impact on the first model, excluding it from the model do have an effect on the results, with the coefficient of the current changes in house prices increasing from 3.7% to 5.7% but the last four quarters house price changes decreasing from 3.6% to 3.1%. Thus, if indeed construction cost is excluded from the model, then supply will increase more following an increase in house price than it would have been if the construction cost variable is included in the model. The coefficient estimates on the changes in interest rate however are similar, have the expected sign and are still not significant. To ensure consistency, the changes in the raw cost of building materials are included in Specifications 3 to 8.

In Specification 3, we estimate Equation 8.11 by adding changes in the time on the market variable to the basic equation (Equation 8.9) in order to examine the impact that the number of days properties stay on the market until they are sold have on new housing starts. Table 8.5 shows that by including this variable, the R-squared increased to 28% and the time on the market have a negative significant effect on housing supply. When the changes in the time on the market increase by 1%, all other things being equal, housing starts fall by some 1.7%. This negative sign is expected because as discussed in the third section, when the time on the market increases, it sends a signal to builders that demand is slow and since the builders are rational and want to maximise profit, they will slow down new construction. The magnitude is, however, smaller as compared to some national studies in the USA like Topel and Rosen (1988), DiPasquale and Wheaton (1994) and Mayer and Somerville (2000). The changes in house prices in periods t and $t - 1$ are still statistically significant on a 5% level.

The impact of planning regulation on housing supply is examined in Specification 4 (Equation 8.12) by adding the changes in the ratio of building warrants approved to the total number of building applications to Equation 8.9. The results from Specification 4 show that inclusion of the variables increases the R-squared to 32% and planning regulation have a significant positive effect on housing starts. With a 1% increase in the changes in the ratio of building warrants

Table 8.5 Empirical regression results using the IV approach

Variables	Models							
	1	2	3	4	5	6	7	8
ΔP_t	3.6968	5.7094	5.4268	5.2192	3.9785	3.6356	3.4829	5.3031
	(1.98)**	(2.02)**	(2.51)**	(1.99)**	(2.36)**	(2.01)**	(2.06)**	(1.96)**
ΔP_{t-1}	1.7094	1.6492	-0.4917	1.6041	1.3144	-0.2992	-1.4057	-2.9000
	(0.37)	(0.36)	(-0.10)	(0.34)	(0.28)	(-0.27)	(-0.35)	(-0.69)
ΔP_{t-2}	5.3569	6.0152	2.5728	5.4101	4.9309	4.9858	3.6417	1.3381
	(1.13)	(1.36)	(0.55)	(1.14)	(1.03)	(2.12)**	(1.98)**	(2.02)**
ΔP_{t-3}	6.2540	5.6949	6.0439	6.0250	5.8211	3.1606	2.5399	2.5240
	(1.34)	(1.25)	(1.34)	(1.30)	(2.04)**	(0.72)	(0.62)	(0.63)
ΔP_{t-4}	3.6430	3.1235	2.8725	3.4056	3.2141	1.2568	-0.9240	-1.3906
	(2.08)**	(1.98)**	(1.97)**	(2.01)**	(1.68)	(0.28)	(-0.22)	(-0.34)
ΔR_t	-0.1450	-0.1401	-0.1451	-0.1489	-0.1421	-.0825	-0.1486	-0.1506
	(-1.13)	(-1.11)	(-1.16)	(-1.16)	(-1.09)	(-0.67)	(-1.31)	(-1.36)
ΔR_{t-1}	0.1679	0.1834	0.1478	0.1747	0.1728	0.2041	0.2448	0.2246
	(1.27)	(1.41)	(1.16)	(1.32)	(1.29)	(1.65)	(1.11)	(1.90)
ΔC_t	4.3465		-6.2964	4.0002	4.6270	-.8823	-2.0332	-11.1866
	(0.39)		(-0.46)	(0.36)	(0.42)	(-0.08)	(-0.21)	(-0.94)
ΔT_t			-1.7470					-1.4722
			(-1.97)**					(-1.99)**

(continued)

Table 8.5 Empirical regression results using the IV approach (*continued*)

Variables	Models							
	1	*2*	*3*	*4*	*5*	*6*	*7*	*8*
$\Delta(BWG_t/BWA_t)$				0.0324 (2.06)**				0.2290 (2.46)**
ΔS_{t-1}					8.2431 (2.41)**			
I_{t-1}						0.3422 (3.42)**		
$aEI_{t-1} + I_{t-1}$							0.3085 (5.04)**	0.2948 (4.83)**
Constant	5.6451 (26.66)**	5.6402 (26.72)**	5.6349 (27.41)**	5.6411 (26.55)**	130.2937 (4.58)**		2.1874 (3.05)**	2.3393 (3.30)**
AR(1)	0.3289 (1.29)	0.3409 (1.43)	0.3259 (1.25)	0.3301 (1.30)	0.3158 (1.13)	0.0092 (0.09)	-0.2798 (-1.78)	-0.2438 (-1.39)
Adjusted R^2	23.63%	24.26%	28.18%	32.46%	22.06%	32.88%	42.37%	47.08%

Note: The t-values are in parentheses and ** shows significancy on a 5% significant level. The dependent variable is the logarithm of quarterly single-family housing starts. Seasonal dummies and trend variable are included in all regressions. They are however insignificant and so are not reported in the table.

approved to building warrant applications, housing starts increase in Aberdeen City District Council by approximately 0.03%. This positive impact is not surprising because an increase in the changes in the ratio means that more land has been made available to private developers for development and hence housing starts will increase. The impact of planning regulation on housing starts is also evidenced in a number of local studies in the UK (see for example Bramley, 1993a, 1993b; Cheshire and Sheppard, 1995; Pryce, 1999). In the national studies examined, this variable has been ignored despite its significance as evidenced in these results. This is because planning is more localised and differs from one district council to the other. The impact of planning regulation on housing construction is more appropriate to be examined at the local level and this provides more support for housing studies to be conducted at the local levels rather than the national and regional levels. Again, the changes in house prices in periods t and $t - 4$ are still statistically significant on a 5% level.

In Specification 5 (Equation 8.13), we include lagged stock to Equation 8.9 in order to control for the role of depreciation in explaining housing starts. As already indicated, starts should increase with stock as more units depreciate and need to be replaced, assuming depreciation rate is constant. The results show that the previous period's housing stock does have a significant effect on housing starts but also reduces the model's explanatory power to 22%. A 1% increase in the previous quarter's housing stock increases the current period's housing starts by about 8%, all other things being equal. In all the other models, we assume that the time trend and the constant successfully capture the effect of depreciation (see Mayer and Somerville, 2000). The change in house prices in period t is still significant but instead of period $t - 4$ as found in the first four models, the price changes in period $t - 3$ are now significant with the other lagged periods being insignificant.

In Specification 6, we estimate Equation 8.14 where the lagged value of the starts variable is added to Equation 8.9. As expected there is a positive significant relationship between the current starts and the lagged starts with a 1% increase in the lagged starts increasing the current starts by approximately 0.34%. Again, the change in house prices in period t is still significant and that of period $t - 2$ is also significant.

In Specification 7, the adjustment costs hypothesis by Topel and Rosen (1988) is tested with Equation 8.15 with the local data by including an addition of both the previous period's and next period's new construction, $EI_{t+1} + I_{t-1}$, to Equation 8.9. The results show that the inclusion of the variable increases the explanatory power of Specification 1 to a little over 42% and an increase in $EI_{t+1} + I_{t-1}$ does have a positive impact on the current period's construction starts. When $EI_{t+1} + I_{t-1}$ increases by 1%, the current period's housing starts increase by 0.31%. This positive effect is consistent with the finding by Topel and Rosen (1988) and suggests that the adjustment cost hypothesis is significant in building activities. That is, marginal costs rise with both level of and changes in new construction activity and so following a positive demand shock, the building firms lower costs by smoothing their increase in output over a number of periods rather than building all units at a time. The changes in house prices in periods t and $t - 2$ are still significant.

Finally, in Specification 8, all the variables from each of the previous seven specifications, except the lagged stock variable, are included to estimate housing starts. The lagged stock is excluded so that adjusted the multicollinearity problem likely to arise as a result of the inclusion of both lagged stock and lagged starts will be avoided. The inclusion of price changes together with the time trend and the constant term are assumed to successfully control for the role of depreciation (Mayer and Somerville, 2000). That is, we estimate Equation 8.16. The model produces the highest explanatory power of about 47%. The results show that the changes in house prices in periods t and $t - 2$, the current period's time on the market, the ratio of building warrants granted to building warrant applications and the previous period's and next period's new construction are all statistically significant on a 5% level. Changes in the raw cost of building materials and interest rate still remain insignificant. Since the significant variables are all local variables, it suggests that local factors do influence housing starts at the local level more than national variables.

Price elasticities of supply

In this sub-section, the price elasticity of supply estimated from the eight models is presented in Table 8.6. Like DiPasquale and Wheaton (1994) and Mayer and Somerville (2000), there is a distinction between the price elasticity of housing stock and that of housing starts. The formula for the price elasticity is presented in Equation 8.17:

$$PES = \frac{\partial I}{\partial P} \times \frac{P}{I} \qquad (8.17)$$

where PES is the price elasticity of supply, ∂I is the change in housing starts,[1] ∂P is the change in price, P is the mean value of the real property price index which is 97.57 and I is the mean value of housing starts which is 172.89. As a convention, when the price elasticity of supply is greater than one, ($PES > 1$), then supply is sensitive to price changes and so supply is elastic. However, when $PES < 1$, then supply is not sensitive to price changes and so it is not elastic. Also, when $PES = 1$, then supply is unit elastic, with a unit increase in house prices producing the same unit increase in supply. $PES = 0$ means that supply is fixed and does not respond to changes in price.

Table 8.6 shows that the price elasticities of starts range from 2.0 to 3.2 depending on the model used. That is a 10% increase in house prices increases housing starts by between 20% and 32%. These supply elasticities are within the 0–4 range of supply elasticities found by Malpezzi and Maclennan (2001) for the UK market. They are also similar to the supply elasticities estimated by Ball et al. (2010). Compared to the other local market supply elasticities, the supply elasticities for the Aberdeen local authority district are higher than the 0.29 for the Birmingham market but similar to the Worcester market (3.11) estimated by Bramley (1993a, 1993b). The results are also higher than the supply elasticities of 0.58 in 1988 and 1.03 in 1992 estimated by Pryce (1999) for 162 local authority districts in England.

The model that produces the highest price elasticity of supply is the second model. This is not surprising because the second model assumes that private developers are not faced with construction costs. If this is to be the case, then a little shock in demand will see a large change in new construction. In this case, 1% increase in house price will increase new construction by 3.2%. On the contrary, in Specification 1, where we assume that private developers are faced with construction cost, the same 1% change in house prices increases new construction by only 2.1%.

Specification 6, which assumes that private developers face adjustment cost, produces the lowest supply elasticity. This is also expected because when there is a demand shock and private developers face adjustment costs, in order to maximise their profits, they will have to spread construction over several periods and hence the small starts elasticity of only 2.0.

In estimating the stock elasticities, however, the I is replaced by S, the average volume of stock, which is 96055.87. Since housing stock is stable in the short run and changes only after some time, the coefficients of changes in the current and lagged values of house prices are summed up to replace ∂I in estimating the stock elasticities. The results from Table 8.5 show that it takes about five quarters (one year and three months) for the housing stock to move following a demand shock, and then returns to equilibrium. The price elasticity of stock ranges from 0.01 to 0.02 meaning that a 10% increase in house prices would increase the entire stock by between 0.1% to 0.2%. The stock elasticities seem relatively small as compared to the starts elasticities but given that starts are a small percentage of the stock, only 0.18%, the results are not surprising.

Table 8.6 Price elasticities of supply in Aberdeen

Models	Price elasticities of supply	
	Starts	*Stock*
1	2.1	0.02
2	3.2	0.02
3	3.1	0.02
4	2.9	0.02
5	2.2	0.02
6	2.1	0.01
7	2.0	0.01
8	3.0	0.01

Conclusion

This chapter has examined the determinants of new residential construction and has estimated the price elasticity of supply for the housing market of Aberdeen local authority district council. Eight different models are estimated using the instrumental variable (IV) approach, with the basic model treating single-family housing starts as a function of the changes in the current and lagged values in house prices, raw building material costs and interest rate.

The other variables incorporated in the other models include the number of days properties stay on the market until they are sold (time on the market) as a measure of the condition of the local housing market, changes in the ratio of building warrants granted as a measure of the effect of planning regulations on housing supply, the previous total dwelling stock as a control variable for depreciation and lagged and future changes in single-family housing starts to measure the adjustment cost model propose by Topel and Rosen (1988).

It has become clear from the empirical results that serial correlation is absent in all the eight specifications. It is also found that changes in house prices, time on the market, planning regulation, lagged stock and lagged and future housing starts are the main factors that influence new residential construction in Aberdeen. Changes in house prices have a large positive coefficient of about 3.7% in the basic model in the current period and a coefficient of about 3.6% in the previous fourth quarter.

Also, when time on the market increases by one day, housing starts also decrease by 1.7%. Changes in the ratio of the building warrants granted to the building warrant applications made also have a positive effect on housing starts: with a 1% increase in the ratio starts increase by approximately 0.03%. The results also show that when the previous period's single-family housing starts increase by 1%, all other things being equal, the current period's single-family housing starts increase by almost 0.34%. The adjustment cost hypothesis by Rosen and Topel (1988) is also found to significantly influence housing starts with a 1% increase in the lagged and future housing starts increasing current starts by approximately 0.3%.

The changes in raw building material costs and interest rates are found to be insignificant in all the models. These variables are national variables and so suggest that when modelling the local housing market, local variables are more useful than the national variables. These influential local variables would not be measured properly or would be ignored entirely when the national or regional housing markets are modelled. That is, it is more suitable and better to conduct housing studies at the local levels because important local factors that are specific to specific local markets would be shrouded when national and regional markets are used.

The price elasticities of supply estimated are in the range of 2.0–3.2 for housing starts, and 0.01–0.02 for housing stock. The starts elasticities are within the range of supply elasticities for a few local housing markets but, on average, higher than most of the local housing markets elasticities in the UK. Thus, private developers in Aberdeen respond more to a change in house prices by initiating new construction than most of the local authority districts in the UK.

Note

1 The coefficient estimate for the current change in house price is used to represent ∂I since the lagged price changes are not consistently significant in all the models.

9 The last word

Real estate forms the greater part of total assets in the world and constitutes a significant portion of the wealth of households. Information about real estate prices is therefore very important to households, investors and decision-makers. Even though the real estate market is most frequently analysed at the national and regional levels, the need to understand the dynamics of the local property market has been stressed by real estate analysts. This book has examined the dynamics of the Aberdeen housing market.

Several issues have been examined in this book. The book has discussed the various traditional property valuation methods. These include the comparisons sales approach, the replacement cost method, the income method, the profits method and the development or residual method. Some of the existing appraisal-based indices around the world like the NCREIF, JLW and the IPD appraisal indices area also presented. The book has also provided a global tour of the existing transaction-based property price indices. The importance of property price indices and the attributes which determine the quality of a property price index are all discussed. The scope, methodology and the level of index construction of various existing transaction-based indices are discussed. Previous empirical studies measuring property price trends in the form of indices have been reviewed with the aim of identifying any gaps in the literature. The study employs five index construction models based on the hedonic, repeat-sales and hybrid methods to construct indices with data from the study area. The implicit prices of the hedonic characteristics are tested to see if they are constant over time. The accuracy of the various index construction models is assessed and the issue of temporal aggregation effect on the construction of house prices is also examined. Finally, the constant-quality house price indices are applied to examine the determinants of housing construction and to estimate the price elasticity of supply for Aberdeen City District Council.

The aim of the book was to demonstrate how to construct and apply property price indices so as to benefit academics, practitioners and policy-makers. In order to accomplish this aim, three objectives were set out. To wit: *(i) to establish the state of current knowledge on house price index construction methods and identify areas where further knowledge or research is required. (ii) to apply the different methods to the same dataset, empirically examine the accuracy of the various methods and examine* the effect of aggregating observations on house prices across time. (iii) to use the house price index series to learn more about the supply side of the Aberdeen housing market.

A quantitative research framework has been applied to achieve these objectives. This involves a theoretical analysis stage, a descriptive statistics analysis stage and an empirical modelling stage.

Major findings

Chapters 2, 3, 4 and 5 contain the main theoretical aspects of measuring house price indices. In Chapter 2, the various traditional property valuation methods are discussed. These include the comparisons sales approach, the replacement cost method, the income method, the profits method and the development or residual method. It is clear from the chapter that a lot of assumptions are made when employing any of the traditional valuation methods and so the objectivity of the methods is compromised. A global tour of the existing transaction-based property price indices are provided in Chapter 3. The chapter highlights that most of the existing indices are provided at the national and regional levels even though city-specific indices are desirable. Also identified is the importance of house price indices. House price indices are used to target inflation and monetary policy: in making regional, national and international comparisons of house price trends, as an input for estimating the value of housing as a component of health, as an input into buying (or selling) decision-making, as a macroeconomic indicator for economic growth and as a financial stability indicator. The chapter has also highlighted five desirable properties of an index construction method. A good index construction method should: (i) require less data in its implementation; (ii) use data which is representative of the inventory; (iii) be standardised for quality (constant-quality); (iv) be easy to implement; and (v) not change historical numbers when revised.

In Chapter 4, hedonic pricing theory is discussed. This is an advanced property valuation method that seeks to estimate the specific contribution that each of the property attributes make to the value or price of the property. Accurate development of the hedonic equation, functional form selection and availability of a large database are necessary to ensure that the hedonic model is correctly applied.

Four index construction methods were discussed in Chapter 5. These are the average method, the hedonic method, the repeat-sales method and the hybrid method. The average method is the simplest way of constructing house price indices. However, the method does not control for the differences in quality of properties that are transacted over time and so the indices constructed with this method are not standardised or adjusted for these differences in quality.

The hedonic method recognises that a property is a composite product: while the attributes are not sold separately, regressing the attributes on the sale price of the composite product yields the marginal contribution of each attribute to the sale price. The physical and locational characteristics of the properties are all considered in the method. In constructing house price indices, the hedonic regression method can be applied in two main ways. These are the explicit time variable hedonic model, where the data is pooled together and time dummies are included to estimate the indices, and the strictly cross-sectional hedonic model, where separate regressions are estimated each period to estimate the index. The method corrects for the effects of the heterogeneity of properties by taking the characteristics of the properties into consideration. The implementation of the method however requires an extensive dataset of house price observations together with the details on the physical and locational attributes of the properties concerned. It is difficult and expensive, in terms of finance, time and other resources, to collect this dataset and some of the variables are omitted in most cases.

The repeat-sales method avoids the problem of omitted variable bias by confining the analysis to properties which have been sold at least twice in the sample. Sample selectivity bias is the main problem that affects the repeat-sales method. The properties that sell more frequently are 'starter homes' which are also relatively cheaper. The method is therefore criticised for understating the true price. The sample size that is used to estimate the index is relatively small since the properties that are typically sold more than ones may be small. The hybrid method works by combining elements of the hedonic and the repeat-sales methods to estimate the index. With this method, all the transaction data, both single- and repeat-sales, are used to estimate the indices. Different models have been developed by Case and Quigley (1991), Quigley (1995), Hill et al. (1997) and Englund et al. (1998). Like the hedonic method, the hybrid method corrects for the effects of heterogeneity of properties by taking the characteristics of the properties into consideration. The problem of small sample size is also avoided. The method however requires an extensive dataset in its implementation. The chapter also compared the various methods based on previous empirical studies. It is found that none of the index methods consistently outperform the others in terms of their accuracies. Apart from the fact that these studies use different datasets and that the differences in study areas and datasets could cause this inconsistency, two other reasons that have been identified as the possible cause for this inconsistency are: (i) absence of appropriate proxy for the unobservable "true" house price trend to measure index accuracy; (ii) scarcity and pooling of data across time. These issues have been noted as areas where further research is required and form the basis for the second objective.

The second objective was addressed in Chapters 6 and 7. The local house price indices are constructed using the Aberdeen housing market as the case study area. The reason for choosing this study area is explained in Chapter 6. The area was chosen because of the availability of readily and accessible transaction data at the time of the empirical analysis as well as the proximity to and familiarity with the area. The chapter has also highlighted that Aberdeen contributes significantly to both Scotland's and the UK's GDP, has a higher proportion of economically active adults and a lower unemployment rate as compared to Edinburgh and Glasgow, even though the population in Aberdeen is relatively small.

The availability, sources and limitations of the data were also discussed and it was decided that the transacted properties recorded by ASPC from January 2000 to December 2010 would be used for the study. The sale prices, various structural property characteristics and the easting (X) and northing (Y) locational variables are all included in the dataset. The dataset was prepared in this chapter to make it a workable one and also to identify the repeat-sales. The final dataset contained a total of 57,150 observations but 40,971 unique properties. Only 34.9% of this are repeat-sales and most of the repeat-sales are flats. The descriptive statistics show that, generally, the data meet the criteria of normality and variability of values for index construction.

In Chapter 7, five different house price index construction models based on the hedonic, repeat-sales and the hybrid methods have been used to construct several indices with the data described above. The models employed are the explicit time variable (ETV) hedonic, the strictly cross-section (SCS) hedonic, the ordinary repeat-sales (ORS), the weighted repeat-sales (WRS) and the Quigley's hybrid (Q-hybrid) model. The indices are constructed at the annual, semi-annual, quarterly and monthly temporal level of aggregation. Several empirical tests and analysis relating to house price index construction have been conducted. The first test conducted relates to the assumption that the implicit prices of the housing attributes are constant over time. This is the main assumption that distinguishes the ETV hedonic model from the SCS hedonic model. Using the Chow test, the null hypothesis that the implicit prices are the same over the various years is rejected at a 1% level. Thus, the implicit prices of the housing attributes differ from year to year.

In examining the indices constructed from the various models, the SCS hedonic model is found to produce the most volatile index and the repeat-sales indices track house prices below the other index types. The accuracy of the various models is also examined by using the mean squared errors (MSE) technique based on out of sample forecast evaluation. The SCS hedonic model is found to be the most accurate model to construct house price indices at the broader level of temporal aggregation (annual or semi-annual). At the lower level of temporal aggregation (quarterly or monthly), however, either the ETV hedonic model or the Q-hybrid model is superior. The ETV hedonic model is, however, suitable in constructing house price indices at the lower level of temporal aggregation given the technical and cumbersome nature of implementing the Q-hybrid model. The MSE differences among most of these models are found to be statistically significant on a 1% level.

The next test conducted relates to the issue of temporal aggregation in constructing house price indices. The F-test is employed to test the null hypothesis that house price indices generated at different levels of temporal aggregation are the same. We find that at a 1% level, the tests conducted consistently reject the null hypothesis that the indices are the same. We also find that the F-ratios at the lower levels (like the monthly and quarterly levels) of temporal aggregation are smaller than at the broader levels (like the yearly and semi-yearly levels), suggesting that time should be represented using the lower levels of aggregation as much as possible when constructing house price indices. This finding is very consistent across all the models and the differences among the calculated returns at the various level of temporal aggregation are really small and insignificant. Thus, even though temporal aggregation is statistically important and so the lower level of temporal aggregation should be used, economically, the level of temporal aggregation does not really matter.

The third objective addressed in Chapter 8. The chapter examined the determinants of new residential construction and has estimated the price elasticity of supply for the housing market of Aberdeen Local Authority District Council. This was important because the supply side of the housing market is still under-researched and most of the supply studies are conducted at the national and regional levels. Eight different models are estimated using the instrumental variable (IV) approach, with different sources of data at both the national and local levels including the house price indices. Twenty-five-year quarterly time series data are used for the analysis. The basic model treats single-family housing starts as a function of the changes in the current and lagged values in house prices, raw building material costs and interest rate.

The other variables included in the other models include the number of days a property stays on the market until they are sold (time on the market) as a measure of the condition of the local housing market, changes in the ratio of building warrants granted as a measure of the effect of planning regulations on housing supply, the previous total dwelling stock as a control variable for depreciation and lagged and future changes in single-family housing starts to measure the adjustment cost model propose by Topel and Rosen (1988). All these variables are also modelled together in a single equation.

It became clear from the chapter that the housing starts variable is stationary and integrated in order of zero but most of the other variables are non-stationary and are integrated in order of one, using both the ADF and KPSS stationary tests. Also, serial correlation is absent in all the eight models. It is also found that changes in house prices, time on the market, planning regulation, lagged stock and lagged and future housing starts are the main factors that influence new residential construction in Aberdeen. Changes in house prices have a large positive coefficient of about 3.7% in the basic model in the current period and coefficient of about 3.6% in the previous fourth quarter.

Also, when time on the market increases by one day, housing starts also decrease by 1.7%. Changes in the ratio of the building warrants granted to the building warrant applications made also have a positive effect on housing starts, with a 1% increase in the ratio, increasing starts by approximately 0.03%. The results also show that when the previous period's single-family housing starts increase by 1%, all other things being equal, the current period's single-family housing starts increase by almost 0.34%. The adjustment cost hypothesis by Rosen and Topel (1988) is also found to significantly influence housing starts with a 1% increase in the lagged and future housing starts increasing current starts by approximately 0.3%.

The changes in raw building material costs and interest rates are found to be insignificant in all the models. These variables are national variables and so suggest that when modelling the local housing market, local variables are more useful than the national variables. These influential local variables would not be measured properly or would be ignored entirely when the national or regional housing markets are modelled. That is, it is more suitable and better to conduct housing studies at the local levels because important local factors that are specific to specific local markets would be shrouded when national and regional markets are used.

The price elasticities of supply estimated are in the range of 2.0–3.2 for housing starts, and 0.01–0.02 for housing stock. The starts elasticities are within the range of supply elasticities for few local housing markets but, on average, higher than most of the local housing markets elasticities in the UK. Thus, private developers in Aberdeen respond more to a change in house prices by initiating new construction than most of the local authority districts in the UK.

Implications for policy and theory

This book has added value to the construction and application of property price indices in several ways. In this section, the contributions of the book are discussed and the implications of the findings for policy are also highlighted.

One major significant contribution of this book is the use of UK data at the local level in comparing the various index construction methods. In most of the previous index construction studies, the analysis has been done with national and regional level data. Using local house price data is clearly one of the contributions. The results obtained with the data also confirm the need to limit housing market analysis to the local level. The dataset used for constructing the house price indices is also very rich with a large number of observations and variables that relate to physical and locational characteristics of the properties, thereby producing robust results.

Again, this book is one of the few studies that extensively compares the various house price index construction methods. In comparing the accuracy of the various index construction methods, previous studies have mostly used either the goodness of fit statistics reported by the various models under investigation or the average price to represent the true house price. This book has highlighted the problems involved in using these criteria to compare the index methods and instead applies an out of sample forecast evaluation to compare the accuracy of the various methods based on their MSE.

Furthermore, this book tackles a major issue that most index construction studies in the literature ignore – that is, the issue of pooling data across time. Most studies in the literature have arbitrarily pooled data together across time to estimate indices. The perception is that pooling data together helps to overcome the problem of small sample size, a common problem encountered in studies using real estate transaction data. In doing this, however, they implicitly assume that the pooled sample will produce index numbers that are statistically equivalent to those that would have been obtained from their constituent sub-samples, without any empirical tests. The book moves a step further to test the validity of this assumption and so contributes to knowledge regarding house price index construction.

In addition, this book examines the relationship between house prices and housing construction. The demand side of the housing market is more researched than the supply side and this book provides further evidence about housing supply in the UK. Also, unlike most of the housing supply studies in the UK that are conducted at the national and regional levels, in this book, this relationship is examined at the local level, providing more evidence about local housing market analysis.

In the few previous local housing supply studies, a cross-sectional dataset has been employed for the empirical modelling. This book has highlighted the problems involved in employing a cross-sectional dataset for modelling housing supply and estimating price elasticity of supply. The book avoids this problem by employing consistent quarterly time series data for a twenty-five-year period. This long period of time series data coupled with the robust methodology employed is one of the strengths of this book.

Finally, the comparison of eight different models using local data to explain the determinants of new construction is clearly an additional contribution of this book. More especially, planning regulation variables have mostly been ignored in time series modelling of housing supply. The inclusion of the percentage of building warrants granted in explaining new construction is therefore a contribution to the housing supply literature. Also, there has not been previous evidence of price elasticity of supply for Aberdeen City District Council and this book has provided such evidence and thus filled that gap in the literature.

The book has not only provided theoretical and empirical analysis, but the results and findings also have some policy and practical applications. Some of the relevant policy and practical implications are highlighted below.

Firstly, one major significant and practical contribution of this book is the construction of house price indices for the Aberdeen housing market and the other major areas within the North East of Scotland. Due to the important role housing plays in the socioeconomic development of every country, the availability of a robust, reliable and timely house price indices is crucial. However, due to the lack of constant-quality house price indices for the various local areas in the UK, either average price signals or constant-quality regional house price indices produced by the Nationwide and/or Halifax Building Society are usually relied on for decision-making in the local housing market. Constructing a constant-quality local house price index for the Aberdeen Housing Market and the other areas in the North East of Scotland, therefore, provides market participants and policy-makers with better information about house price changes in the local area upon which they can base their decisions. For example, when house prices increase in a certain period, households in Aberdeen and the surrounding areas will be able to know that their total wealth has increased and so can plan their consumption expenditure accordingly. Also, with updated data, the city council will get to know that there is an increase in house prices in the private market and so can assess its impact on housing demand for council housing which can be incorporated into their planning policy.

Another practical and policy implication of the book relates to the factors that affect new housing construction and the price elasticities of supply that have been estimated in the book. The book has highlighted that the factors that determine private new housing construction in Aberdeen are changes in house prices, time on the market, planning regulation, lagged stock and lagged and future housing starts. When there is a change in any of these variables, private housing construction will also change and this will affect social housing and so the city council which is tasked with providing social housing for the inhabitants will know whether to increase or decrease housing construction. For example, when house prices reduce, time on the market increases and planning regulation becomes tighter, and all other things remain the same, new housing construction by the private factor will reduce. In this case, if population has increased and is expected to remain high, then the city council will have to build new houses to accommodate the growing population. The estimated price elasticity of supply will also help the private developers, the city council and other stakeholders in their decision-making. If house prices increase for instance, the estimated elasticities will help private developers to know exactly what volume of house construction to start in order to increase the stock in the future. This will also guide the city council to know how many houses the private developers will bring to the market so that they can incorporate it in their decision-making.

The methodologies and models that have been developed in the book could also be used to construct house price indices in other local markets which will promote transparency and ensure accurate reporting of house price changes.

Limitations and direction for future research

Even though the book has made several contributions to the literature on house price index construction and modelling of housing supply, and also has some major policy and practical relevance, there are some limitations in the book. This section discusses the limitations of the book and also suggests potential areas for future research.

The first limitation of the book relates to the dataset that has been used for the empirical analysis and demonstration. The author had access to the dataset up to the year 2010 when he was a researcher at the University of Aberdeen. Due to the data right protection policy between the University of Aberdeen and the data providers (ASPC), the author could not get any updated data beyond 2010 since had left the University by then. Nevertheless, since the purpose of the empirical analysis in this book is just to illustrate how to construct property price indices so that readers can use the models and techniques developed in the book for their own work, the lack of updated data beyond 2010 do not compromise the relevance of the book.

Also, the ASPC dataset contains some of the variables needed for hedonic modelling and an attempt has been made to include these physical and locational characteristics of the properties as fully as possible. However, missing variables are unavoidable in this book due to the unavailability of data on these variables.

Important variables like the size (area), building quality and age of the property are absent in the ASPC dataset. While the number of rooms (bedrooms, public rooms and bathrooms) can measure the effect of property size on house prices, there is no variable to represent age. Data on age of the building are usually used to measure depreciation associated with a property and hence the building quality. Indeed, the absence of age of the property has made it impossible to construct indices with Hill et al.'s (1997) and Englund et al.'s (1998) hybrid models. Another limitation of the ASPC data is the lack of new dwellings. The new developments tend to be sold through developers in Scotland, and therefore are not sold through the Property Solicitors Centre. The inclusion of these transactions in the dataset would have controlled for the effect of depreciation and indices related to new houses would have been developed for the housing supply modelling.

The data limitations do not only relate to the ASPC dataset but also the data used for modelling housing supply. Information about the material cost index, interest rate, inflation, income or GDP could not be obtained consistently for the 25-year period at the local level. There are no measures of the material cost index, interest rate and inflation at the local level and so the national measures are used in the empirical modelling, assuming that these variables are similar across all areas in the UK. Even though information about income or GDP per head are available at the local level, the data is not available for the 25-year period under study. The regional GDP is therefore used in the empirical modelling but will not significantly bias the results since it is used as an instrument together with other local variables for house price.

Another limitation is the book's inability to examine the effect of geographical aggregation on house price index construction. The book has examined the effect of aggregating data across time in the construction of house price indices but the issue of geographical aggregation effect on house price index construction is not examined.

Based on the limitations above, the following recommendations are made as directions for future research concerning house price index construction and housing supply studies. One practical area that should be explored further is the construction of house price indices for other cities or districts in the UK. The book has clearly demonstrated that using national or regional house price indices to take decisions at the local levels due to the absence of constant-quality local house price indices will be misleading. The construction of house price indices for the various local housing markets in the UK will therefore promote efficiency in the housing market. Currently, the Land Registry collects house price data at the local levels in the UK. However, the dwelling characteristics are not included. If effort is made to augment this database with the various dwelling characteristics, the construction of constant-quality house price indices in the UK would be possible.

Another direction that should be explored is the examination of the effect of geographical aggregation in the construction of house price indices. Because statistically temporal aggregation has an effect on house price indices, it could be the case that geographical aggregation will also affect the construction of house price indices. Location has been widely acknowledged as the major determinant of housing values and the price of residential properties typically vary across space. Therefore, the pooling of data from different areas within the housing market, even at the local level, could have an influence on the indices constructed, and this issue could be empirically explored.

More housing supply studies are needed especially in the UK. These studies should, however, be conducted at the local level and the dataset should be time ses instead of cross-sectional. In this case, the long-run relationship between housing supply and its determinants could be explored further and house price elasticity of supply could be estimated for the other housing markets. Also, the inclusion of planning variables in examining the determinants of housing supply should be encouraged since this is expected to differ from one local area to the other. Furthermore, more structural models like the vector autoregressive (VAR) and error correction (VEC) models could be applied to examine the housing supply variables.

Finally, this book has only applied house price indices to examine the supply side of the housing market. However, there could be other uses of price indices. These include empirical tests of housing market efficiency, the role of housing in portfolio management, mortgage market analysis, hedging mechanism for house price volatility and estimating of real estate derivatives and home equity insurance. These issues could be examined further using house price indices.

References

Abdulai, R.T. (2010) *Traditional Landholding Institutions in Sub-Saharan Africa – The Operation of Traditional Landholding Institutions in Sub-Saharan Africa: A Case Study of Ghana* (LAP Lambert Academic Publishing, Germany).

Aberdeen City and Shire Strategic Development Planning Authority (2011) Available at https://www.aberdeenshire.gov.uk/media/11871/hnda2011_000.pdf, accessed 24th March, 2012.

Abraham, J. and Schauman, W. (1991) 'New evidence on home prices from Freddie Mac repeat sales', *Real Estate Economics*, vol. 19, no. 3, pp. 333–352.

ACC (2011) Housing Need and Demand Assessment, Aberdeen City and Shire Strategic Development Planning Authority, March 2011.

Adair, A.S., Berry, J.N. and McGreal W.S. (1996) 'Hodonic modelling, housing submarkets and residential valuation', *Journal of Property Research*, vol. 13, pp. 67–83.

Ambrose, B. and Peek, J. (2008) 'Credit availability and the structure of the home-building industry', *Real Estate Economics*, vol. 36, no. 4, pp. 659–692.

Anglin, P. and Gencay, R. (1996) 'Semiparametric estimation of a hedonic price function', *Journal of Applied Econometrics*, vol. 11, no. 6, pp. 633–648.

ASPC (2011a) City and Suburbs. Available at www.aspc.co.uk/Search/HomesForSale, accessed 10th July, 2011.

ASPC (2011b) House Price Information. Available at www.aspc.co.uk/Documents, accessed 12th August, 2011.

Baer, W.C. (1986) 'The dynamics of the nation's housing stock', *Scientific American*, vol. 255, pp. 29–35.

Bajari, P. and Khan, E.M. (2005) 'Estimating housing demand with an application to explaining racial segregation in cities', *Journal of Business and Economic Statistics*, vol. 23, no. 1, pp. 20–33.

Bailey, M.J., Muth, R.F. and Nourse, H.O. (1963) 'A regression method for real estate price index construction', *The American Statistical Association*, vol. 58, no. 304, pp. 933–942.

Ball, M.J. and Kirwan, R.M. (1977) 'Accessibility and supply constraints in the urban housing markets', *Urban Studies*, vol. 14, pp. 11–32.

Ball, M., Meen, G. and Nygaard, C. (2010) 'Housing supply price elasticities revisited: Evidence from international, national, local and company data', *Journal of Housing Economics*, vol. 19, no. 4, pp. 255–268.

Bartlett, W. (1988) *The Economics of Housing Supply: A Review of the Theoretical and Empirical Literature* (Joseph Rowntree Foundation, York).

Basu, S. and Thibodeau, T.G. (1998) 'Analysis of spatial autocorrelation in house prices', *Journal of Real Estate Finance and Economics*, vol. 17, no. 1, pp. 61–85.

Bateman, I.J., Day, B., Lake, I. and Lovett, A. (2001) *The Effect of Road Traffic on Residential Property Values: A Literature Review and Hedonic Pricing Study* (UEA, ESRC, UCL).

Bell, K.C. (2006) 'World Bank Support for Land Administration and Management: Responding to the Challenges of the Millennium Development Goals', *Paper presented at the 23rd FIG Congress, Munich Germany.*

Berndt, E.R. (1991) *The Practice of Econometrics: Classic and Contemporary* (Addison-Wesley, Reading, MA).

Berndt, E.R. and Rappaport, N. (2001) 'Price and quality of desktop and mobile personal computers: A quarter-century historical overview', *American Economic Review*, vol. 91, no. 2, pp. 268–273.

Blackley, D.M. (1999) 'The long-run elasticity of new housing supply in the United States: Empirical evidence for 1950 to 1994', *Journal of Real Estate Finance and Economics*, vol. 18, no. 1, pp. 25–42.

Blomquist, G. and Worley, L. (1981) 'Hedonic prices, demands for urban housing amenities, and benefit estimates', *Journal of Urban Economics*, vol. 9, no. 2, pp. 212–221.

Bourassa, S.C., Cantoni, E. and Hoesli, M. (2007) 'Spatial dependence, housing submarkets, and house price prediction', *The Journal of Real Estate Finance and Economics*, vol. 35, pp. 143–160.

Bourassa, S.C., Hamelink, F., Hoesli, M. and MacGregor, B.D. (1999) 'Defining housing submarkets', *Journal of Housing Economics*, vol. 8, no. 2, pp. 160–183.

Bourassa, S.C., Hoesli, M. and Peng, V.S. (2003) 'Do housing sub-markets really matter?', *Journal of Housing Economics*, vol. 12, no. 1, pp. 12–28.

Bourassa, S.C., Hoesli, M. and Sun, J. (2006) 'A simple alternative house price index method', *Journal of Housing Economics*, vol. 15, no. 1, pp. 80–97.

Box, G.E.P. and Cox, D.R. (1964) 'An analysis of transformations', *Journal of the Royal Statistical Society. Series B (Methodological)*, vol. 26, no. 2, pp. 211–252.

Boykin, J.H and Ring, A.A. (1986) *The Valuation of Real Estate* (Prentice Hall, Upper Saddle River, NJ).

Bramley, G. (1993a) 'The impact of land use planning and tax subsidies on the supply and price of housing in Britain', *Urban Studies*, 30, pp. 5–30.

Bramley, G. (1993b) 'Land-use planning and the housing market in Britain: the impact on house-building and house prices', *Environment and Planning A*, vol. 25, pp. 1021–1051.

Breusch, T.S. and Pagan, A.R. (1979) 'A simple test for heteroscedasticity and random coefficient variation', *Econometrica*, vol. 47, no. 5, pp. 1287–1294.

Brigham, E. (1965) 'The determinants of residential land values', *Land Economics*, vol. 41, no. 4, pp. 325–334.

Brooks, C. and Tsolacos, S. (2010) *Real Estate Modelling and Forecasting* (Cambridge University Press, Cambridge).

Brueggeman, W.B. and Fisher, J.D. (2001) *Real Estate Finance and Investments (11th ed.)* (McGraw Hill, New York).

Calhoun, C.A., Chinloy, P. and Megbolugbe, I.F. (1995) 'Temporal aggregation and house price index construction', *Journal of Housing Research*, vol. 6, no. 3, pp. 419–438.

Campbell, J. and Cocco, F.J. (2007) 'How do house prices affect consumption? Evidence from micro data', *Journal of Monetary Economics*, vol. 54, no. 3, pp. 591–621.

Can, A. (1990) 'The measurement of neighbourhood dynamics in urban house prices', *Economic Geography*, vol. 66, no. 3, pp. 254–272.

Case, B., Pollakowski, H. and Wachter, S. (1991) 'On choosing among house price index methodologies', *Real Estate Economics*, vol. 19, no. 3, pp. 286–307.

Case, B. and Quigley, J.M. (1991) 'The dynamics of real estate prices', *The Review of Economics and Statistics*, vol. 73, no. 1, pp. 50–58.

Case, B. and Szymanoski, E.J. (1995) 'Precision in house price indices: Finding of a comparative study of house price index methods', *Journal of Housing Research*, vol. 6, no. 3, pp. 483–496.

Case, K.E. (1986) 'The market for single-family homes in Boston area', *New England Economic Review*, May, pp. 38–48.

Case, K.E. and Shiller, R.J. (1987) 'Prices of single-family homes since 1970: new indexes for four cities', *New England Economic Review*, Sep, pp. 45–56.

Case K.E. and Shiller, R.J. (1988) 'The behavior of home buyers in boom and post-boom markets', *New England Economic Review*, Nov/Dec, pp. 29–46.

Case, K.E. and Shiller, R.J. (1989) 'The efficiency of the market for single-family homes', *American Economic Association*, vol. 79, no. 1, pp. 125–137.

Case, K.E., Shiller, R.J. and Weiss, A.N. (1993) 'Index-based futures and options markets in real estate', *Journal of Portfolio Management*, vol. 19, no. 2, pp. 83–92.

Cassel, E. and Mendelsohn, R. (1985) 'The choice of functional forms for hedonic price equations: Comment', *Journal of Urban Economics*, vol. 18, no. 2, pp. 135–142.

Cheshire, P. and Sheppard, S. (1995) 'On the price of land and the value of amenities', *Economics*, vol. 62, no. 246, pp. 247–267.

Chow, G.C. (1960) 'Tests of equality between sets of coefficients in two linear regressions', *Econometrica*, vol. 28, no. 3, pp. 591–605.

Clapham, E., Englund, P., Quigley, J. and Redfearn, C. (2006) 'Revisiting the past and settling the score: Index revision for house price derivatives', *Real Estate Economics*, vol. 34, no. 2, pp. 275–302.

Clapp, J.M. (2003) 'A semiparametric method for valuing residential location. Application to automated valuation', *Journal of Real Estate Finance and Economics*, vol. 27, no. 3, pp. 303–320.

Clapp, J. (2004) 'A semiparametric method for estimating local house price indices', *Journal of Real Estate Economics*, vol. 32, no. 1, pp. 127–160.

Clapp, J.M. and Giaccotto, C. (1992a) 'Estimating price indices for residential property: A comparison of repeat sales and assessed value methods', *The American Statistical Association*, vol. 87, no. 418, pp. 300–306.

Clapp, J.M. and Giaccotto, C. (1992b) 'Estimating price trends for residential property: A comparison of repeat sales and assessed value methods', *Journal of Real Estate Finance and Economics*, vol. 5, no. 4, pp. 357–374.

Clapp, J.M. and Giaccotto, C. (1998) 'Price indices based on the hedonic repeat-sale method: Application to the housing market', *Journal of Real Estate Finance and Economics*, vol. 16, no. 1, pp. 5–26.

Clapp, J.M. and Giaccotto, C. (1999) 'Revisions in repeat-sales price indexes: Here today, gone tomorrow?', *Real Estate Economics*, vol. 27, no. 1, pp. 79–104.

Clapp, J.M., Kim, H.-J. and Gelfand, A.E. (2002) 'Spatial prediction of house prices using LPR and Bayesian smoothing', *Journal of Real Estate Economics*, vol. 30, no. 4, pp. 505–532.

Cleveland, W.S. and Devlin, S.J. (1988) 'Locally weighted regression: An approach to regression analysis by local fitting', *Journal of the American Statistical Association*, vol. 83, pp. 596–610.

Cleveland, W.S., Devlin, S.J. and Grosse, E. (1988) 'Regression by local fitting: Methods, properties, and computational algorithms', *Journal of Econometrics*, vol. 37, pp. 87–114.

Cocco, F.J. (2004) 'Portfolio choice in the presence of housing', *The Review of Financial Studies*, vol. 18, no. 2, pp. 535–567.

Colwell, P.F. and Dilmore, G. (1999) 'An examination of an early hedonic study', *Land Economics*, vol. 75, no. 4, pp. 620–626.

Costello, G. and Watkins, C. (2002) 'Towards a system of local house price indexes', *Housing Studies*, vol. 17, no. 6, pp. 857–873.

Coulson, N.E. and Kim, M.S. (2000) 'Residential investment, non-residential investment and GDP', *Real Estate Economics*, vol. 28, no. 2, pp. 233–247.

Court, A. (1939) Hedonic price indexes with automotive examples. In: American Statistical Association (Ed.). *The Dynamics of Automobile Demand* (General Motors Corporation, New York).

Cover, T.M. (1968) 'Estimation by the nearest neighbour rule', *IEEE Trans. Information Theory IT*, vol. 14, no. 1, pp. 50–55.

Cover, T.M. and Hart, P.E. (1967) 'Nearest neighbour pattern classification', *IEEE Trans. Information Theory IT*, vol. 13, no. 1, pp. 21–27.

Creswell, J.W. (2003) *Research Design: Qualitative, Quantitative and Mixed Methods Approaches* (Sage Publications, California).

Creswell, J.W. (2007) *Qualitative Inquiry and Research Design: Choosing Among Five Approaches* (Sage Publications, California).

Crone, T. and Voith, R. (1992) 'Estimating house price appreciation: A comparison of methods', *Journal of Housing Economics*, vol. 2, no. 4, pp. 339–357.

Cropper, M., Deck, B. and McConnell, M. (1988) 'On the choice of functional form for hedonic price functions', *The Review of Economics and Statistics*, vol. 70, no. 4, pp. 668–675.

Cullingworth, J. (1997) *Planning in the USA* (Routledge, New York).

Davidian, M. and Carroll, R. (1987) 'Variance function estimation', *Journal of American Statistical Association*, vol. 82, pp. 1079–1091.

Day, B. (2003) *Submarket Identification in Property Markets: A Hedonic Housing Price Model for Glasgow*, University of East Anglia, England: The Centre for Social and Economic Research on the Global Environment School of Environmental Sciences.

Dehring, C. and Dunse, N. (2006) 'Housing density and the effect of proximity to public open spaces in Aberdeen, Scotland', *Real Estate Economics*, vol. 34, no. 4, pp. 553–566.

De Jong, F. and Driessen, J. and Van Hemert, O. (2008) Hedging House Price Risk: Portfolio Choice With Housing Futures (July 31, 2008). Available at http://dx.doi.org/10.2139/ssrn.740364.

DeLeeuw, F. and Ekanem, N. (1971) 'The supply of rental housing', *American Economic Review*, vol. 61, no. 5, pp. 806–817.

Diewert, E.W. (2008) *Index Numbers. The New Palgrave Dictionary of Economics. 2nd Eds* (Palgrave Macmillan, Basingstoke).

Diewert, W., Heravi, S. and Silver, M. (2007) 'Hedonic imputation versus time dummy hedonic indexes', *International Monetary Fund Working Paper No. 07/234*.

DiPasquale, D. (1999) 'Why don't we know more about housing supply?', *Journal of Real Estate Finance and Economics*, vol. 18, no. 1, pp. 9–23.

DiPasquale, D. and Wheaton, W.C. (1994) 'Housing market dynamics and the future of housing prices', *Journal of Urban Economics*, vol. 35, no. 1, pp. 1–28.

Dubin, R.A. (1992) 'Spatial autocorrelation and neighborhood quality', *Regional Science and Urban Economics*, vol. 22, pp. 433–452.

Dubin, R.A. and Sung, C. (1987) 'Spatial variation in the price of housing: Rent gradient in non-monocentric cities', *Urban Studies*, vol. 24, no. 3, pp. 193–204.

Eberts, R. and Gronberg, J.T. (1982) 'Wage gradients, rent gradients, and the price elasticity of demand for housing: An empirical investigation', *Journal of Urban Economics*, vol. 12, no. 2, pp. 168–176.

Eichholtz, P. (1997) 'A long run house price index: The Herengracht index', *Real Estate Economics*, vol. 25, no. 2, pp. 175–192.

Englund, P. (2010) Trading on home price risk: Index derivatives and home equity insurance. In: *The Blackwell Companion to the Economics of Housing: The Housing Wealth of Nations* (pp. 499–511) (Wiley-Blackwell, Hoboken NJ).

Englund, P., Hwang, M. and Quigley, J.M. (2002) 'Hedging housing risk', *Journal of Real Estate Finance and Economics*, vol. 24, no. 1/2, pp. 167–200.

Englund, P., Quigley, J.M. and Redfearn, C.L. (1998) 'Improved price indexes for real estate: Measuring the course of Swedish housing prices', *Journal of Urban Economics*, vol. 44, no. 2, pp. 171–196.

Englund, P., Quigley, J.M. and Redfearn, C.L. (1999) 'The choice of methodology for computing housing price indexes: Comparisons of temporal aggregation and sample definition', *Journal of Real Estate Finance and Economics*, vol. 19, no. 2, pp. 91–112.

Eurostat (2011) *Residential Property Price Handbook*. In: de Haan, J. and Diewert, W.E. (eds.), Luxembourg: Eurostat, November 8 version. Available at http://epp.eurostat.ec.europa.eu/portal/page/portal/hicp/methodology/hps/rppi_handbook, accessed 15th September, 2013).

Evans, A. (1996) 'The impact of land use planning and tax subsidies on the supply and price of housing in Britain: A comment', *Urban Studies*, vol. 33, no. 3, pp. 581–585.

Fenwick, D. (2013) 'Uses of Residential Property Price Indices', in OECD, et al., *Handbook on Residential Property Price Indices*, Eurostat, Luxembourg.

Fan, J. and Gijbels, I. (1996) *Local Polynomial Modelling and Its Applications* (Chapman and Hall, New York).

Fergus, J. (1999) 'Where, when, and by how much does abnormal weather affect housing construction', *Journal of Real Estate Finance and Economics*, vol. 18, no. 1, pp. 63–87.

Figueroa, R.A. (1999) 'Modelling the value of location in Regina using GIS and spatial autocorrelation statistics', *Assessment Journal*, vol. 6, no. 6, pp. 29–37.

Fik, T.J., Ling, D.C. and Mulligan, G.F. (2003) 'Modeling spatial variation in housing prices: A variable interactions approach', *Real Estate Economics*, vol. 31, pp. 623–646.

Financial Times (2017) 'UK housing stock value soars to a record £6.8tn'. Available at https://www.ft.com/content/4906a246-dcb7-11e6-86ac-f253db7791c6, accessed 14th June, 2017.

Fix, E. and Hodges, L.H. (1951) Discriminatory analysis-nonparametric discrimination: Consistency properties. Project 21-49-004, Report No. 4, USAF School of Aviation Medicine, Randolph Field, Texas, pp. 261–279.

Fleming, M.C. and Nellis, J.G. (1984) The Halifax House Price Index: Technical Details (Halifax Building Society, Halifax).

Fletcher, M., Gallimore, P. and Mangan, J. (2000a) 'Heteroscedasticity in hedonic house price models', *Journal of Property Research*, vol. 17, no. 2, pp. 93–108.

Fletcher, M., Gallimore, P. and Mangan, J. (2000b) 'The modelling of housing submarket', *Journal of Property Investment and Finance*, vol. 18, no. 4, pp. 473–487.

Fletcher, M., Mangan, J. and Raeburn, E. (2004) 'Comparing hedonic models for estimating and forecasting house prices', *Property Management*, vol. 22, no. 3, pp. 189–200.

Follain, J. (1979) 'The price elasticity of the long run supply of new housing construction', *Land Economics*, vol. 55, no. 2, pp. 190–199.

Follain, R.J. and Jimenez, E. (1985) 'Estimating the demand for housing characteristics: A survey and critique', *Regional Science and Urban Economics*, vol. 15, no. 1, pp. 77–107.

Follain, J.R. and Malpezzi, S. (1980) *Dissecting Housing Values and Rent* (The Urban Institute, Washington DC).

Fox, J. (2004) 'Nonparametric regression'. Available at http://socserv.mcmaster.ca, accessed 12th December, 2009.

Frew, J. and Wilson, B. (2002) 'Estimating the connection between location and property value', *Journal of Real Estate Practice and Education*, vol. 5, no. 1, pp. 17–26.

Gallimore, P., Fletcher, M. and Carter, M. (1996a) *GIS-based Response-surface Refinements to House-price Modelling* (RICS, London).

Gallimore, P., Fletcher, M. and Carter, M. (1996b) 'Modelling the influence of location on value', *Journal of Property Valuation and Investment*, vol. 14, no. 1, pp. 6–19.

Garrod, G.D. and Willis, K.G. (1992) 'Valuing goods' characteristics: An application of the hedonic price method of environmental attributes', *Journal of Environmental Management*, vol. 34, no. 1, pp. 59–76.

Gatzlaff, D. and Haurin, D. (1997) 'Sample selection bias and repeat-sales index estimates', *Journal of Real Estate Finance and Economics*, vol. 14, nos. 1–2, pp. 33–50.

Gatzlaff, D. and Ling, D. (1994) 'Measuring changes in local house prices: an empirical investigation of alternative methodologies', *Journal of Urban Economics*, vol. 35, no. 2, pp. 221–224.

Gelfand, A.E., Ghosh, S.K., Knigh, J.R. and Sirmans, C.F. (1998) 'Spatio-temporal modeling of residential sales data', *Journal of Business and Economics Statistics*, vol. 16, no. 3, pp. 312–321.

Gibbons, S. and Machin, S. (2005) 'Valuing rail access using transport innovations', *Journal of Urban Economics*, 57, no. 1, pp. 148–169.

Gillen, K., Thibodeau, T. and Wachter, S. (2001) 'Anisotropic autocorrelation in house prices', *Journal of Real Estate Finance and Economics*, vol. 23, no. 1, pp. 5–30.

Glaeser, G., Gyourko, J. and Saiz, A. (2008) 'Housing supply and housing bubbles', *Journal of Urban Economics*, vol. 64, no. 2, pp. 198–217.

Glejser, H. (1969) 'A new test of heteroskedasticity', *American Statistical Association*, vol. 64, no. 325, pp. 316–323.

Goetzmann, W. and Spiegel, M. (1997) 'A spatial model of housing returns and neighbourhood substitutability', *Journal of Real Estate Finance and Economics*, vol. 14, no. 1–2, pp. 11–31.

Goldfeld, S.M. and Quandt, R.E. (1965) 'Some tests for homoskedasticity', *American Statistical Association*, vol. 60, no. 310, pp. 539–547.

Goodman, A.C. (1978) 'Hedonic prices, price indices and housing markets', *Journal of Urban Economics*, vol. 5, no. 4, pp. 471–484.

Goodman, A.C. (1988) 'An econometric model of housing price, permanent income, tenure choice, and housing demand', *Journal of Urban Economics*, vol. 23, pp. 327–353.

Goodman, A.C. (1998) 'Andrew Court and the invention of hedonic price analysis', *Journal of Urban Economics*, vol. 44, no. 2, pp. 291–298.

Goodman, A.C. and Thibodeau, T.G. (1995) 'Age-related heteroskedasticity in hedonic house price equations', *Journal of Housing Research*, vol. 6, no.1, pp. 25–42.

Goodman, A.C. and Thibodeau, T.G. (1997) 'Dwelling-age-related heteroskedasticity in hedonic house price equations: An extension', *Journal of Housing Research*, vol. 8, no. 2, pp. 299–317.

Goodman, J.L. (1987) 'Housing and the weather', *Real Estate Economics*, vol. 15, no. 1, pp. 638–663.

Goodman, J.L. (1998) 'Aggregation of local housing markets', *Journal of Real Estate Finance and Economics*, vol. 16, no. 1, pp. 43–53.

Government Statistical Service (2010) National Statistician's Review of House Price Statistics. Available at www.statisticsauthority.gov.uk/archive/national-statistician/ns-reports--reviews-and-guidance, accessed 15th September, 2013.

Granger, C.W.J. and Newbold, P. (1977) *Forecasting Economic Time Series* (Academic Press, Orlando, FL).

Graves, P., Murdoch, J., Thayer, M. and Waldman, D. (1988) 'The robustness of hedonic price estimation: Urban air quality', *Land Economics*, vol. 64, no. 3, pp. 220–233.

Green, R.K. (1997) 'Follow the leader: How changes in residential and non-residential investment predict changes in GDP', *Real Estate Economics*, vol. 25, no. 2, pp. 253–270.

Greene, W.H. (2000) *Econometric Analysis* (Prentice Hall, Upper Saddle River, NJ).

Greene, W. (2005) *Econometric Analysis (4th ed.)* (Macmillan, New York).

Griliches, Z. (1958) 'The demand for fertilizer: An econometric reinterpretation of a technical change', *Journal of Farm Economics*, vol. 40, no. 3, pp. 591–606.

Haas, G.C. (1922) *Sale Prices as a Basis for Farm Land Appraisal*, Technical Bulletin 9. St. Paul: The University of Minnesota Agricultural Experiment Station.

Hakfoort, J. and Matysiak, G. (1997) 'Housing investment in the Netherlands', *Economic Modelling*, vol. 14, no. 4, pp. 501–516.

Hale, D. (2008) *The Global Driver: How Housing is Driving the World Economy* (Cengage Learning, Gale).

Halvorsen, R. and Pollakowski, H.O. (1981) 'Choice of functional form for hedonic price equations', *Journal of Urban Economics*, vol. 10, no. 1, pp. 37–49.

Han, L. (2008) 'Hedge house price risk in the presence of lumpy transaction costs', *Journal of Urban Economics*, vol. 64, no. 2, pp. 270–287.

Han, L. (2010) 'The effects of price risk on housing demand: Empirical evidence from U.S. markets'. *Review of Financial Studies*, vol. 23, no. 11, pp. 3889–3928.

Harding, J.P., Rosenthal, S.S. and Sirmans, C.F. (2003) 'Estimating bargaining power in the market for existing homes', *The Review of Economics and Statistics*, vol. 85, no. 1, pp. 178–188.

Härdle, W. (1990) *Applied Nonparametric Regression* (Cambridge University Press, New York).

Härdle, W., Müller, M., Sperlich, S. and Werwatz, A. (2004) *Nonparametric and Semiparametric Models* (Springer-Verlag, Heidelberg, Berlin).

Harris, C.D. and Ullmann, E. (1945) 'The nature of cities', *Annal of American Academy of Political and Social Science*, vol. 242, no. 4, pp. 7–17.

Harter-Dreiman, M. (2004) 'Drawing inferences about housing supply elasticity from house price responses to income shocks', *Journal of Urban Economics*, vol. 55, no. 2, pp. 316–337.

Harvey, A.C. (1976) 'Estimating regression models with multiplicative heteroskedasticity', *Econometrica*, vol. 44, pp. 461–465.

Hastie, T. and Loader, C. (1993) 'Local regression: Automatic kernel carpentry', *Statistics Science*, vol. 8, no. 2, pp. 120–143.

Hastie, T., Tibshirani, R. and Friedman, J. (2001) *Elements of Statistical Learning: Data Mining, Inference, and Prediction* (Springer, New York).

Haurin, D.R. and Hendershott, P.H. (1991) 'Local house price indexes: 1982–1991', *Real Estate Economics*, vol. 19, no. 3, pp. 451–472.

Hendry, D.F. (1995) *Dynamic Econometrics* (Oxford University Press, Oxford).

Hilber, C.A.L. and Vermeulen, W. (2010) *The Impacts of Restricting Housing Supply on House Prices and Affordability: Final Report* (Department for Communities and Local Government, London).

Hill, R.C., Knight, J. and Sirmans, C. (1997) 'Estimating asset price indexes', *The Review of Economics and Statistics*, vol. 79, no. 2, pp. 226–233.

Hoesli, M. and Hamelink, F. (1997) 'An examination of the role of Geneva and Zurich housing in Swiss institutional portfolios', *Journal of Property Valuation and Investment*, vol. 15, no. 4, pp. 354–371.

Hoesli, M. and MacGregor, B.D. (2000) *Property Investment: Principles and Practice of Portfolio Management* (Pearson Education, Harlow).

Hofmann, B. (2006) 'EMU and the transmission of monetary policy: Evidence from business lending rates', *Empirica*, vol. 33, no. 4, pp. 209–229.

Holland, A. (1991) 'The baby boom and the housing market: Another look at the evidence', *Regional Science and Urban Economics*, vol. 21, no. 4, pp. 565–571.

Horowitz, L.J. and Lee, S. (2002) 'Semiparametric methods in applied econometrics: Do the models fit the data?', *Statistical Modelling*, vol. 2, pp. 3–22.

Hoyt, H. (1938) *The Structure and Growth of Residential Neighbourhoods in American Cities* (Government Printing Office, Washington DC).

Huang, S. (1973) 'Short run instability in single family housing starts', *Journal of American Statistical Association*, vol. 68, no. 334, pp. 788–792.

Hughes, W.T. and Sirmans, C.F. (1993) 'Adjusting house prices for intra-neighbourhood traffic differences', *Appraisal Journal*, vol. 61, no. 4, pp. 99–119.

Hwang, M. and Quigley, J. (2006) 'Economic fundamentals in local housing markets: Evidence from US metropolitan regions', *Journal of Regional Science*, vol. 46, no. 3, pp. 425–453.

Iacoviello, M. and Ortalo-Magne, F. (2003) 'Hedging housing risk in London', *The Journal of Real Estate Finance and Economics*, vol. 27, no. 2, pp. 191–209.

Ioannides, Y.M. and Zabel, J.E. (2008) 'Neighbourhood effects and housing demand', *Journal of applied Econometrics* vol. 18, no. 5, pp. 563–584.

Jarocinski, M. and Smets, F. (2008) 'House prices and the stance of monetary policy', *Review, Federal Reserve Bank of St. Louis*, vol. 90, no. 4, pp. 339–366.

Jones, C. (2002) 'The definition of housing market areas and strategic planning', *Urban Studies*, vol. 39, no. 3, pp. 549–564.

Jones, J. and Casetti, E. (1992) *Applications of the Expansion Method* (Routledge, London).

Kauko, T.J. (2002) 'Modelling the locational determinants of house prices: Neural network and value tree approaches', PhD thesis, Utrecht University, The Netherlands.

Kearl, J. (1979) 'Inflation, mortgages and housing', *Journal of Political Economics*, vol. 87, no. 5, pp. 1115–1138.

Kenny, G. (2003) 'Asymmetric adjustment costs and the dynamics of housing supply', *Economic Modelling*, vol. 20, no. 6, pp. 1097–1111.

Lancaster, K.J. (1966) 'A new approach to consumer theory', *Journal of Political Economy*, 74, no. 2, pp. 132–157.

Lardaro, L. (1992) *Applied econometrics (2nd ed.)* (Macmillan, New York).

Lee, G.S. (1999) 'Housing investment dynamics. Period of production and adjustment costs', *Journal of Housing Economics*, vol. 8, no. 1, pp. 1–25.

Leishman, C. (2001) 'House building and product differentiation: An hedonic price approach', *Journal of Housing and the Built Environment*, vol. 16, no. 2, pp. 131–152.

Leishman, C. and Watkins, C. (2002) 'Estimating local repeat sales house price indices for British cities', *Journal of Property Investment and Finance*, vol. 20, no. 1, pp. 36–58.

Li, Ker-Chau (1984) 'Consistency for cross-validated nearest neighbour estimates in nonparametric regression', *The Annals of Statistics*, vol. 12, no. 1, pp. 230–240.

Linneman, P. (1980) 'Some empirical results on the nature of the hedonic price function for the urban housing market', *Journal of Urban Economics*, vol. 8, no. 1, pp. 47–68.

Linneman, P. (1986) 'An empirical test of the efficiency of the housingmarket', *Journal of Urban Economics*, vol. 20, no. 2, pp. 140–154.

Lokshin, M. (2006) 'Difference-based semiparametric estimation of partial linear regression models', *The Stata Journal*, vol. 6, no. 3, pp. 377–383.

Maclennan, D. (1977) 'Some thoughts on the nature and purpose of house price studies', *Urban Studies*, vol. 14, no. 1, pp. 59–71.

Maclennan, D., Muellbauer, J. and Stephens, M. (1998) 'Asymmetries in housing and financial market institutions and EMU', *Oxford Review of Economic Policy*, vol. 14, no. 3, pp. 54–80.

Malpezzi, S. (2003) Hedonic pricing models. A selective and applied review. In: T. O'Sullivan and K. Gibb (Eds.), *Housing Economics and Public Policy* (Blackwell, Oxford).

Malpezzi, S. and Maclennan, D. (1994) *The Long Run Price Elasticity of Supply of New Residential Construction in the United States and the United Kingdom* (Mimeo, University of Wisconsin).

Malpezzi, S. and Maclennan, D. (2001) 'The long-run price elasticity of supply of new residential construction in the United States and the United Kingdom', *Journal of Housing Economics*, vol. 10, no. 3, pp. 278–306.

Malpezzi, S. and Mayo, S. (1987) 'The demand for housing in developing countries', *Economic Development and Cultural Change*, vol. 35, no. 4, pp. 687–721.

Mark, J.H. and Goldberg, M.A. (1984) 'Alternative housing price indices: An evaluation', *Real Economics*, 12, no. 1, pp. 30–49.

Mayer, C.J. and Somerville, C.T. (2000) 'Residential construction: Using the urban growth model to estimate housing supply', *Journal of Urban Economics*, vol. 48, no. 1, pp. 85–109.

McCluskey, W.J. and Borst, R.A. (2007) 'Specifying the effect of location in multivariate valuation models for residential properties', *Property Management*, vol. 25, no. 4, pp. 312–343.

McCluskey, W.J., Deddis, W.G., Mannis, A., Lamont, I.G. and Borst, R.A. (2000) 'The application of surface generated interpolation models for the prediction of residential property values', *Journal of Property Investment and Finance*, vol. 18, no. 2, pp. 162–176.

Meen, G. (1999) 'Regional house prices and the ripple effect: A new interpretation', *Housing Studies*, vol. 14, no. 6, pp. 733–753.

Meen, G. (2002) 'The time-series behavior of house prices: A transatlantic divide?', *Journal of Housing Economics*, vol. 11, no. 1, pp. 1–23.

Meese, R. and Wallace, N. (1991) 'Nonparametric estimation of dynamic hedonic price models and the construction of residential housing price indices', *Real Estate Economics*, vol. 19, no. 3, pp. 308–332.

Meese, R. and Wallace, N. (1994) 'Testing the present value relation for house prices: Should I leave my house in San Francisco?', *Journal of Urban Economics*, vol. 35, no. 3, pp. 245–266.

Meese, R. and Wallace, N. (1997) 'The construction of residential housing price indices: A comparison of repeat-sales, hedonic-regression, and hybrid approaches', *Journal of Real Estate Finance and Economics*, vol. 14, nos. 1–2, pp. 51–73.

Mertens, D.M. (2003) Mixed methods and the politics of human research: The transformative- emancipatory perspective. In: Tashakkori, A. and Teddlie, C. (Eds.) *Handbook of Mixed Methods in the Social and Behavioural Sciences* (Sage Publications, California).

Michaels, R.G. and Smith, V.K. (1990) 'Market segmentation and valuing amenities with hedonic models: A case of hazardous waste sites', *Journal of Urban Economics*, vol. 28, no. 2, pp. 223–242.

Monk, S. and Whitehead, C. (1999) 'Evaluating the economic impact of planning controls in the United Kingdom: Some implications for housing', *Land Economics*, vol. 75, no. 1, pp. 74–93.

Morgan, W.A. (1939) 'A test for the significance of the difference between the two variances in a sample from a normal bivariate population', *Biometrika*, vol. 31, no. 1/2, pp. 13–19.

Munro, M. and Maclennan, D. (1986) 'Intra-urban changes in housing prices: Glasgow 1972–83', *Housing Studies*, vol. 2, no. 2, pp. 65–81.

Muth, R.F. (1960) The Demand for Non-farm Housing. In: A.C. Harberger, ed., *The Demand for Non-durable Goods* (University of Chicago Press, Chicago, IL).

Nadaraya, E.A. (1964) 'On estimating regression', *Theory of Probability and its Applications*, vol. 9, no. 1, pp. 141–142.

Nadaraya, E.A. (1965) 'On non-parametric estimates of density functions and regression curves', *Theory of Probability Application*, vol. 10, pp. 186–190.

Nellis, J. and Longbottom, J. (1981) 'An empirical analysis of the determination of house prices in the United Kingdom', *Urban Studies*, vol. 18, no. 1, pp. 9–22.

Neto, M.S. (2005) 'Analysis of the determinants of new housing investment in Spain', *Housing, Theory and Society*, vol. 22, no. 1, pp. 18–31.

Nguyen, N. and Cripps, A. (2001) 'Predicting housing value: A comparison of multiple regression analysis and artificial neural networks', *Journal of Real Estate Research*, vol. 22, no. 3, pp. 313–336.

Nicol, C. (1996) 'Interpretation and compatibility of house-price series', *Environment and Planning A*, vol. 28, pp. 119–133.

ONS (2004) New mortgages: average mortgage repayment as a percentage of average income. Available at www.statistics.gov.uk, accessed 11th November, 2011.

ONS (2011) Wealth in Great Britain. Main Results from the Wealth and Assets Survey: 2008–2010, URL www.statistics.gov.uk, accessed 9th February, 2012.

Orford, S. (1999) *Valuing the Built Environment: GIS and House Price Analysis* (Ashgate Publishing Ltd, Aldershot).

Owusu-Ansah, A. (2011) 'A review of hedonic pricing models in housing research'. *Journal of International Real Estate and Construction Studies*', vol. 1, no. 1, pp. 19–38.

Owusu-Ansah, A. (2012a) 'The dynamics of residential property values in developing markets. The case of Kumasi, Ghana', *Journal of International Real Estate and Construction Studies*, vol. 2, nos. 1–2, pp. 19–35.

Owusu-Ansah, A. (2012b) 'Measuring and understanding the house price dynamics of the Aberdeen housing market', PhD thesis, University of Aberdeen, Aberdeen.

Owusu-Ansah, A. (2013) 'Construction of property price indices: Temporal aggregation and accuracy of various index methods', *Property Management*, vol. 31, no. 2, pp. 115–131.

Owusu-Ansah, A. (2014) 'Modelling the supply of new residential construction in Aberdeen, UK', *International Journal of Housing Markets and Analysis*, vol. 7, no. 3, pp. 346–362.

Owusu-Ansah, A. and Abdulai R.T. (2014) 'Producing hedonic price indices for developing markets: Explicit time variable versus strictly cross-sectional models', *International Journal of Housing Markets and Analysis*, vol. 7, no. 4, pp. 444–458.

Owusu-Ansah, A., Adolwine W.M., and Yeboah E. (2017) 'Construction of real estate price indices for developing housing markets. Does temporal aggregation matter?' *International Journal of Housing Markets and Analysis*, vol. 10, no. 3, pp. 371–383.

Pace, R.K., Barry, R., Clapp, J.M. and Rodgriguez, M. (1998) 'Spatiotemporal autoregressive models of neighbourhood effects', *Journal of Real Estate Finance and Economics*, vol. 17, no. 1, pp. 15–33.

Pagourtzi, E., Assimakopoulos, V., Hatzichristos, T. and French, N. (2003) 'Real estate appraisal: A review of valuation methods', *Journal of Property Investment and Finance*, vol. 21, no. 4, pp. 383–401.

Pakes, A. (2003) 'A reconsideration of hedonic price indexes with an application to PCs', *American Economic Review*, vol. 93, no. 5, pp. 1576–1593.

Palmquist, R.B. (1980) 'Alternative techniques for developing real estate price indexes', *Review of Economics and Statistics*, vol. 62, no. 3, pp. 442–448.

Palmquist, R.B. (1982) 'Measuring environmental effects on property values without hedonic regressions', *Journal of Urban Economics*, vol. 11, no. 3, pp. 333–347.

Palmquist, R.B. (1992) 'Valuing localized externalities', *Urban Studies*, vol. 31, no. 1, pp. 59–68.

Park, R.E. (1966) 'Estimation with heteroscedastic error terms', *Econometrica*, vol. 34, p. 888.

Pavlov, A.D. (2000) 'Space-varying regression coefficients: A semi-parametric approach applied to real estate markets', *Real Estate Economics*, vol. 28, pp. 249–283.

Pholphirul, P., Rukumnuaykit, P. (2010) 'Economic contribution of migrant workers to Thailand', *International Migration*, vol. 48, no. 5, pp. 174–202.

Pollakowski, O.H. and Ray, T.S. (1997) 'Housing price diffusion patterns at different aggregation levels: An examination of housing market efficiency', *Journal of Housing Research*, vol. 8, no. 1, pp. 107–124.

Poterba, J.M. (1984) 'Tax subsidies to owner occupied housing: An asset market approach', *Quarterly Journal of Economics*, vol. 99, no. 4, pp. 729–752.

Poterba, J.M. (1991) 'House price dynamics: The role of tax policy and demography', *Brookings Papers on Economic Activity*, vol. 2, pp. 143–183.

Pryce, G. (1999) 'Construction elasticities and land availability: A two-stage least-squares model of housing supply using the variable elasticity approach', *Urban Studies*, vol. 36, no. 13, pp. 2283–2304.

Quigley, J.M. (1995) 'A simple hybrid model for estimating real estate price indexes', *Journal of Housing Economics*, vol. 4, no. 1, pp. 1–12.

Rapaport, C. (1997) 'Housing demand and community choice: An empirical analysis', *Journal of Urban Economics*, vol. 42, no. 2, pp. 243–260.

Reinhart, M.C. and Rogoff, S.K. (2009) 'The aftermath of financial crises', *American Economic Review*, vol. 99, no. 2, pp. 466–472.

Reinsch, C. (1967) 'Smoothing by spline functions', *Numerische Mathematik*, vol. 10, pp. 177–183.

Riddel, M. (2004) 'Housing-market disequilibrium: An examination of housing-market price and stock dynamics 1967–1998', *Journal of Housing Economics*, vol. 13, pp. 120–135.

Robinson, P.M. (1987) 'Asymptotically efficient estimation in the presence of heteroskedasticity of unknown form', *Econometrica*, vol. 55, pp. 875–891.

Rodriguez, D.A. and Targa, F. (2004) 'Value of accessibility to Bogota's bus rapid transit system', *Transport Reviews*, vol. 24, pp. 587–610.

Rosen, S. (1974) 'Hedonic prices and implicit markets: Product differentiation in pure competition', *Journal of Political Economy*, vol. 82, pp. 34–55.

Rosenthal, S.S. (1999) 'Housing supply: The other half of the market', *Journal of Real Estate Finance and Economics*, vol. 18, pp. 5–8.

Rosiers, D.F. and Theriault, M. (1992) 'Integrating geographic information systems to hedonic price modelling: An application to the Quebec region', *Property Tax Journal*, vol. 11, pp. 29–57.

Schwann, G.M. (1998) 'A real estate price index for thin markets', *Journal of Real Estate Finance and Economics*, vol. 16, pp. 269–287.

Shaul, K., Bar-Lev, B.B. and Enis, P. (1999) 'On the mean squared error, the mean absolute error and the like,' *Communications in Statistics – Theory and Methods*, vol. 28, no. 8, pp. 1813–1822.

Shiller, R.J. (1993) 'Measuring set values for cash settlement in derivative markets: Hedonic repeated measures indices and perpetual futures', *Journal of Finance*, vol. 48, pp. 911–931.

Shiller, R. and Weiss, N.A. (1999) 'Evaluating real estate valuation systems', *The Journal of Real Estate Finance and Economics*, vol. 18, no. 2, pp. 147–161.

Shiller, R. and Weiss, N.A. (2000) 'Moral hazard in home equity conversion', *Real Estate Economics*, vol. 28, no. 1, pp. 1–31.

Shiller, J.R. (2008) 'Derivatives markets for home prices', NBER Working Paper Series, No. 13962. Available at www.nber.org/papers/w13962.pdf, accessed 20th August, 2017.

Sirmans, G.S., Macpherson, D.A. and Zietz, E.N. (2005) 'The composition of hedonic pricing models', *Journal of Real Estate Literature*, vol. 13, pp. 3–43.

So, H.M., Tse, R.C.Y. and Ganesan, S. (1997) 'Estimating the influence of transport on house prices: Evidence from Hong Kong', *Journal of Property Valuation and Investment*, vol. 15, pp. 40–47.

Sommervoll, D.E. (2006) 'Temporal aggregation in repeat sales models', *Journal of Real Estate Finance and Economics*, vol. 33, pp. 151–165.

Sousa, R.M. (2014) 'Wealth, asset portfolio, money demand and policy rule', *Bulletin of Economic Research*, vol. 66, no. 1, pp. 95–111.

Standard and Poor (2012) 'Case-Shiller Home Price Index Report'. Available at https://africa.spindices.com/index-family/real-estate/sp-corelogic-case-shiller, accessed 20th March, 2013.

Stern, D. (1992) 'Explaining UK house price inflation 1971–89', *Applied Economics*, vol. 24, pp. 1327–1333.

Stevenson, S. (2004) 'New empirical evidence on heteroscedasticity in hedonic housing models', *Journal of Housing Economics*, vol. 13, pp. 136–153.

Stewart, J. and Gill, L. (1998) *Econometrics (2nd edn)* (Prentice Hall, Upper Saddle River, NJ).

Stock, J.H. (1989) 'Nonparametric policy analysis', *Journal of American Statistical Association*, vol. 84, pp. 567–575.

Stock, J.H. (1991) 'Confidence intervals for the largest autoregressive root in U.S. economic time series', *Journal of Monetary Economics*, vol. 28, pp. 435–460.

Stone, C.J. (1977) 'Consistent nonparametric regression (with discussion)', *Annual Statistics*, vol. 5, pp. 595–645.

Stover, M.E. (1986) 'The price elasticity of the supply of single-family detached urban housing', *Journal of Urban Economics*, vol. 20, pp. 331–340.

Thibodeau, T.G. (1997) 'Introduction', *Journal of Real Estate Finance and Economics*, vol. 14, pp. 5–9.

Tiesdell, S. and Allmendinger, P. (2004) 'City profile: Aberdeen', *Cities*, vol. 21, pp. 167–179.

Topel, R. and Rosen, S. (1988) 'Housing investment in the United States', *Journal of Political Economy*, vol. 96, pp. 718–740.

Tsatsaronis, K. and Zhu, H. (2004) 'What drives housing price dynamics: Cross-country evidence?', *BIS Quarterly Review*, March, pp. 65–78.

Tsoukis, C. and Westaway, P. (1994) 'A forward looking model of housing construction in the UK', *Economic Modelling*, vol. 11, pp. 266–279.

Tu, Y. (2003) Segmentation, Adjustments and Equilibrium. In: O'Sullivan and K Gibbs, eds, *Housing Economics and Public Policy* (Blackwell, Oxford).

Ullah, A. (1988) 'Non-parametric estimation of econometric functional', *Canadian Journal of Economics*, vol. 21, no. 3, pp. 625–658.

Wand, M.P. and Jones, M.C. (1995) *Kernel smoothing* (Chapman and Hall, New York).

Wang, F.T. and Zorn, P.M. (1997) 'Estimating house price growth with repeat sales data: What's the aim of the game?', *Journal of Housing Economics*, vol. 6, pp. 93–118.

Watkins, C. (2001) 'The definition and identification of housing submarkets', *Environment and Planning A*, vol. 33, pp. 2235–2253.

Watson, G.S. (1964) 'Smooth regression analysis'. *Sankhya Series A*, 26, pp. 359–372.

Waugh, F. (1928) 'Quality factors influencing Vegetable prices', *Journal of Farm Economics*, vol. 10, pp. 185–196.

White, H. (1980) 'A heteroskedasticity-consistent covariance matrix estimator and a direct test for heteroskedasticity', *Econometrica*, vol. 48, pp. 817–838.

White, M. and Allmendinger, P. (2003) 'Land-use planning and the housing market: A comparative review of the UK and the USA', *Urban Studies*, vol. 40, pp. 953–972.

White, M., Dunse, N., Wilson, P. and Zurbruegg, R. (2009) 'Modelling price movements in housing micro-markets: Permanent and transitory components in local housing market dynamics', *RICS Research Papers*, July 2009.

Whitehead, C. (1974) *The UK Housing Market: An Econometric Model* (Lexington Books, Lexington, MA).

Wigren, R. and Wilhelmsson, M. (2007) 'Housing stock and price adjustments in 12 west European countries between 1976 and 1999', *Housing, Theory and Society*, vol. 24, pp. 133–154.

Wilhelmsson, M. (2000) 'The impact of traffic noise on the values of single-family houses', *Journal of Environmental Planning and Management*, vol. 43, pp. 799–815.

Wilhelmsson, M. (2002) 'Spatial model in real estate economics', *Housing Theory and Society*, vol. 19, pp. 92–101.

Wilhelmsson, M. (2004) 'A method to derive housing sub-markets and reduce spatial dependency', *Property Management*, vol. 22, no. 4, pp. 276–288.

Wilhelmsson, M. (2009) 'Construction and updating of property price index series. The case of segmented markets in Stockholm', *Property Management*, vol. 27, no. 2, pp. 119–137.

Wooldridge, J.M. (2009) *Introductory Econometrics – A Modern Approach* (Thomson, South-Western, Mason, OH).

Wu, J., Gyourko, J. and Deng, Y. (2015) Evaluating the Risk of Chinese Housing Markets: What We Know and What We Need to Know. *NBER Working Paper*. National Bureau of Economic Research.

Yao, R. and Zhang, H.H. (2004) 'Optimal consumption and portfolio choices with risky housing and borrowing constraints', *The Review of Financial Studies*, vol. 18, no. 1, pp. 197–239.

Yatchew, A. (1997) 'An elementary estimator of the partial linear model', *Economic Letters*, vol. 57, pp. 135–143.

Yatchew, A. (1998) 'Nonparametric regression techniques in economics', *Journal of Economic Literature*, vol. 36, pp. 669–721.

Index

Printed in the United States
by Baker & Taylor Publisher Services